D0691282

BLUE RIBBON OF THE AIR

BLUE RIBBON OF THE AIR

THE GORDON BENNETT RACES

52275

Henry Serrano Villard

SMITHSONIAN INSTITUTION PRESS
Washington, D.C.   London
1987

©Smithsonian Institution 1987
All rights reserved
Printed in the United States

Library of Congress Cataloging-in-Publication Data
Villard, Henry Serrano, 1900-
   Blue ribbon of the air.
   Bibliography: p.
   Includes index.
   1. Gordon Bennett Cup Race—History.   2. Air
pilots—Biography. I. Title.
GV 759.2.G67V55   1987   797.5'2   87-4709
ISBN 0-87474-942-5

∞The paper in this book meets the guidelines for permanence and
durability of the Committee on Production Guidelines for Book
Longevity of the Council on Library Resources

Cover image is the Hanriot monoplane of Alfred Frey. Courtesy the
author's collection.

Edited by Jan Danis

To my daughter Alexandra
with gratitude for her help and encouragement

Oh! you of the present generation, to whom flight is a commonplace, and the sight of an aeroplane in the sky scarce more than a motor on a road, can you possibly conceive what it was . . . to see those first white wings lift from the ground, and actually to behold man's new conquest of an element till then—from the foundations of the world—unconquered? Whatever the future may hold of wonder and invention, it is impossible to conceive that anything more spectacular, and thrillingly momentous, can be vouchsafed us than the birth of flight—and lucky are they who have beheld it.

Land of Sky and Water
Gertrude Bacon

Contents

Acknowledgments

The author is deeply indebted to the staff of the National Air and Space Museum in Washington, D.C., particularly to Jay P. Spenser, former Curator for Aeronautics, and to Philip Edwards, Librarian, for assistance in research; to A. W. L. Nayler, Librarian of the Royal Aeronautical Society, and John A. Bagley, Curator of the National Aeronautical Collection in the Science Museum, London; to the staffs of the Aéro Club de France in Paris, the Musée de l'Air in Paris and in the museum's new headquarters at Le Bourget, and, through the Air Attaché of the French Embassy in Washington, of the Service Historique de l'Armée de l'Air in Versailles; and to the editors of the *International Herald Tribune* in Paris for making their files available. The unfailing readiness of these sources to respond to inquiries is what makes a book such as this possible. Finally, for her eagle-eyed editing of the manuscript go my warm thanks to Jan S. Danis of the Smithsonian Institution Press.

Introduction

Nothing ever caught the public imagination as did the exploits of a few heroic men—and a handful of women—who pioneered the art of flying during the five or six years before the outbreak of World War I in 1914. Passionately in love with the idea of flight, they built their flimsy machines of wood, canvas, and wire, then climbed into the cockpits and took off with no one to turn to for instructions, with no instruments to guide them, and with motors that as often as not would suddenly quit in midair. Difficulties, yes; disappointments, of course; and danger, ever-present, were accepted without question as part of the game.

Those who stared in amazement—some with tears in their eyes—at the wonderful craft that could carry a human being into the atmosphere were moved by a mixture of awe and exultation at seeing a dream come true—a dream millenniums old, repeatedly pronounced by scientific authorities as impossible of fulfillment. All at once there was a new dimension to the universe. People sensed that what was happening would profoundly affect their lives—it had an impact far greater than a blast-off into space or a landing on the moon today—and their reactions were deeply emotional.

As a rule, the pioneers had no particular incentive to try their wings other than a dogged resolve to master the problem of flight and an unshakable conviction that a motor-driven machine could be made to fly. It wasn't long, however, before they began to derive encouragement from the offer of cash prizes and trophies. Ernest Archdeacon, a well-to-do Paris lawyer and ardent proponent of mechanical flight, set the precedent with a prize of 3,000 francs for the first flyer to cover 25 meters; it was won handily on 23 October 1906 by the Brazilian Santos-Dumont with a hop of twice that distance in a box-kite, tail-first contraption dubbed *The Bird of Prey*, which resembled nothing so much as duck in flight.

Once off the ground and airborne, the flying machine began to develop with phenomenal rapidity. As airmen gained confidence, motors became more reliable, and manufacturers increased their know-how, competitions and tournaments pitted one type of machine against another, bringing out the best qualities in each. When it was realized that inhabitants of the earth had truly acquired the capability to navigate through the air, a wave of indescribable enthusiasm swept over the civilized world. To the cheers of the multitude, with a variety of prizes luring the flyers on, records fell in quick succession—for altitude, for endurance, for speed, for passenger carrying, for cross-country flying. Prominent firms like the Michelin Brothers donated awards that coincidentally advertised their products. Enterprising newspapers boosted circulation by sponsoring long-distance events that held out the prospect of big winnings. Wealthy benefactors lent glamour to achievement by establishing valuable trophies in their own names. In the year 1911 alone more than a million dollars worth of prizes were given away.

Of the various early contests, the most prestigious by far was the annual race for the Gordon Bennett Cup, indisputably the most exacting, the most exciting aerial event of its day, universally acclaimed and recognized as the Blue Ribbon of the Air. The mystique of the Gordon Bennett lay not in the ability of an airman to ascend higher, stay up longer, or travel farther but in his ability to fly faster than anyone else. Whoever won the Gordon Bennett was the champion of the world. Symbol of speed and object of jealous international rivalry, it was the single most important aviation event on the calendar, the test supreme not only of a pilot's skill but of the machine he flew—on the wings of which rode the paramountcy of the country where the craft was built.

James Gordon Bennett, the donor of the trophy, was the multimillionaire publisher of the New York *Herald* and its Paris edition, renowned as a yachtsman, a bon vivant, and a zealous supporter of racing on land and sea and in the air. It would be hard to find a more extraordinary figure in an age that was in itself extraordinary. His life, with his whims and foibles, would fill a separate book. "Names, names, names—that's what makes a paper" was his credo; yet he discouraged mention of his name in print and never allowed it to appear in the pages of his own publications. To the French, he was invariably "Monsieur Gordon-Bennett," despite his insistence that he be known only as Bennett and that his name not be hyphenated, and notwithstanding the fact that he always signed himself J. G. Bennett. The cup which he inaugurated for airplanes—known officially as the Coupe Internationale d'Aviation—would nevertheless be indissolubly linked to the name James Gordon Bennett whether he liked it or not, and the race would be known best as the Gordon Bennett Contest.

Launched in 1909, captured twice by the United States and once by England, the coveted trophy came into the permanent possession of France after three successive wins by that nation. In the eleven years of its existence, the victor's speed had risen from 47.65 to 168.5 miles per hour. A world war had intervened, giving enormous impetus to the design and construction of aircraft. A whole new way of life had begun for populations everywhere. And the airplane had evolved from a rudimentary, undependable machine into the forerunner of today's commercial airlines. The contribution of Gordon Bennett, by being the first to promote the concept of speed—and therefore of all-round excellence—in the air, is an unforgettable part of aviation history.

Chapter 1 THE AIRPLANE COMES OF AGE · 1908

All France was agog with the news that summer: man had at last learned how to fly! At the small Hunaudières racecourse near the ancient town of Le Mans, where a marble monument would one day be erected to his memory, Wilbur Wright and his Model A biplane were confounding the skeptics with astonishing demonstrations of controlled and powered flight.

To the reporter who covered Wilbur Wright's initial ascent on 8 August 1908 for the Paris edition of the New York *Herald,* the plane "looked frail in relation to its bulky motor," which balked at starting on the first two or three trys. A tear in the lower wing had been patched and glued. The aviator himself, unconcerned with the tension that gripped a throng of Saturday afternoon spectators, was dressed as if going for a stroll: gray business suit, high starched collar with tie, gray cap. When the weight attached to a pulley suddenly dropped from a derrick-like launching device, the airplane darted forward "like an arrow from a cross bow shot into the air."

Within seconds the machine attained "a height of between eight and ten meters, circled twice around the race track, taking corners almost terrifying in their sharpness, and descended . . . at its starting point as

1

safely as any bird." The flight lasted exactly 1 minute 45 seconds, but it was enough to convince the experts that the aerial age was at hand.

Frenchmen had never seen anything like it; and their enthusiasm was boundless. "A new era in mechanical flight has begun . . . it is marvelous!" exclaimed the still struggling inventor Louis Blériot. "Wright is a genius! He is the master of us all!" Throwing up his hands, the sculptor-turned-airman Léon Delagrange cried, "We are beaten! We simply don't exist!" *Le Figaro,* the conservative daily, pronounced the exhibition "not merely a success but a triumph, a conclusive trial and a victory for aviation, the news of which will revolutionize scientific circles throughout the world."

No wonder the French were surprised. The best their inventor-pilots had been able to achieve had been short, straight hops or wavering circles of a few seconds duration, performed for the most part on the military parade ground at Issy-les-Moulineaux just outside the old Paris fortifications, from the grassy tops of which onlookers could watch the abortive attempts to fly. (Among them was a Russian revolutionary named Vladimir Ulyanov, better known later as Lenin, who would bicycle over from his tiny apartment at 4, rue Marie-Rose.) Reports of what Wilbur Wright and his brother Orville had accomplished in America were frankly disbelieved if not openly ridiculed. "Of course, it is impossible to say out and out that they have not flown," cautioned the secretary of the Aéro Club de France, "but until suitable evidence arrives, I think it is at least wise to hold one's judgment in suspense." The Americans were regarded as *bluffeurs.* And that, the noted balloonist Edouard Surcouf observed dryly, was to prove *le plus grand erreur du siècle* (the greatest mistake of the century).

Now the evidence was here, and it was irrefutable. First at the Hunaudières track, then at the artillery grounds of Auvours 10 miles away, Wilbur Wright executed a series of perfect flights. His machine, thanks to the Wright system of wing warping for lateral stability, could maneuver like a bird and, as the *Herald*'s correspondent put it, make turns at "almost terrifying" angles. By contrast, the Voisin biplane—the only airplane in Europe then capable of sustained flight for more than a

2

minute—had no way to control bank or roll. It was compelled to yaw itself around turns and could fly only in a calm, outclassed in practically every respect by the versatile American machine.

Much longer flights, with breathtaking banks, circles, and figure eights followed the early trials. Venturesome passengers were given a ride, including George Dickin of the *Herald* staff and Monsieur Reichel of *Le Figaro*, the first journalists to fly, and Mrs. Hart O. Berg, the first woman in the world to go up. On 21 September Wilbur Wright dazzled the continent by remaining aloft for more than 1½ hours. Maj. B. F. S. Baden-Powell, secretary of the British (later Royal) Aeronautical Society, after flying as a passenger expressed a sentiment that would soon become widespread: "That Wilbur Wright is in possession of a power which controls the fate of nations, is beyond dispute."

The Wright biplane was indeed a revelation. Politicians, statesmen, journalists, artists, writers, thinkers, and those moved simply by curiosity flocked to Le Mans to examine it at close range and to gaze open-mouthed at the miracle of human flight. Sir Arthur Balfour, former prime minister of Great Britain, crossed the Channel especially to see its birdlike evolutions in the air. It gave the lie to what most people, along with Simon Newcomb, the astronomer and mathematician, believed: "Aerial navigation is one of that class of problems with which man can never cope."

The hawk-faced, taciturn Wilbur Wright had gone abroad to win the recognition denied him and his brother at home. When they were said to have flown at Kitty Hawk in 1903 the news was generally ignored. Anyone who claimed he could fly was considered a lunatic or a liar. Largely because no official observers attended their experiments, doubters far outnumbered believers. Even casual bystanders who happened to glimpse their strange craft in flight seemed unable to grasp the significance of what they saw. Twice the War Department rebuffed their attempts to sell a flying machine to the government, viewing it as perpetual motion devices or flying saucers might be regarded today. But the French had shown signs of interest. France and Germany appeared headed for a clash over a sphere of influence in Morocco, and an "air

3

The Gordon Bennett Cup,
Aero Club de France.
Courtesy National Air and
Space Museum.

ship," thought certain elements in the army, might be useful as a scout in that disputed African territory.

During the next few weeks Wilbur Wright continued regularly to set records for distance and duration. Others, like Blériot and Henry Farman, the son of a British journalist based in Paris, took heart from his example and redoubled their efforts. On the wide open spaces at Buc, not far from Versailles, Robert Esnault-Pelterie was trying out the R.E.P., a red fabric-covered monoplane of semi-metal construction, while an engineer named Léon Levavaseur was testing the Gastambide–Mengin, prototype of the Antoinette, whose graceful contours belied its ungainly name. By the end of the year Farman had made the first town-to-town flight in history, covering 27 kilometers (16¾ mi) from Bouy to

4

Rheims, and Blériot had flown from Toury to Artenay and back, some 28 kilometers (about 17 mi) with two landings en route, in 22 minutes flying time. In England the flamboyant Colonel Cody—no relation to Buffalo Bill—had contrived to fly 1,390 yards in 27 seconds, and in Germany Hans Grade was making promising hop-flights. At the Grand Palais in Paris that fall, a section of the annual automobile show featured the first Salon de l'Aéronautique, where a fair sampling of fledgling aircraft, including three different types presented by Blériot, was displayed to an awed and fascinated public. And on 31 December Wilbur Wright again stole the headlines with a brilliant flight of 2 hours 20 minutes. To all intents and purposes, one of those problems with which man could "never cope" had been solved. The dream of flying had become reality.

Even so, few would have believed that only months later, the art of flying would have progressed to the point where an international race in the air could take place, the prize a resplendent trophy offered by the Paris *Herald*'s enterprising publisher, the astute, farseeing, and aviation-conscious James Gordon Bennett.

Wilbur Wright's dramatic performance had been a shot in the arm to the French, whose national pride had been wounded by defeat in the Franco-Prussian War. It awakened the nation as nothing had before, giving the military something to think about and focusing attention on the flying machine instead of the dirigible balloon as the coming vehicle of the air. People were enraptured by the advent of the airplane. The idea of soaring and swooping in space with the ease of an eagle—even if the sport was too dangerous for the ordinary citizen—was positively intoxicating. Picture postcards of Wright and his biplane sold briskly in kiosks and bookstalls throughout the land, touching off a craze that would shortly provide collectors with a likeness of every plane and pilot in the country. In the general excitement following Wilbur Wright's success, scoffers gave way to enthusiasts, and popular interest in flying grew apace. It was entirely in character that Gordon Bennett, who was famous for being first in the field as a newspaperman, should capitalize on the possibilities of powered flight by founding a cup for world compe-

5

tition. The news value of such a contest was obvious. It was also good business, for it sold more papers.

Bennett had a knack for being ahead of the news. Napoleon's boast "I live always one year in advance" might well have been applied to him. His name was already a household word in the realm of motorcar racing—his Coupe Internationale de l'Automobile, established at the turn of the century and competed for annually until 1905, was a sporting event of the first magnitude. So was his Coupe Internationale de l'Aéronautique, an annual long-distance contest for spherical balloons, inaugurated in 1906 when the world was beginning to turn from races on land to exploration of the air. Of less lasting fame were his prizes for bicycle, motorboat, and yacht racing—such as the New York–Bermuda race, first staged in 1907. "Surely," wrote the editor of *The Motor* in 1903, "never before has the name of a single individual rushed through the world's printing presses, spread broadcast around the earth, and been scanned by so many millions of readers as the name of Gordon Bennett." The new trophy, the Coupe Internationale d'Aviation, would add immensely to his reputation for it brought to the fore man's conquest of the air—the most thrilling sport of all.

Bennett had come to Paris in 1877 as the result of an embarrassing incident that ostracized him from straitlaced New York society. His name had been linked to that of Caroline May, the beautiful daughter of a distinguished Baltimore family, whose home he reached on a round of calls on New Year's Day in a state of advanced inebriation. Seized by an uncontrollable need to urinate, he relieved himself in the fireplace—an act that caused Caroline's brother Frederick to horsewhip him in front of the Union Club two days later and to challenge him to a duel. The duel took place on 7 January at Slaughter's Gap on the Maryland–Delaware line, happily without injury to either party. But Bennett exiled himself to France where, ten years later, he started the Paris edition of the *Herald*.

Born in New York in 1841 and educated abroad, in part at the College of Versailles, James Gordon Bennett had succeeded his father of the same name as editor of the *Herald,* then near the apogee of its power

James Gordon Bennett.
Courtesy National Air and
Space Museum.

and prosperity. To a marked talent for news-gathering he added a bent
for exclusive stories—especially the foreign, novel, or bizarre. It was the
younger Gordon Bennett who in 1870 financed the expedition to Central Africa led by Henry Morton Stanley to search for the missing
explorer David Livingstone, the discovery and rescue of whom was a
scoop that electrified the world. Four years later he again sent Stanley
to Africa, this time to look for the sources of the Nile. In 1875 he
turned his attention to the Arctic. With the steamer *Jeannette,* purchased in England and named for his sister, he organized the De Long
polar expedition to seek a northwest passage. The tragic loss of that vessel, crushed in the ice pack, and the death from starvation of all its crew,
made a story not easily forgotten.

7

Despite the barrier of distance, Bennett from Paris continued to direct in minute detail the affairs in New York of the parent paper and its less-respected companion, the *Evening Telegram*. His task was facilitated by the Commercial Cable Company, which he put together with John W. Mackay. To a great extent he concentrated on shipping news, reporting at length on arrivals and departures. In the theatrical field, as in that of sports, the New York *Herald* was long without a rival. Every naval officer, yachtsman, and lover of horses read it, as did every sporting man. Much of this focus spilled over into the Paris edition, which with the advent of the flying machine added a coverage of aeronautical events unsurpassed even by the *Daily Mail* of air-minded Alfred Harmsworth, Lord Northcliffe, in England. Bennett's interest in aeronautics began at an early date and took tangible form in 1880, when he gave Thomas Alva Edison 1,000 dollars to make experiments "in the direction of flying." Edison constructed a primitive helicopter powered by stock-ticker tape made into guncotton, which was fed into the cylinder of an engine and exploded with a spark, but the contrivance was not light enough. "I reported to Mr. Bennett," said the inventor, "that when an engine could be made that would weigh only three or four pounds to the horsepower, the helicopter would be a success." Edison claimed to have "got good results," but he had burned one of his men "pretty badly" in the process and singed off some of his own hair. It would be many more years before the Wright brothers developed their version of a lightweight internal combustion engine, making the airplane practical and convincing Bennett that the day of powered flight had arrived.

A bachelor who could afford whatever he wanted—he didn't marry until he was seventy-three—the *Herald*'s tall, slim publisher cut a handsome figure with his heavy black moustache, hair parted on the side, and gray eyes tinged with blue, shaded by bushy eyebrows. He was frequently seen on the boulevards with bowler hat—the ubiquitous *chapeau melon*—cane, spats, and a pair of Pekingese, especially cherished pets whom he would bury eventually in an ornate mausoleum. Egocentric, strong-willed, blunt, hot-tempered and tyrannical to those who worked for him, he nevertheless delighted friends with his wit, his brilliance, his propensity for outrageous pranks, and his spontaneous bursts of generosity. There were as many opinions about him as he had acquaintances. To some he was always the hospitable patron, courteous and free-handed; to others, he was stern, cold, and harshly satirical. He never, it was said, stifled an impulse. Legends flourished concerning his extravagances and escapades: about the time he drove his four-in-hand up the Champs-Elysées at midnight, sitting naked in the coachman's box; about the furor caused at Maxim's when he abruptly yanked the tablecloth and everything on it to the floor, paying for the damage on the spot; about parties on his yacht *Lysistrata,* where a nude dancer might appear after dinner, borne by crewmen on a huge silver platter. His behavior was at times scandalous, but he was unmoved by disapproval or ridicule. He minded only if people didn't talk about his papers.

Devotion to the sea claimed a large part of Bennett's life, not to mention his wealth, and he indulged this devotion by acquiring expensive steam yachts. As a young man he had skippered his sloop *Dauntless* across the Atlantic to arrive in England on Christmas Day—an exploit that led to his being called Commodore. He looked the part and took pains to cultivate the nickname. Soon after coming to Paris and settling into quarters on the avenue des Champs-Elysées, he made himself at home on the Riviera, winter habitat of royalty and the aristocrats whose company he often preferred to forgo in favor of private entertaining afloat. From Nice, Cannes, Menton, Villefranche, or Beaulieu he embarked on cruises that took him and favored guests to such exotic places as Venice, Suez, Ceylon, the East Indies, or South America. First there was *Namouna,* with a crew of seventy, followed by the smaller *Serena.* Then *Lysistrata,* the ultimate in luxury, whose great funnel and single mast aft made her unmistakable, carried a crew of ninety and two Guernsey cows to supply fresh milk for the voyage.

At Beaulieu, his Villa Namouna—irreverently named Pneumonia by his employees—as well as the yachts were embellished with owls, an idiosyncrasy that dated, so the tale goes, from his service as a correspondent with the Union Army in the Civil War. Asleep one night under a tree, he was awakened by an owl's persistent hooting—barely in time,

9

too, for the Confederate cavalry was fast approaching. The wise old bird had saved his life, something Bennett never forgot. A different account has it that he fell asleep while standing watch on his yacht, which he had tendered to President Lincoln as a revenue cutter at the outbreak of the war. The hooting of an owl awoke him just in time to save the ship from running ashore on a sandy reef. Believing if she had not been lost, he would have been, he adopted the solemn bird of Minerva as an emblem of good luck. Whatever the truth, bronze owls—their wings outstretched, electric eyes blinking at night—adorned the cornices of the *Herald* building in New York. Owls decorated his tableware, his linen, his stationery, his gifts. So far, in fact, was the motif carried that the *Herald*'s four-man despatch boat used by its ship reporters to board incoming steamers in New York Harbor was named the *Owlet*—derisively referred to by critics as the Omelet.

In later years Bennett's long face seemed impassive and austere, his manner arbitrary and authoritarian. The clothes became more informal, the hat more often a soft fedora, the graying moustache more free flowing. In a typical pose, he stood with right arm crooked at the elbow, thumb hooked into the top of his vest, left leg thrust forward, left hand in trouser pocket—an imperial stance. With good reason he gave the appearance of a tough and forceful person, tempered by his winning social ways. Bennett was a modern Caliph of Baghdad, spending lavishly, combining the pursuit of pleasure with the desire to reward high endeavor or achievement with his impressive trophies. He liked to lunch at the smart Tour d'Argent put preferred the plebeian métro in getting there. "He created the American-in-Paris image," wrote Eric Hawkins, his longtime managing editor. "He was the most colorful American expatriate the French had ever laid eyes on. For forty years he enchanted Europe as publisher and playboy." Dynamic, farsighted, and shrewd, there is little question that he could have played a great part in his country's destiny had he wished to live another life than he chose.

The world of James Gordon Bennett was the world of *la Belle Epoque*, a glittering period that would be remembered nostalgically as the calm before the storm. Paris was the "City of Light," of high spirits

10

and innovation. The Moulin Rouge, with the risqué cancan, became the center of an animated night life. Debussy was leading a revolt against the somber music of Wagner, Sarah Bernhardt dominated the theater, the great Chaliapin was singing at the Opéra, and the main literary figures were Anatole France and Marcel Proust. But the best-selling science fiction of Jules Verne was prodding the imagination with such fantasies as *Twenty Thousand Leagues Under the Sea, From the Earth to the Moon,* and *Around the World in Eighty Days.* Against the lingering conservatism and provincialism of the nineteenth century, the newfangled flying machine made a greater impact than other revolutionary inventions—the wireless telegraph, the motion picture, the X-ray, the electric light—even greater than the automobile, an intriguing new toy that Bennett foresaw would have wide popular appeal once it developed speed and power. In more ways than one, 1908 was a watershed; it not only gave Europe its first look at the Wrights' biplane but it proved the worth of the automobile by a sensational race around the world, won by America's Thomas Flyer.

Gordon Bennett had a particular interest in one significant sign of the times, a newfound concern with sports. Taking their cue from the energetic British, the French were going in for rugby and soccer, boxing and swimming, running, tennis, and gymnastics. The roads were swarming with bicycles, and contenders in the hugely successful Tour de France were popular idols. Journals consecrated to outdoor life were beginning to multiply, and an illustrated magazine titled *La Vie au Grand Air* drew subscribers by the thousands whether they were active athletes or not. Others, specializing in the "mechanical sports," sold almost as well: *Le Vélo* for bicycle fans, *L'Auto* for motor buffs, and presently *L'Aéro* for the air-oriented.

Like many others in a position of authority, Gordon Bennett was a firm believer in man's competitive instinct, and he never failed to capitalize on it. As a contemporary newspaper would say at his death, he knew it was sport that "created the intense energy that in peacetime wins races and in wartime wins battles." One of the reasons for the growing popularity of sports was the prospect of war. It behooved

France to shape up—soldiers couldn't afford to be weaklings. "War," asserted Georges Clemenceau, "is inevitable." Across the ocean came a bellicose echo from Theodore Roosevelt. "Only war will allow us to acquire the virile qualities necessary to be victorious in the merciless battles which these times impose." Wittingly or not, the press played upon the theme of military fitness by eulogizing the champions, by trumpeting every new record, by stressing the qualities of courage and fortitude, by extolling that extra effort needed to win. Bennett contributed to the spirit of competition by sponsoring international races, and the French—by temperament bold, brash, combative—took naturally to racing on the road and in the air.

Bennett's faith in the horseless carriage led him in 1894 to regard the first road race—an elementary, crude affair between Paris and Rouen—as a newsworthy event. The following year he subscribed to funds raised for a Paris–Bordeaux race; in 1896 he added 10,000 francs to the purse for a race from Paris to Marseilles and back. In 1899 Bennett decided to offer a trophy for annual competition by the budding motor clubs of the world. A massive bronze objet d'art mounted on a marble base was executed by André Aucoc of the fashionable rue de la Paix. It portrayed a winged "Goddess of Victory" holding a sheaf of palm leaves, poised on the driver's seat of the most frequent winner of the day—a 12-horsepower chain-driven Panhard. She was guided by a "Spirit of Progress" carrying a lighted torch. The artifact cost 12,500 francs. In accordance with the donor's inflexible rule, it was always described in the pages of his New York and Paris publications as the Coupe Internationale de l'Automobile. To the rest of the world it was simply the Gordon Bennett Cup.

From the initial race on 14 June 1900, won by the Frenchman Fernand Charron on a Panhard, to the last on 5 July 1905, when Leon Thery was the victor on a Brasier, the great series was packed with emotional tension. Speeds rose from an average of 31.8 to 54.5 miles per hour for the winner. The Gordon Bennett became the major event on the racing calendar. But in six short years the game changed. From a sport for amateurs that helped to further an infant industry it had become a show of commercial rivalry, with professionals competing to gain publicity for the firms that employed them. Perversely, although a founding member of the Automobile Club de France, Bennett did not care especially about motoring, preferring his coach-and-four. He never drove a car and never attended any of the races known by his name. It wasn't hard for him to read the handwriting on the wall. The "Spirit of Progress" was quietly allowed to expire; the trailblazing trophy was permanently enshrined in the foyer of the Automobile Club in Paris, and its originator raised his sights from racing on land to competition in the skies.

The swan song of the auto cup had scarcely died away when Bennett announced his intention of presenting a trophy "for the purpose of creating a great aeronautical contest on somewhat similar lines to those in accordance with which the . . . automobile races have been organized." What he had in mind was a race for balloons, which, with its unusual news potential, seemed a logical shift of interest. Ever since Pilâtre de Rozier and the Marquis d'Arlandes made the first ascent in their elegantly decorated Montgolfier in 1783, adventure-seeking aeronauts had been floating over the landscape in hot-air or gas-filled bags. Balloons had been a useful means of sending mail and occasional passengers out of besieged Paris during the Franco–Prussian War of 1870–71. In 1897 Bennett's imagination had been caught by the quixotic attempt of Maj. Salomon August Andrée, the Swedish explorer, to cross the North Pole in a balloon. He offered Andrée 27,000 dollars to include a *Herald* reporter in the craft, which Andrée did not accept—fortunately for whoever might have been chosen, since the explorer and his two companions perished on the flight. At the Paris Universal Exposition in 1900 meetings were organized in which more than 150 balloons took part. That same year Comte Henri de la Vaulx, another explorer and sportsman, traveled a prodigious 1,922 kilometers in 35¾ hours to Korostyshew, about 100 kilometers west of Kiev, setting a record for balloons that would stand for more than a decade. For a time Bennett entertained the idea of using balloons to speed news coverage but gave up the project when he realized how unreliable they were, apt to travel miles away from their destination.

The toast of the town at the time was Alberto Santos-Dumont, whose one-man dirigibles, or "steerable balloons," would as often as not deposit him in the branches of a tree or on a rooftop. Slight of stature and agile as a cat, the affluent Brazilian endeared himself to his public by his audacious exploits. In October 1901 he had piloted one of his little ships around the Eiffel Tower, winning a Deutsch de la Meurthe Prize of 100,000 francs, which he lost no time in distributing among his employees and the poor. Also to be seen were the "navigable airships" constructed for the government by the Lebaudy brothers, rich sugar refiners who had turned to aeronautics, until the newest and largest, *La Patrie,* tore loose from her moorings and was swept out to sea in a gale. A regular sight, too, was the yellow silhouette of the *Ville de Paris,* first of several lighter-than-air craft built by the Société Astra at Billancourt-sur-Seine and the forerunner of various nonrigid types produced by other French firms. Nor could anyone ignore across the Rhine the large, cigar-shaped, rigid dirigibles of Count Ferdinand von Zeppelin. The dirigible and the free balloon, it was thought, using hydrogen gas, were the wave of the future. Gordon Bennett, with his infallible sense of timing, was prepared to exploit the development by a competition open to all the aero clubs of the world.

The silver trophy that Bennett again ordered from Aucoc was an elaborate and original work of art. The elongated gas bag, rudder and propeller at the rear, suggested the powered dirigibles rather than the conventional spherical balloons. It was supported by a winged female figure, with bared breasts and flowing hair, holding the torch of progress. On the envelope of the dirigible were etched a biplane glider, two free balloons, and the figure of a man surveying the distant horizon. The base was a complex of scrolls and laurel leaves, athwart which lay a ribbon with the legend "Coupe Aéronautique J. Gordon Bennett 1906." Like its predecessor, it cost 12,500 francs. It disappeared from the Aero Club de France during the German occupation of Paris in the war of 1939–45, though a somewhat damaged replica survives today.

The first race got under way from Paris on the afternoon of 30 September 1906. In the presence of an applauding crowd that included the

14

donor of the trophy, sixteen gas-filled balloons from seven nations lifted off from the gardens of the Tuileries, where in 1783 Charles and Nicolas Robert had launched their historic hot-air journey of 36 kilometers. A cash prize of 12,500 francs was earmarked for first place, 5,000 francs for second, 3,250 francs for third, 2,500 francs for fourth, and 1,250 francs for fifth. One by one the spheres rose skyward and disappeared in the distance, their pilots and passengers fortified by a banquet given the night before by the Aéro Club de France. There were no television crews to record the lift-off, no weather reports or radio to follow the aeronauts—it was anyone's guess where or when they would come down. Suspense engulfed the city until news of the landings began to come in. When all had been accounted for, Bennett found to his unconcealed satisfaction that an American Army balloon, the *United States,* flown by Lt. Frank P. Lahm of the Sixth Cavalry and Maj. Henry B. Hersey of Teddy Roosevelt's Rough Riders, which had started twelfth, had won over the entries of Great Britain, France, Belgium, Germany, Italy, and Spain. Crossing the English Channel by night, it had journeyed 647 kilometers to land in Yorkshire.

The balloon race inaugurated by James Gordon Bennett gained instant popularity. With the exception of the war years 1914 through 1920 and the year 1931, it was held regularly until 1939 when World War II intervened. During that period it was won ten times by the United States, seven times by Belgium, four times by Poland, three times by Germany, once by Switzerland, and—ironically—only once by France, the country where the balloon was invented.

Floating over the countryside at the whim of the winds was, however, not the same as winging a path through the clouds in free and unfettered flight. Something far more exciting than the placid balloon was in the offing, and as usual Gordon Bennett was ahead of events. With the wonderful Wright biplane before it, the public was ready and eager to be introduced to another form of aerial endeavor. Already the New York *Evening Globe* had dismissed the dirigible. "Airship experiments have gone far enough," it declared in 1904. "There is not the slightest evidence of any genuine progress made toward constructing an

15

airship of the smallest practical use." In London the *Daily Mail* was equally skeptical about the balloon. It "has now been known to the world for more than a century," observed an editorial in June 1907, "but in that long period no real progress has been achieved in the art of directing or controlling it. . . . The conclusion is irresistible that no progress is possible with it, and that attempts to adapt it for use in war are a mere waste of time." The *Herald* of Gordon Bennett struck a more optimistic note. "There is an universal belief," it affirmed, also in 1907, "that we are on the eve of the most important discoveries ever made in aeronautics and that the answer long sought to the problems of complete mastery by man of aerial navigation is about to be had."

In December 1908, scarcely four months after Wilbur Wright's debut on the aeronautical stage in France, Bennett announced his latest and most imaginative prize competition, intended to hasten "the answer long sought" to the problems of human flight. To this end, he had again gone to the rue de la Paix and commissioned André Aucoc to create the Coupe Internationale d'Aviation. As in the case of his other "Coupes," the Gordon Bennett aviation trophy was not a cup at all but a magnificent silver artifact, whose design was inspired by the stunning success of the Model A biplane at Le Mans. It depicted a winged, lightly clad androgynous figure about to spring into the air from a massive, elaborately adorned base; the right foot is already clear of the ground, the left arm is reaching for the sky. Surmounting this representation of the spirit of flight was a meticulously executed model of the machine that had caused such a sensation that year. Every significant detail was clear: the double front elevator with semicircular vanes or "blinkers"; skids for an undercarriage instead of wheels; twin chain-driven propellers; a maze of uprights and bracing wires; rudder, engine, radiator—even a pilot wearing jacket and visored cap, a control lever in each hand. Below was a cluster of oak leaves and the inscription "Coupe Gordon Bennett." Again, the cost was 12,500 francs.

Originally, the contest was thought of as one for distance, "but," said the charter, "this may be changed into one of duration, subject to atmospheric conditions." It was to be open "in principle, in accordance with the progress of aeronautics, and according to the judgment of the Fédération Aéronautique Internationale, to all kinds of apparatus of aerial locomotion, and especially on its first offering to motor aerostats." Not much attention was given to the matter of speed—at that stage it was enough to rise at all—yet the term "flying machine" implied a swiftness greater than anything yet seen. It was inevitable, considering the rapid progress following Wilbur Wright's demonstrations, that the question should become not how far or how high a "motor aerostat" could go, or how long it could stay up, but how fast it could travel through the air. It was soon evident that the only kind of "apparatus of aerial locomotion" that could qualify would be the power-driven, heavier-than-air flying machine. By the time the first contest could be scheduled, the accepted criterion would be speed.

Rules were drawn up under the auspices of the Fédération Aéronautique Internationale, the recognized authority founded by the Comte de la Vaulx in 1905, with headquarters in Paris, to represent the aero clubs of those nations that elected to become members. Each club was allowed to enter a team of not more than three pilots and their machines, supported by an equal number of substitutes. The cup would go to the country of the winner, which would be under obligation to play host the following year. The first country to win three times in succession would become the permanent owner of the trophy. For the first contest a purse of 25,000 francs awaited the victorious pilot.

The Gordon Bennett Cup presented a direct challenge to inventive talent and genius, as well as to proficiency and technique in that uncharted element, the air. No more suitable setting could have been devised for its unveiling than the first international aviation meet in history, to be held on the plain of Bétheny near the old cathedral town of Rheims in the province of Champagne during the last eight days of August 1909. Deservedly, the contest was billed as the main drawing card at an event whose avowed objective was to bring together the principal birdmen of the day in the greatest exhibition of flying the world had ever witnessed. Initiated, promoted, and financed by the champagne industry, under the patronage of Armand Fallières, president of the

Republic, and the Aéro Club de France, the Rheims meeting was put together by a local committee directed by the Marquis de Polignac. It was a period piece in the most eloquent tradition of *la Belle Epoque.*

To the barons of the champagne business the extraordinary new sport of flying offered an exercise in public relations too good to miss. Veuve-Clicquot, Ponsardin, Heidsieck et Olry, Moët et Chandon, Pommery et Greno, Roederer, G. H. Mumm—producers of all the famous brands contributed to a staggering total of 200,000 francs in prizes. There would be awards for distance, nonstop; for speed, over courses of 10, 20, and 30 kilometers; for altitude; for endurance; and for passenger carrying. There was even a prize for dirigible balloons. The meet was to run from 22 to 29 August, and the pièce de résistance, after a week of appetizers, was the race for the Gordon Bennett trophy on the next to the last day, Saturday the twenty-eighth, when attendance by out-of-town visitors was likely to be at its height and an extra day remained in case the event had to be put off. An open air restaurant was stocked with 3,500 bottles of champagne where, to the popping of corks and the strains of a gypsy orchestra, the drama of flight could be watched. For newsmen, the drinks were on the house. As the British air historian Charles H. Gibbs-Smith would write later, "The aeroplane was thus finally brought into civilization by courtesy of the most civilized, urbane and sophisticated industry of France."

The site selected for this aerial extravaganza had been the scene of a military review for the czar of Russia in 1901. To create an adequate flying area, unmarred for miles by houses or hills, woods or villages, more than 1,500 parcels of land were requisitioned, most of it culti- vated. The only drawback was the roughness of the ground, with its stubble and its stacks of wheat sheaves and root crops. The layout included a race track of 32 hectares, on which pylons painted white were erected to mark the turns. Hangars were constructed for an entry list of thirty-eight machines. Grandstands and adjacent enclosures were readied; barber, beauty, and florist shops were installed. A photo studio was set up, capable of printing picture postcards overnight of each day's flights; and a branch post office was established, where reporters would telegraph more than a million words in the course of the meet and thirty thousand cards would be despatched on one day alone. To restrain the impetuous from invading the field, an infantry battalion had been recruited, twelve hundred strong, reinforced by two hundred mounted dragoons and four hundred gendarmes. And linked to the area by a special railway siding was the city of Rheims, filled with a cosmopolitan cross-section of society, beside itself with excitement.

Formidable strides had been made in powered flight since Wilbur Wright had shown the way at Le Mans. During the first six months of 1909 the number of aviators and constructors—including a sizeable lunatic fringe—had appreciably increased. Aircraft factories, albeit on a small scale, had begun to sprout; a burgeoning government concern with aviation was manifest. France, indisputably at the center of progress in Europe, was clearly out to win the Gordon Bennett. By the middle of August no less than seventeen French airplanes had been entered in the qualifying trials to be held for the cup: two Blériots, three R.E.P.'s, three Antoinettes, three French-built Wrights, five Voisins, and the diminutive Demoiselle of Santos-Dumont. The week of flying that led up to the race itself was a rapturous experience for those who made the acquaintance of the flying machine for the first time. Record after record was broken as intrepid birdmen steered their frail machines around the course. Henry Farman won the Grand Prix, reeling off the astonishing distance of 112 miles (180 km) in a flight of 3 hours 4 minutes 56⅝ seconds, ending in darkness. In the altitude contest, Hubert Latham reached what the editor of *The Aeroplane* described as the "awe-inspiring and perilous" height of 155 meters, a little over 500 feet. At one point seven machines were in the air at once. "The people who gathered at the aerodrome were treated to the most magnificent exhibition of flying ever witnessed," the *Herald* reported. "No language is adequate to convey the idea of the unprecedented spectacle." "The mad enthusiasm of the watchers was a feature unforgettable," wrote the *Daily Mail* correspondent. "Men and women stood on tables and shouted and screamed for joy, completely carried away by the ecstasy of the moment. It is only once in a lifetime that one sees a great crowd so utterly beneath the influence of a single common and uncontrolled emotion." Others ran out of adjectives describing the daily events. "To the rescue!" pleaded a writer for *Le Figaro,* trying to scale new heights of rhetoric with the aid, perhaps, of the free-flowing champagne. "Help! send us words, qualifiers, modifiers! Send us a supply of hyperboles! But please send us something! We've reached the limit, we're drained, our nerves shattered, we've nothing left!"

Excitement increased as the day for the cup race drew near. The main topic of conversation was whether these miraculous machines would be given a chance to show what they could do by their archenemy, the wind, and its ally, inclement weather. The opening day had nearly been rained out, and on many occasions a pesky breeze had interfered with the program. "That detestable wind!" fumed one exasperated journalist, deprived of copy for twenty-four hours. "You want to strangle it, to imprison it, to punish it like a wild animal escaped from its cage!" On the eve of the race, the chief question remained unanswered. Would the weather favor the fliers or would wind force a postponement?

Chapter 2 RHEIMS · 1909

A heavy mist hung over the plain of Bétheny in the early hours of 28 August, but it was soon dissipated by the sun. Only a few white clouds flecked the blue of the summer sky, there was little or no wind; it was going to be a hot day. Conditions were perfect—as perfect as the champagne of the region—for the event everyone was waiting for, the international race for the Gordon Bennett trophy. The day was to be long remembered.

The crowds streaming out of Rheims on the dusty road to the airfield came by bicycle, by carriage, by wagon, and on foot. Threading a path among them were the touring cars—the Panhards, the Peugeots, the De Dion–Boutons and the Delaunay-Bellevilles of the rich. In the flag-bedecked stands, behind boxes of daisies and geraniums, sat the notables, shoulder to shoulder. Military uniforms mingled with morning coats and striped trousers, binoculars with boutonnières, straw boaters and Panamas with derbies, canes with umbrellas, bow ties with fancy cravats. Women wore gargantuan plumed hats, dresses down to the ankle, and tightly laced corsets and were further adorned with feathery boas, scarves, veils, gloves, and parasols. Diplomats from half a dozen interested nations toasted one another at the bar—in champagne, naturally. For those coming down from Paris the salons, the *vernissages,* the

21

"ballets russes" of Diaghilev with Nijinsky and Pavlova, the promenades on the boulevards and the races at Longchamps were forgotten in the incredible novelty of seeing men fly. If one counted the people in the lower-priced enclosures and standing on the sidelines, the crowd totaled closed to one hundred thousand.

Earlier in the week white-bearded President Armand Fallières and his buxom spouse had paid a ceremonial visit to the meet, accompanied by the new premier, Aristide Briand. Young Prince Albert, about to succeed his father as king of the Belgians, had been a constant spectator, firmly determined to make a flight some day. The Right Honorable Lloyd George, chancellor of the exchequer, had also been present, asserting that "flying machines are no longer . . . dreams." He felt, "as a Britisher, rather ashamed to be so completely out of it." Lord Alfred Northcliffe, the newspaper tycoon, had not only published the chancellor's views but had a special edition of the *Daily Mail* hawked about the streets of Rheims for the benefit of English-speaking visitors. The *Morning Post* wished that all Englishmen might have a chance to be present. "The nation is supposed to be lacking in imagination but the flight of aeroplanes . . . cannot but stir the dullest of minds and force them to realize the meaning and importance of a movement which may well affect a revolution in the conditions of life."

But the guests of honor today were Mrs. Theodore Roosevelt, whose husband had recently concluded his second term as president of the United States, her two sons, and her daughter Ethel. With them were the American ambassador, patrician Henry White of New York, his wife, and the newly appointed ambassador to Turkey, Oscar Strauss. Nearby was the travelogue lecturer then much in vogue, Burton Holmes. They and some three thousand other Americans were there to watch a dark horse, a tall, thirty-one-year-old compatriot with a bristling moustache named Glenn Hammond Curtiss, the sole entry from the United States in the race. Aero Club of America officials, as well as Gordon Bennett himself, had looked to the Wrights to carry the American colors. But the Wrights were not interested; while they would do anything to promote the science of aeronautics, they had no time to waste on "sporting events or prize competitions." Wilbur was busy with his demonstrations, Orville had gone to Berlin to negotiate the contract for a German Wright company and, as part of the bargain, to give instructions to Capt. Paul Engelhard of the army. Nominated belatedly, Curtiss had arrived in Rheims at the eleventh hour with a small, untested biplane, having barely caught the S. S. *Savoie* from New York on 5 August. Customs officials at Le Havre, entering into the spirit of the occasion, had sped him on his way. Waving rules aside, they had allowed him to check the three crates containing his machine on the train as personal baggage. "I am taking with me the most powerful motor ever put into an aeroplane," he had told the press before leaving the United States, " . . . an eight-cylinder motor that has developed sixty horsepower in tests, and will give a speed of a mile a minute. I hope to give the Frenchmen a surprise." It had had only one hurried block test.

Gordon Bennett was unimpressed and plainly showed his dissatisfaction. Was this all America had to offer? Although Curtiss had made a name for himself back home as a potential rival of the Wrights, no one in Europe knew much about him. On the Fourth of July 1908, at his native village of Hammondsport, New York, he had won the first leg on a silver trophy put up by the *Scientific American* for the first public flight to exceed 1 kilometer (3,281 ft) in a straight line. This, because of the secrecy with which the Wrights had conducted their experiments, became the first officially recorded flight of a heavier-than-air machine in the United States. The winner three times in succession would become the permanent owner of the trophy, and in 1909 Curtiss tried again. On 17 July he flew 25.002 miles over a 1.3 mile course in competition for the trophy, which this time was offered to the aviator covering the greatest distance during the year; it would give him the prize for the second time. No other airman had come near that performance in public. Curtiss had set his sights on the upcoming meeting at Rheims: realizing the importance of the Gordon Bennett contest, the Aero Club had named him as its entry, leaving the other two places on the team unfilled. It had virtually no other choice.

The night before the race there was not a bed to be had in Rheims.

23

Hotels and *pensions* were charging whatever the traffic would bear; a closet-sized room went for fifty francs. André Aucoc had inserted an advertisement in the *Herald* directing the public's attention to Bennett's unique cup; a shop window where it was displayed was the center of attraction, a constant procession of people pressing forward to have a look. The streets were illuminated, filled with a lively throng. A general air of festivity prevailed. Theaters with Paris companies were drawing huge houses, while the restaurant of the Hotel Lion d'Or resembled that of a big New York hotel, so full was it with Americans. Like the *Daily Mail,* the *Herald* was being hawked on the streets. "Fresh batches of Americans are arriving by every train," it reported, "and today the diners overflowed into the courtyard. . . . Five tables out of six were occupied by visitors from the United States come . . . to see the aviation contest." A day earlier the paper had reported the international enthusiasm for the contest, which "must wonderfully increase popular interest in the twentieth century art and give a stimulus to its mentors and practitioners." The airplane was the invention of the century, beside which the automobile sank into insignificance. "Truly," said Martin W. Littleton, a leading New York lawyer, "it is a week of marvels we have been living through."

If the name of James Gordon Bennett was on every tongue, so was that of Louis Blériot, the odds-on favorite to win the cup. Only a month before, he had startled Europe by flying across the English Channel— a hazardous hop of 23½ miles in 36½ minutes—in a quite unsuitable monoplane of his own construction powered by a three-cylinder 25-horsepower Anzani engine to win a prize of 1,000 pounds offered by the *Daily Mail.* No pilot today, no matter how great, averred the French authority Charles Dollfuss before his death in 1982, could repeat that exploit with such an engine (though seventy-five years afterwards Patrick Lindsay, a director of the London auction house Christie's, duplicated the feat exactly in a pioneer style Manning– Flanders monoplane). For Frenchmen, the epic crossing from Calais to Dover over a body of water that had always been thought impregnable by the British was unquestionably the greatest event of the year: it eclipsed Peary's discovery of the North Pole, overshadowed Shackelton's reports from the Antarctic, and transcended news of Germany's strikingly accelerated naval building program.

Blériot's flight could not have been more fortunately timed for the tournament at Rheims. The announcement that the conqueror of the Channel would participate not only ensured a high attendance but helped spread an interest in aviation that would sweep France like a prairie fire. "There are no islands any more!" was the cry—surprise mixed with alarm—in Britain. On his return to Paris, decorated with the Legion of Honor by Jules Cambon, the French ambassador in London, Blériot found his countrymen in a frenzy of patriotic feeling. *Le Francais Blériot Vient de Traverser la Manche en aéroplane!* blared a banner headline across the entire front page of *Le Matin.* Nobody could beat a champion like this in the Gordon Bennett.

When the meet opened on Sunday with elimination trials to determine the make-up of the French team, flying conditions could scarcely have been worse. DEFYING THE FURY OF THE ELEMENTS, AVIATORS WILL BEGIN FIGHT FOR SUPREMACY OF THE AIR TODAY was the lead story in the *Herald.* A heavy rain had turned the airfield into a sodden, muddy expanse. Lowering clouds, intermittent showers, and a treacherous, gusting wind greeted the first comers. Planks had to be laid to help pedestrians cross the puddles, stalled automobiles had to be hauled out of ruts, and a forbidding black pennant flew from a yardarm on the judges' stand signifying that flights were impossible. But when the rain let up around eleven o'clock it was decided to go ahead with the trials as scheduled.

An elliptical course of 10 kilometers (6.21 mi) had been laid out, running 3,750 meters (about 2⅓ mi) parallel to the grandstand, 1,250 meters on the backstretch, and 2,500 meters at each end. To qualify for a place on their team, French pilots were required to make a flight of 20 kilometers, or two laps (nearly 12½ mi), the same distance as that for the race itself and one that made them think twice when a cross-wind was blowing. It would be a battle between monoplanes and biplanes, thought the *Herald.* "The biplane holds the endurance record but has

25

ceased to be a favorite, the recent exploits of the Antoinette and the Blériot machines having brought the monoplane into the front rank." Blériot's craft was a monoplane; Curtiss, the challenger from across the Atlantic and the only one likely to provide serious competition, operated a biplane. Which type would prevail?

Lots had been drawn for the order of start and priority had fallen to the R.E.P. establishment of Robert Esnault-Pelterie. A dark-haired man of great personal magnetism, he was a graduate of the Sorbonne and a sculptor, engineer, and inventor whose thoughts were often in the clouds. He had been born in Paris on 8 November 1881 and was the fourth person to obtain a pilot's license in France. In 1904 he had started to experiment with gliders, and by late 1907 he was making brief essays on a monoplane of advanced design with internally braced wings and enclosed fuselage of steel tubing. He had also invented a four-bladed propeller and a lightweight motor whose fan-shaped "magic seven" cylinders delivered from 30 to 35 horsepower. But Esnault-Pelterie's career as a pilot had ended in a crash on 18 June 1908. After that, fearing the effect of his injuries might cause him to make an involuntary movement of the controls, he flew only as passenger. The red muslin-covered monoplane that was now dragged from its shed hitched to a horse and escorted by a small band of helpers was in the hands of Maurice Guffroy, a company mechanic.

The contrast between a plodding horse and the winged vehicle it had in tow must have struck the spectators. Although the trend toward mechanization was under way, life was still dominated by the horse: horse-drawn carriages and carts, horse-drawn trams, omnibuses and fiacres, plough horses and horses that drew bathing cabins into the sea. To be a cavalry officer was a mark of distinction, to own a riding horse was suggestive of status and wealth. Man might aspire to fly, but horses were obviously indispensable in pulling a flying machine to the starting line or in extricating motorcars from the muck when it rained.

The R.E.P., its motor coaxed into a sullen roar, wallowed grotesquely in an effort to take off. It moved on a single large bicycle wheel; a smaller wheel at the tail and a wheel at the end of each wing maintained balance as it tipped from one side to the other. But no amount of persuasion would get the machine into the air. Burdened by the metal in its fuselage, it lacked the power to rise from the quagmire of the field. Esnault-Pelterie's product would fly later at Rheims, but it would not distinguish itself until the following year when an improved version flown by the test pilot Pierre-Marie Bournique would establish speed records and win praise for general excellence of construction.

Each entrant was allowed 15 minutes to get away. The next to try was Paul Tissandier on a Wright biplane manufactured under license by the French-formed Société Ariel. It was equipped with a four-cylinder, 24-horsepower Bariquand et Marre motor copied from the Wrights and with curved skids in place of wheels. Launched by derrick, falling weight, and monorail, it had an immense advantage on the sticky soil of Bétheny, taking off with obvious ease and landing light as a feather. The same type as that finally accepted by the U.S. Army for its Signal Corps, the standard Model A was built of spruce and ash and was covered with unbleached cotton; it had a wing area of 415 square feet, a span of 36½ feet, and a length from front elevator to rudder of 29 feet. Its twin propellers were of spruce. Tissandier, tall, lean, and seriously devoted to the sport, had been born in Paris on the same day as Esnault-Pelterie. He came naturally to aeronautics. His father, Gaston Tissandier, was one of the best-known balloonists of the nineteenth century, a writer on scientific subjects and a chemist as well. Paul Tissandier had gone up in a balloon for the first time at the age of twenty-one and would go on to make more than a hundred ascents, accumulating a total of 618 hours in the air, traveling a distance of nearly 15,000 kilometers and winning a number of prizes along the way. But lighter-than-air craft lost their appeal as soon as there was talk of mechanical flight—nothing would deter him from becoming an aviator instead of an aeronaut. At the flying school established by Wilbur Wright early in 1909 at Pau, a sheltered winter resort at the base of the Pyrenees, he learned to solo after three hours of instruction. In March he won an Aéro Club prize for a flight of 250 meters, covering ten times that distance, and on 20 May he became the first European to stay up one hour. He was awarded a license with the supposedly unlucky number 13 but soon took steps to have it changed; after the Rheims meeting it would be reissued as No. 10 *bis.*

Tissandier's bid to be included on the Gordon Bennett team lasted less than a minute. Motor trouble, that familiar nemesis of the pioneers and the cause of many fatal accidents, intervened. The Bariquand et Marre engine spluttered, coughed, and died—an inauspicious start indeed for the trials preceding a speed contest.

Blériot himself now entered the lists, warming up the engine of the Channel-crossing monoplane XI that had made him famous, then getting into the air without undue difficulty to the *bravos!* of the crowd. The Type Onze was next to last in a series of experimental craft that for the most part were disheartening failures. It had a wing span of 25 feet 7½ inches, was 26 feet 3 inches in length, and weighed 462 pounds when empty. Total wing area was 150 square feet, and lateral stability was obtained by wing warping. The rectangular fuselage of four main members, tapering toward the tail and half covered with rubberized fabric, was of ash supported at intervals by vertical struts, all trussed together by diagonally running wires. The Chauvière propeller was of laminated walnut.

Holder of French pilot's license No. 1, Blériot was born in Cambrai on 1 July 1872 and started his career as a manufacturer of acetylene lamps for automobiles. A stocky man with a walrus moustache, brooding eyes, and an aquiline nose, he had begun his efforts to fly in 1901 by building an ornithopter, or flapping wing machine. He had been close to the end of his resources in the spring of 1909 when the Type XI was constructed. With a wife and child to support, he seemed to have only one alternative to giving up the game: to win as many prizes as possible, especially the *Daily Mail*'s thousand pounds. At that critical juncture, with the motor not yet paid for, Fate came to the rescue. On 1 July his wife Alice was visiting friends when she saved the life of a young boy, the son of a Haitian planter named Laroque, whom she caught teetering on the edge of a balcony. That evening, when the Laroques called on the Blériots to express their gratitude, it developed that the Haitian was deeply interested in aeronautics. When he learned how pressed the inventor was for funds, Laroque spontaneously wrote him a check for 25,000 francs, asking only a receipt until settlement could be made. Blériot promised Laroque half the *Daily Mail* prize if he won, and he successfully went after a number of local prizes in preparation for the Channel try.

Expectations that the newfound hero would put on a masterly performance in the Gordon Bennett trials were, however, dashed almost at once. After sweeping past the grandstand in fine style, Blériot was brought down by a clogged carburetor. Never had the unreliability of airplane engines been more apparent: he had covered only 2½ kilometers. It seemed to bear out a widely quoted remark of Lord Kelvin, the mathematician and physicist: "I have not the smallest molecule of faith in aerial navigation other than ballooning."

Nor did the next attempt help to refute Kelvin's caustic observation. Close to Blériot in popularity was the chief pilot of Léon Levavaseur's elegant Antoinette, the debonair Hubert Latham. Slender, pale, reported to be tubercular, Latham had been born in Paris on 19 January 1883, the scion of a wealthy British family long settled in France, and had taken a degree at Balliol College, Oxford. Still fresh in everyone's mind was his duel with Blériot to be first across the Channel. Two attempts had landed him in the water: the first, seven miles off the French coast, where the destroyer *Harpon* had plucked him, smoking a cigarette, from the wreckage of his plane; the second within sight of the cliffs at Dover. Both descents were due to motor failure. Latham had previously crossed the Channel by balloon with his cousin Jacques Faure. A bachelor sportsman who moved in aristocratic circles, Latham indulged a love of adventure by hunting wild animals in Abyssinia and racing fast motorboats at Monaco. In February 1909 he was asked by the Société Antoinette, maker of Antoinette motors—sentimentally named for the daughter of Jules Gastambide, the company's director— whether he would be interested in becoming its standard-bearer in the air. Latham needed no urging. After a brief period of instruction at Châlons-sur-Marne he made a perfect flight of 10 minutes, and on

29

Hubert Latham taking off on a trial flight with his Antoinette at Rheims in 1909. Courtesy Roger-Viollet, Paris.

5 June broke the French record for duration by remaining aloft 1 hour 7 minutes 37 seconds. Further successes followed; by 23 June he was able to take off in a breeze of 25 kilometers per hour, illustrating the Antoinette's stability as well as his own natural skill as a pilot. He took his license, No. 9, on 17 August, five days before the Rheims meet.

The Antoinette on which Latham now rose into the gusty air was probably the most glamorous airplane ever built. Its imposing, delicately arched wings had a span of 42 feet. Its slender, boatlike body, 37 feet 8¾ inches in length, looked like a racing shell, with cedar panels and twin radiators of burnished copper tubing comprising the forward section. Rubberized fabric by Michelin covered the wings and trapezoidal ailerons, the rear of the fuselage, and the sweeping birdlike tail assembly. Its steel-shafted propeller had aluminum blades. The wing area totaled 538 square feet—more than three and a half times that of Blériot's XI—and the machine weighed twice as much. Levavaseur had been an artist before he designed the Antoinette and his creative instinct showed in every line. An English journalist rhapsodized at the sight: "Before the background of a rising thunder cloud, the beautiful white wings and flashing propellor stood out as a dream of pure loveliness." The noise of the motor was almost swallowed up in wild cheers, but the applause was short-lived. Latham had flown a mere 500 yards, mud clinging to undercarriage, tail, and underside of his wings, when the 50-horsepower V-8 Antoinette engine began to misfire, then slowed and stopped altogether. Some ascribed his bad luck to a shower of rain, others shrugged their shoulders and pointed to the ill-omened 13 painted in black on the fuselage.

Eugène Lefèbvre, with a Wright biplane exactly like Tissandier's, was the last to try to qualify on that difficult morning; all other entrants in the trials, which closed at two o'clock, were unable to raise their machines from the ground. Like Tissandier, Lefèbvre could afford to disregard the morass. Gliding smoothly along his monorail, he climbed swiftly to a height of 75 feet. The crowd shrieked its delight: another biplane of the type that in miniature graced the Gordon Bennett cup. The passage through the air of a Wright was unlike that of any other flying machine: at an average speed of 38 miles per hour it was described by Gertrude Bacon as "fussy, fidgety and flickering." This in no way detracted from its well-earned laurels.

One of the youngest—he was not yet twenty-one—and one of the least-experienced aviators at Rheims, Lefèbvre would become the most popular because of his personality, flair, and daring. Born on 4 October 1879 at Corbie in the Department of the Somme, educated as an engineer at the Polytechnic Institute at Lille, he began work installing cold-storage facilities on ships in Russia and Algeria but soon abandoned that line to open an automobile agency in Paris. Energetic, disciplined, fond of boxing, bicycling, and motorcars, Lefèbvre displayed an in-born talent as a flier. Early in 1909 he joined the Ariel company, which appointed him the Wright representative in Holland. At an airfield near

The Hague, with patience and ingenuity, he taught himself to fly, heading his biplane into the wind and rising dexterously from the rail without help from the customary derrick. On 8 July he made flights of 100, 200, and 300 meters; eight days later he stayed up for 17½ minutes. In the presence of Prince Henry of the Netherlands he made two flights on 4 August, one of 5 minutes, the other of 17 minutes duration. On the strength of that short record and no more, he departed for Rheims, where he was one of the first to inscribe his name for the Gordon Bennett trials. Lefèbvre would be remembered for the audacious manner with which he handled his machine, putting it through clownish antics that made everyone gasp—the first stunt pilot in history. Like all the other participants in the tournament, he would come through the Rheims week unscathed—only to have the unhappy distinction a few days afterward of being the first airplane pilot in the world to lose his life.

Lefèbvre completed the first lap without incident. Everything seemed to be going well when, on the second round just short of the required 20-kilometer distance, he too was forced down. Fortunately, these flawed attempts would not be typical of what the *Grande Semaine d'Aviation de la Champagne* and its eagerly awaited climax had in store. On the contrary, the sequence of events with their "wonderful evolutions," "brilliant figure eights," and record-breaking achievements would tell a different story. But, since no one had bettered the attempts of Lefèbvre and Blériot–such as they were—it was announced that these two would represent France in the Gordon Bennett. The third member of the team would be chosen in accordance with the results of the regular afternoon's program.

As the day waned, conditions improved. At five o'clock a sharp squall cleared the air and flying activity commenced at once. Latham was first off and made such a favorable impression that the judges decided to give him third place on the team. There remained the selection of substitutes.

Of five pilots who succeeded in negotiating a 30-kilometer course late in the day, Tissandier ended up with the fastest time and became first choice. Another Wright made the next best showing, with a difference of only $1\,^3/_5$ seconds; it was piloted by Comte Charles de Lambert, a distinguished figure of Russian origin with a reddish moustache and steel-gray eyes, who at the beginning of 1909 had enrolled as Wilbur Wright's first pupil in the school at Pau. Both his father and grandfather had been generals in the army of the czar, the family having emigrated to Russia during the French revolution in 1789; he himself was born on the island of Madeira on 30 December 1865. At the age of eighteen he became fascinated with the gigantic steam-propelled flying machine of Sir Hiram Maxim, which never got off the ground but traveled experimentally on rails. An irresistible urge to fly seemed to flow in de Lambert's blood. After 5 hours 22 minutes of instruction he won the Aéro Club's Prix des Débutantes on 24 March, and on 15 May he gave his first public exhibition on the La Napoule racetrack near Cannes. On 27 June he flew a closed circuit of 1 kilometer at Essen, Germany, and on 4 and 5 July he entertained a crowd at Juvisy-sur-Orge, Paris's *Port-Aviation*. He then took his machine to the town of Wissant on the English Channel with the intention of competing for the *Daily Mail* prize. Forestalled by Blériot's success, he demonstrated its capabilities from the beach.

Although de Lambert did not obtain his license until after the Rheims meet, his proficiency as a pilot was enough to earn him second place among the substitutes. He would achieve lasting fame on 18 October with an unannounced flight around the Eiffel Tower—a feat that did more than anything else at the time to convince Parisians that the airplane had a future.

Third place as a substitute went to Louis Paulhan, an amiable, impecunious mechanic with a small moustache, pilot of a biplane built by Gabriel Voisin that he had won in a competition for model airplanes. Paulhan's experience was minimal. Born on 19 July 1884 at Pézenas in the south of France, he planned to follow the sea and had served as a sailor on the Marseilles–Yokohama run of the Messageries Maritimes steamship company. During his military service at Chalais-Meudon he caught the attention of the flight pioneer Capt. Ferdinand Ferber, who was then experimenting with gliders. Struck by the young man's inventiveness, Ferber made Paulhan his assistant. After completing his military duties as mechanic aboard the Astra dirigible *Ville de Paris,* Paulhan founded a toy company that specialized in scale models of gliders, one of which took the biplane prize. Only an engine and propeller were lacking; with borrowed funds Paulhan acquired a 50-horsepower rotary Gnôme motor and began trials, first at Bar-sur-Aube, then at Issy-les-Moulineaux, where he learned to put *Octavie,* as he fondly called the plane, through her paces. He qualified for his license on 17 August, the same day as Latham. Paulhan had yet to walk into the pages of history, though with his cumbrous Voisin—from which speed couldn't really be expected—he would set several records for distance and duration in the course of the Rheims meet.

Barring an accident to one of the principals, it was unlikely that any of the substitutes would be called upon to take part in the race, but France was taking no chances. A fourth substitute was held in reserve—trim-bearded, slightly built Roger Sommer, son of a felt manufacturer from the village of Mouzon in the Ardennes, who had wrested the world record for duration from Wilbur Wright by flying for 2 hours 27 minutes 15 seconds on 7 August, two weeks before the opening of the meet. Born on 4 August 1877, Sommer had studied at the renowned Ecole des Arts et Métiers in Paris and had become a cycling champion at the age of eighteen. Turning to the automobile in the early stages of its development, he built two voiturettes and by 1908 had completed a six-cylinder model—an innovative vehicle for the time. Then, fired by the exploits of the Wrights, he decided to become an aviator; with a home-built biplane and its twin chain-driven propellers, he managed a number of short hops. In 1909 he ordered a biplane from Henry Farman, installed a 40-horsepower Vivinus automobile motor, and on 4 July made a flight of 6 kilometers. The next day he remained airborne for half an hour, subsequently increasing his time aloft until he had captured the record. Before the meet he had won the Prix de la Ville de Suippes, for linking that community with Mourmelon, but he would not receive his license until 15 January 1910.

With a full complement of pilots and substitutes, France dominated the prospects for the first Gordon Bennett contest. It had been hoped and expected that other nations would take part. Italy had indicated it would send a team headed by Mario Calderara, a young naval lieutenant who had been ordered to Paris to study aviation in 1908. (Later he was to be named air attaché at the Italian embassy in Washington, D.C.) In the spring of 1909 he had been given twenty-three lessons by Wilbur Wright at the Centocelle flying field near Rome as part of a contract for a Wright-licensed company in Italy. Calderara had access to a Wright machine acquired by the Club Aviatori di Roma; with a fellow pupil, Lt. T. U. Savoia of the Military Engineers, he was the leading aspirant for aerial honors in Italy and the first to obtain a license in that country. Italy's chances vanished, however, when it proved impossible for Calderara to join the gathering at Rheims; instead, he would be the chief Italian entrant in an open meeting at Brescia immediately following the French *Grande Semaine.*

Preoccupied with the dirigible, Germany had not gone far with heavier-than-air flight. The nation had hitched its wagon to the star of Count Zeppelin's mammoth airships and Major von Parseval's nonrigid types. With the exception of one or two serious experimenters such as Hans Grade, no established airplane companies could be found; practiced aviators were numbered on the fingers of one hand. It was Orville Wright who opened the eyes of Kaiser Wilhelm II and his court to the potential of the flying machine when he came to Berlin, coincidentally with the meeting at Rheims, to demonstrate a standard Model A built in Dayton and assembled in Germany at the Tempelhof military parade ground. Though there were German entrants in the Gordon Bennett balloon races from the start, airplane racing was still in the future.

While no German entry was forthcoming for the Coupe Internationale d'Aviation, the possibility seems to have existed of an Austro-Hungarian competitor in an aviator named Lorenc. More than a dozen organizations, especially the Wiener Aero Club, later the Oesterreicherscher Aero Club, were actively interested in the developing art of aviation. One of the world's earliest pioneers, Igo Etrich, was working at Wiener-Neustadt on the design and construction of the Taube, a dovelike monoplane with wing tips curved upward for stabil-

35

ity, to be taken over eventually by the German Rumpler firm and turned into a famous warbird. But in the end no Austrian entry materialized. It would be left to Great Britain and the United States to give the race its international flavor.

Enthusiasts had confidently looked to the Royal Aero Club of the United Kingdom, the responsible body through which competitors for the international cup could enter from Britain, to furnish a team of three in accordance with the rules of the race. But England in 1909 was notoriously behind in aviation. There were no licensed aviators, and except for Geoffrey de Havilland, Frederick Handley Page, and A. V. Roe, experimenters were few. A subcommittee on Aerial Navigation, of the Committee of Imperial Defense, appointed to investigate the triumphant Wright demonstrations of October 1908, had concluded lamely that "it had not been able to obtain any trustworthy evidence to show whether great improvements may be expected in the immediate future, or whether the limit of practical utility had already been reached." Such shortsightedness did not encourage private enterprise. Would-be fliers turned to France for training or experience, to the Wrights, Voisin, or Farman for their machines.

One of these was George B. Cockburn (pronounced Có-bun), a lank-haired, nervy, powerfully built Scotsman, noted as a rugby player, who had bought a biplane from Farman a little more than a month before the Rheims tournament. He was the first Briton to do so and the first pupil at the recently opened Farman school on the outskirts of Châlons-sur-Marne. On 20 July he made three flights with his new machine, in the best of which he covered 10 kilometers in 11 minutes 28 seconds. A few days later, the magazine *Flight* reported that Cockburn had remained in the air for 18 minutes. That, apparently, was enough for the Royal Aero Club to nominate him as a member of its team for the Gordon Bennett race on 28 August. No other candidates seem to have been available. In preparation for the international contest, Cockburn flew again at Châlons on 9 August, this time for a full 20 minutes. He would not qualify for a license until 26 April of the following year, when the Aero Club would issue him its No. 5.

Cockburn's Farman, identical to that of Roger Sommer and bearing the number 32, was of a type that within a year would become the best-selling biplane in the world. It had a wing span of 32 feet 9¾ inches, it was 39 feet 4½ inches in length, and its total wing area was 430 square feet. The airframe was of ash and mahogany, the covering of unbleached cotton. It weighed 1,213 pounds at takeoff. Four converging outrigger spars formed the fuselage, leading backward to a square tail with two vertical rudders; four other outriggers carried forward to an elevator plane 15 feet in length. Farman did not go in for wing warping; large aileron flaps hung from the rear of both upper and lower planes—like washing on a line, somebody said. On the lower plane was mounted the engine with its pusher propeller—most commonly the lightweight, seven-cylinder, 50-horsepower Gnôme with its air-cooled flanges, revolving with the propeller around a fixed crankshaft, the foremost choice of aviators in Europe. On the plane's leading edge was a basket seat for the pilot, five feet above the ground. The whole was supported by a chassis between the four wheels of which, strapped to their axles by broad elastic bands, were long wooden skids. Very quickly, the biplane's maze of struts and wires gained it a nickname—the *cage à poules* or chicken coop—though compared to the bulk of a machine like the Voisin it was a thing of grace and beauty. Henry Farman's product was not likely to set records for speed with its average of 37 miles per hour (60 km/hr). On the contrary, it would win slow-speed contests, as well as contests for the shortest takeoff. But for general purposes as an airplane, its popularity was unsurpassed.

The first British national to participate in a meet against foreign fliers, Cockburn made one circuit of the course on the opening day. As the week progressed, he made several more flights, all without incident. On one occasion he raced a passing train and circled it after overtaking it easily. Promising pilot though he was, Cockburn seemed to spend more time working on his motor than on practicing in the air. To some of his friends he appeared depressed, for he knew that his chances in the Gordon Bennett were not rated very high.

Unlike any of the other competitors, Glenn Curtiss had made a scientific approach to the problems of flight and had an expertise in motors as well. In 1907 he had joined the Aerial Experiment Association of Alexander Graham Bell, inventor of the telephone, at the latter's summer home in Nova Scotia, the declared purpose of which was "to build a practical aeroplane which will carry a man and be driven through the air on its own power." Curtiss had from youth been addicted to speed, first as a bicycle maker and racer, then as a motorcyclist. On the hard sands of Ormond Beach, Florida, on 29 January 1904 with a two-cylinder machine, he streaked 10 miles at the rate of 89.07 miles per hour—a record that would stand for the next seven years; in 1907 he was back with an eight-cylinder, 40-horsepower monster and set the unofficial—and unheard of—mark of 136.3 miles per hour. It was only a step into the realm of aeronautics. Curtiss started by building engines for the nonrigid dirigibles of Thomas Scott Baldwin, whose *California Arrow* won the airship event at the St. Louis Fair in 1904. When Baldwin delivered a larger craft to the U.S. Army in 1908, operating the controls from the rear of its skeleton nacelle, Curtiss was up forward looking after his latest motor.

With Curtiss as director of experiments and executive secretary, the Aerial Experiment Association conducted trials with motor-driven tetrahedral kites and aerial propellers mounted on boats until the group moved to Hammondsport in the Finger Lakes district of upper New York State, where Curtiss had been born on 21 May 1878. In the winter of 1908, installed in Curtiss's workshop after a session with gliders, the association tried out a pusher biplane named the *Red Wing* on the frozen surface of Lake Keuka; having no lateral stability, the machine crashed on the second attempt to get it into the air. That spring a second biplane, the *White Wing,* flew 1,017 feet from a racetrack at Stony Brook Farm with Curtiss at the controls, while a third—the *June Bug,* so named by Bell because it was built and tested in June—covered 3,420 feet, again with Curtiss as pilot. This machine on 4 July captured the *Scientific American* trophy—and an impressive trophy it was: a stylized column supporting a globe on which was engraved a likeness of the early experimenter Samuel P. Langley's tandem-winged flying

GRANDE SEMAINE D'AVIATION DE CHAMPAGNE (Première Journée)
L'américain Curtiss et son biplan

Phototypie J. Bienaimé, Reim   Librairie L. Michaud, Reim

Glenn H. Curtiss preparing for the first Gordon Bennett, from a postcard printed in France. Courtesy National Air and Space Museum.

machine, surmounted by an eagle in flight, and ornamented at its base with two prancing reproductions of the winged horse Pegasus.

On 1 April 1909 the Aerial Experiment Association was dissolved. In its place appeared a partnership between Curtiss and Augustus M. Herring, an engineer who had experimented in aeronautics for at least half of his forty-three years. Capitalized at 365,000 dollars, the Herring–Curtiss company entered into a contract to build a biplane for the Aeronautic Society of New York. Because the wings were covered with yellow Baldwin rubberized silk, it was christened the *Golden Flyer*. With this machine, powered by a four-cylinder, 25-horsepower Curtiss engine and delivered at the Morris Park racetrack on 29 May, Curtiss made the first airplane flight in New York City. To obtain more space, the society then moved to Hempstead Plains near Mineola, Long Island, an area destined to play a leading part in the development of

39

American aviation. There Curtiss was allowed the use of the machine for practice—right up to the day he sailed for Europe—and there he learned to fly for extended periods.

The pusher biplane with tricycle landing gear that Curtiss brought with him to Rheims, secretly completed in day-and-night shifts in less than four weeks, was a close copy of the *Golden Flyer,* suitably modified for the forthcoming contest. Like its immediate precursor, it had several features that distinguished it from the prize-winning *June Bug*: instead of flaps at each wing tip for lateral stability, it had flat, hinged panels between the outer edges of upper and lower wings to serve as ailerons, with a shoulder yoke to control their movements; it had a double-surfaced forward elevator; and it had a fixed rear horizontal stabilizer. It had a wing span of 26 feet 3 inches, a chord of 4 feet 6 inches, and a gap between the planes of 4 feet 6 inches; its length was 30 feet 4 inches, its height approximately 9 feet, and the total wing area, including aileron panels, was 258 square feet. The airframe was of clear Oregon spruce, with bamboo outriggers fore and aft; the propeller was of spruce; and the gross weight of the machine was seven hundred pounds. The eight-cylinder water-cooled engine had developed 51.2 horsepower in its only test—twice the power Curtiss had used before.

The *Rheims Racer,* or the "Rheims machine" as it was known to the Curtiss firm, would subsequently become identified in the public mind with the more romantic-sounding *Golden Flyer* and was so called in numerous publications; to an astonishing extent the error is perpetuated today. Adding to the confusion, the *Golden Flyer* itself is sometimes referred to as the *Gold Bug*—apparently the result of a careless reporter's coupling the *Golden Flyer* with the *June Bug* to produce the nonexistent hybrid *Gold Bug.* Actually, the wings of the *Rheims Racer* gave off no golden hue whatsoever, being covered with a prosaic gray silk. The name *Golden Flyer* belongs exclusively to the Aeronautic Society's machine and not to the biplane that was to attain fame at Rheims.

Many people were puzzled by Curtiss's failure to participate in the week's preliminary events. Lounging in the entrance to his hangar, which was draped conspicuously with a large American flag, he gave some the impression of being aloof and superior. But, as he explained to all who cared to listen, he was unwilling to risk damage to the racer and thus jeopardize his country's chances before the Gordon Bennett. He had only one machine, one motor, and two mechanics, compared with the ready replacements, the supplies of spare parts, and the bevy of helpers at the call of French airmen. Moreover, he had had one warning: after a rough landing in a field of grain, he had been thrown from his seat and had sprained an ankle. Nonetheless, on Friday, 27 August, he had made the Tour de Piste—10 kilometers once around the course—in 8 minutes $9\frac{1}{5}$ seconds, the fastest time recorded for that distance and clear evidence that his trim little biplane would be a definite challenge to the Blériot monoplane.

The exuberant spirit of Rheims was caught in a fetching poster, the first to portray mechanical flight, which advertised the scene in arresting color. Conceived by the Parisian artist Edouard Montaut, it depicted an armada of aircraft rising like a swarm of bees from the distant outline of the celebrated cathedral, with four balloons and a dirigible hovering in the rear. Soft tints in the sky indicate that sunset is near, when the wind would be expected to drop and flying would be more likely to take place. A svelte female figure in zebra-striped costume, back to the viewer, raises her right arm in salutation to the onrushing horde of biplanes and monoplanes; her left hand grasps a flagpole from which floats a banner hailing the unparalleled amount of prize money—and, from the look on his face, the nearest pilot is in hot pursuit. Aptly expressing the unveiling of a practical flying machine to mankind, the poster is a collector's item today.

From a souvenir program, printed locally, on the cover of which appeared an exotic version of a monoplane and a long-tailed biplane, the public learned of the lineup for the Gordon Bennet (see table 1).

Two types of monoplanes, three types of biplanes—a Blériot, an Antoinette, a Wright, a Farman and a Curtiss—these were surely as representative of the art as could have been found at the time. Only the Curtiss was given a chance against Blériot's proven monoplane. The

Table 1
1909 • Entry List

Country	Pilot	Machine	Motor
France	Louis Blériot	Blériot monoplane	50-hp Gnôme
	Eugène Lefèbvre	Wright biplane	25-hp Bariquand et Marre
	Hubert Latham	Antoinette monoplane alternates	50-hp Antoinette
	Paul Tissandier	Wright biplane	24-hp Bariquand et Marre
	Comte Charles de Lambert	Wright biplane	25-hp Bariquand et Marre
	Louis Paulhan	Voisin biplane	50-hp Gnôme
	(Roger Sommer)	H. Farman biplane	50-hp Gnôme
Great Britain	George B. Cockburn	H. Farman biplane	50-hp Gnôme
United States	Glenn H. Curtiss	Curtiss biplane	50-hp Curtiss

Antoinette, while conceded to be fast, was not considered fast enough. Nor could the Wright or Farman hope to take better than second or third place. The crowd could only wonder at the temerity of the pilots who were about to fly these fragile craft in the great contest. Little more than novices still, only three of them—Blériot, Latham, and Paulhan—had so far been granted licenses. The aviators of that day were a diverse group, but worldly class distinctions were irrelevant in the air. From the mechanic-turned-aviator to the wealthy sportsman, they were united by a love of flying and by the adulation of the earth-bound. Above all, in the case of this particular race, they were ruled by a sense of international rivalry, for they flew not merely for personal glory but for the honor of their country in the skies. Lloyd George would not have felt "so completely out of it" had he known that watching from the enclosures was a future British winner of the event.

At 10:00 A.M. the race was officially declared open. It would close at 5:30 P.M. and between those hours each contestant would be permitted to make one trial flight and a single try for the cup, starting at a time of his own choosing. The winner would be the airman who made the fastest time over the 20-kilometer course, in other words, twice around the circuit. It would be a race against the clock, rather than one airplane against another. Flags of the three competing nations hung limply from their poles but the grandstand was tense with excitement.

Curtiss had been up early, his biplane tuned and ready. He had made several last-minute refinements: to reduce weight and head resistance he had discarded a large fuel tank and substituted a much smaller one, the capacity of which seemed hardly adequate for the two laps. In preference to a Chauvière propeller specially ordered for him as a sporting gesture by Blériot he had chosen what he considered to be the best of three propellers brought from America. Everything was in order; weather conditions could not have been more favorable; and by 10:30 the Yankee flier was in the air on his trial flight.

Under a blazing sun Curtiss found the going much rougher than he had expected, especially over the backstretch, dubbed the "graveyard," where several machines had come to grief during previous events. Thermal drafts boiled up from the warm ground. "The air seemed literally to drop from under me," he commented on coming down; flying was "difficult if not actually dangerous." He finished the trial circuit safely, however, and was heartened to learn that on the second lap he had set a new record for the course—7 minutes 55 seconds.

Now was the moment. Hastily refilling the fuel tank, he notified the judges he was about to start for the cup. To ringing cheers from the Americans present, the *Rheims Racer*—the number 8 painted on its tail—rose swiftly to an altitude of several hundred feet "to take advantage," as the pilot explained later, "of a general descent over the course and thus gain additional speed." Despite the turbulence, Curtiss resolved to keep the throttle wide open: "I cut the corner as close as I dared and banked the machine high on the turns. I remember I caused great commotion among a big flock of birds which did not seem to get out of the wash of my propellor."

The crowd was on its feet as America's entrant sped past, impatient and anxious as the racer dwindled into a small speck in the distance,

43

tumultuous in its applause as the plane finally crossed the finish line and landed in front of its hangar. From the spectator's point of view the course was almost too wide, for when flying at the far end aircraft could scarcely be seen without field glasses. But such flying had never been seen before. A roar went up when the announcement came, through an intricate system of semaphore signals, that the course had been covered in 15 minutes $50\frac{3}{5}$ seconds at an average speed of 47.65 miles per hours (73.6 k/h).

Cockburn was the next to go up, his Farman rising sluggishly in contrast to the nimble ascent of the Curtiss. To the chagrin of two thousand fans who had come from London by special excursion, "the king of aeroplanes and the aeroplane of kings" (as it was touted "because it was the safest and the easiest to fly") was unable to complete the first lap. Britain's chances ended ingloriously when, on landing, a wing tip caught a stack of standing corn; the machine swung round and the unlucky Cockburn was thrown out. The incident recalled an earlier occurrence, when Henri Fournier swerved his Voisin to avoid a haystack and a wing struck the ground, wrecking the machine. "This wouldn't have happened," Fournier had raged, "if those damned *veillotes* had been removed—as we were promised they would be when flying started!"

With Cockburn eliminated, it was France's turn and Lefèbvre was the first to try. Lefèbvre had performed consistently throughout the week and consistency had raised French hopes. But in a speed contest like the Gordon Bennett something more than consistency was needed—a few seconds clipped off at the turns, an extra thrust from engine and propeller, a more daring bank than usual going into the straightaway. The buzzing Wright biplane, sounding like "a cross between a partridge and a reaping machine" to quote one observer, sailed round the circuit in 20 minutes 47 seconds, nearly 5 minutes slower than the Curtiss. It was enough excitement for the morning; a wind was coming up and it was time for a long lunch and a glass of champagne, accompanied by a babble of discussion on the prospects of Latham or Blériot beating the Curtiss record.

Eugene Lefèbvre of the French team with his Wright biplane. Courtesy
National Air and Space Museum.

Louis Blériot inspecting his Model XII before the 1909 race. Courtesy Roger-Viollet, Paris.

A rumor had gone about—totally without foundation—that the Antoinette was capable of 60 miles per hour, and when the great dragonfly of an airplane was trundled out that afternoon the expectations of the crowd were at fever pitch. To his many admirers Latham epitomized the intrepid airman, determined to pursue an objective against all odds. Undaunted by his two Channel failures, the virtuoso of the Antoinette had not only flown higher than anyone else but had ridden his temperamental mount through threatening storm clouds to set a long-distance mark of 154.5 kilometers. So heroic did the combination of man and machine appear that on one occasion some of his emotional female admirers had burst into tears when they saw the monoplane towed back to its hanger with its aluminum propeller bent. Now it was a question of speed. All eyes were riveted on Latham as he climbed into the shell-like fuselage and settled himself between two enormous control wheels, one on either side. Twisting his checked cap backwards, he calmly lit a cigarette. A mechanic turned the propeller, the engine took

46

hold, and moments later, with a rush and a roar, the mechanical beauty was in the air, its wings shimmering in the slanting sunlight.

A cheer erupted from the spectators, but disappointment was in store. Flying at a height of 150 feet, fighting an obstreperous and mounting wind, Latham could not seem to get more than 40 miles an hour out of the Antoinette; at one point he was even blown to the wrong side of a pylon. Clocked at 17 minutes 32 seconds for the course, he was nearly 2 minutes, or 6 miles an hour, slower than Curtiss. It was up to Blériot to save the day for France.

As soon as he learned Curtiss's time that morning, Blériot had made his trial flight—three seconds slower than the American's. All afternoon the national idol had tinkered with the combination of plane, engine, and propeller he thought most likely to bring him victory; it was after five o'clock before he was ready. Well-aware of the record he would have to beat, he decided against his Channel-crossing model XI in favor of its powerful successor, No. XII, a two-seater, high-wing, aileron-fitted monoplane equipped with an eight-cylinder, water-cooled, British-crafted E.N.V. engine rated at 60 horsepower (though it probably delivered less). Model XII carried a four-bladed, chain-driven Intégrale propeller geared to turn at a slightly slower speed than the motor. It had a wing span of 32 feet 8 inches; its length was 31 feet 6 inches; and the total wing area was 170 square feet. The weight empty was 1,320 pounds. A feature of this model, which was to end its career next day in a fiery crash from which Blériot narrowly escaped with his life, was a vertical strip of fabric running atop the fuselage with an additional horizontal plane near the tail. In order to extract the maximum speed Blériot had stripped approximately 16 square feet of covering from the trailing edge of the wings, leaving the ends of the ribs naked and exposed.

To the thousands who applauded the odd-looking craft with its illustrious pilot, Model XII—the number 22 clearly visible on wings and rudder—had an air of utter invincibility as it roared down the field at 5:10 and swept into the air in front of the timekeepers. Two days· before, the machine had been damaged in a needless accident, when

47

Blériot attempted to take off with an E.N.V. engineer as passenger: a file of dragoons in his path had caused him to collide with and knock down a wooden fence holding back the public. No one was hurt, but the time consumed in repairs had precluded a thorough test of the motor. There was no sign of trouble now. "It looked to me as if he must be going twice as fast as my machine had flown," was the impression of Curtiss, who with his mechanics Ward Fisher and Tod ("Slim") Shriver had been driven out near the timers in the open touring car of Cortlandt Field Bishop, the immaculately turned out president of the Aero Club of America, and his brother David. Blériot's time for the first circuit was 4 seconds faster than Curtiss's and the latter's heart sank: "Then and there I resolved that if we lost the Cup I would build a faster aeroplane and come back next year to win it."

Blériot had renounced several opportunities to win a prize at Rheims, letting it be known that his only interest lay in the Gordon Bennett trophy. The consensus was that his country's chances could not be in better hands; on paper, he couldn't lose. It was, therefore, with justifiable confidence mixed with suspense that the assembled multitude saw him charge around the *piste* at a rate that indicated he was sure to win. When the Frenchman skimmed in for a landing after the second lap, he stood up in his seat to acknowledge the ovation that greeted him. But a puzzling silence followed. Curtiss would always remember the next few minutes. A specially made 2,000-dollar watch belonging to Cortlandt Bishop, the only one of its kind in the world, which could run weeks without winding, to his mortification had stopped ten or fifteen seconds before Blériot's finish. Uncertainty surrounded the result. "I had expected a scene of wild enthusiasm," recounted Curtiss afterwards, "but there was nothing of the sort. I sat in Mr. Bishop's automobile, wondering why there was no shouting, when I was startled by a shout of joy from my friend . . . who had gone over to the judges' stand.

"You win! You win!" he cried, all excitement as he ran toward the automobile. "Blériot is beaten by six seconds!"

Blériot's time was 15 minutes 56⅕ seconds. Slowly the Stars and Stripes was hoisted on the main flagstaff and the red, black, and white

Table 2
1909 • Results

Place	Pilot	Country	Time 1st round	Time 2d round	Total time
1	Glenn H. Curtiss	United States	7m57$^{2}/_{5}$s	7m53$^{1}/_{5}$s	15m50$^{3}/_{5}$s
2	Louis Blériot	France	7m53$^{1}/_{5}$s	8m3s	15m56$^{1}/_{5}$s
3	Hubert Latham	France	8m51s	8m41s	17m32s
4	Eugène Lefèbvre	France	9m45$^{4}/_{5}$s	11m1$^{1}/_{5}$s	20m47$^{3}/_{5}$s
5	George B. Cockburn	Great Britain	————		

squares and triangles of the semaphore system were rearranged to show that Curtiss not Blériot was the victor. The band struck up "The Star Spangled Banner" and Curtiss stood at attention, cap in hand. He had won the Gordon Bennett Cup for America—"the most sensational contest in the history of the world" as the *Herald*'s Bétheny correspondent excitably described it—and for himself a purse of 5,000 dollars.

To the French, it seemed incomprehensible that Blériot should be beaten. Too stunned at first to respond, the majority nevertheless joined in the cheers and applause that rose from the throats of all Americans, who staged a spontaneous demonstration in front of Ambassador White's box. "The most marvelous spectacle" he had ever gazed upon, the ambassador said of the race. Blériot himself was in the forefront of those who rushed to extend congratulations to the United States and to the winner personally, giving Curtiss credit for a superior machine and a job well done. He had no excuses, only an explanation: on the second circuit he had heard his engine misfire and had throttled back a little in consequence.

But not all his countrymen were so gallant. Ferdinand Collin, his close friend and mechanic, claimed that Blériot, naively trying to be helpful, had given his American rival the advice that led to the defeat of France. According to Collin, Curtiss had become discouraged after failing "more than ten times" to better Blériot's time over the 10-kilometer course. He had paid a visit to the Blériot camp, flattered the French

49

President Armand Fallières of France congratulating Latham, who placed third in the 1909 race. Courtesy Roger-Viollet, Paris.

inventor, and slyly led him into making useful suggestions: "You should lighten your machine, refine your propellor—shorten it, your motor turning faster will produce more power. . . . Reduce head resistance by putting in quite a small tank with just the necessary amount of fuel, you should gain several seconds." Never, affirmed Collin in a book he published years later, had he seen Blériot so hoodwinked. "That's it!" he had exclaimed as soon as Curtiss left the hangar. "We've been taken . . . and so we were." It was La Fontaine's fable of the fox and the crow and the piece of cheese all over again. Or was it, perhaps, a simple case of sour grapes?

Henri G. Laignier, secretary of the committee that had organized the *Grande Semaine*, would eventually offer an apology for the public's lukewarm reception of America's triumph. The blow was just too severe, he said. International auto races had gone against France—it was hard to make a beginning in aviation with another defeat. The only consolation lay in Blériot's own words: "The Cup is lost, Till next year, then. We're going to win it back."

50

On Sunday, 29 August, the first two pages of the Paris *Herald* were devoted in their entirety to a description of the race, accompanied by photographs. Next day came a cabled report from New York: "All Americans are wild with enthusiasm over capture of Coupe Internationale. Mr. Glenn Curtiss' feat at Rheims causes great rejoicing throughout the country." The *Washington Post* thought "The award of the international trophy to Mr. Curtiss should prove an inspiration to American genius to maintain its supremacy in aviation, as the possession of the America's cup fired ambition to preserve the yachting championship." The *Cincinnati Inquirer* agreed: "Mr. Curtiss' achievement in flying with safety along a fixed course at a speed greater than that of an average express train will stimulate progress in aviation, besides stirring American pride in the capture and retention of the Coupe Internationale." In Paris the *Herald,* and indirectly its owner and publisher, were not above accepting a share of the applause: "*Herald* is Warmly Praised" was the self-congratulatory caption: "Men Most Interested in Aviation Call it Foremost Champion of Aeronautical Development." Professor A. B. Zahm of the Washington Aero Club brimmed over with enthusiasm as the acclaim continued: "The performance is nothing short of marvelous . . . the whole country" owed the *Herald* a vote of thanks.

The race had "rehabilitated" the biplane, in the opinion of the *Herald.* Biplanes were generally believed to be slower than monoplanes and "while the lightness and bird-like lines of the monoplane seemed to the crowd ideally to represent artificial flight, the American aviator proved that the biplane not only possessed qualities of carrying weight and undoubtedly of superior stability, but that, if need be, it can develop speed equal to, if not superior to, its smaller rival." Whatever the technical merits of this argument, it marked the high point of American aeronautical prestige in the years preceding World War I. The Curtiss victory was the only one during that period in which a plane produced in the United States took part successfully in a competition abroad.

Aero Club officials in New York were euphoric when, after exhibitions in Italy and Germany, Curtiss finally came home. Receptions, luncheons, and dinners without end awaited him. But "the real celebra-

51

tion," wrote the bearded balloonist Augustus Post, one of the activists in the club, "took place in Hammondsport, the place where Mr. Curtiss was born and reared, and where he knew every man, woman and child. The men in the factory and all his other warm friends got together and decided that there must be something out of the ordinary when he got back to town. They planned a procession all the way from Bath to Hammondsport, a distance of ten miles, with fireworks along the route. But a heavy rain came on just in time to spoil the fireworks plan, so they engaged a special train and this passed through a glow of red fire all the way home from Bath. At the Hammondsport station there was a carriage to draw him up the hill to his home, and fifty men furnished the motive power. There were arches with 'Welcome' in electric lights, banners, fireworks and speeches. Through the pouring rain there was a continuous procession of his friends and acquaintances—townspeople who had always given him their loyal support and the men from the shop who had made this possible.

"It was after eleven o'clock when the crowd dispersed—an almost unholy hour for Hammondsport."

It was confidently predicted that when the race was transferred across the Atlantic in 1910, as required by the American victory, the cup would be staunchly defended and would ultimately remain in the United States. "Drive an Aeroplane" urged a full-page advertisement for the Curtiss-Herring biplane by the sales agency Wyckoff, Church and Partridge in *Life* magazine on 18 November. "Americans desiring to enter the international contest next year should order machines early to secure prompt delivery" of "the lightest, speediest, and most practical aeroplane yet designed." America would eventually win the Coupe d'Aviation again—but not with a domestic product. Few realized how quickly aviation would develop in Europe after its slow start, or what determined efforts would be made to wrest the trophy from its first winner.

Chapter 3 BELMONT PARK · 1910

Man Birds Swarm at Belmont Park . . . Thousands View Spectacular Rides of 10 Airships . . . New Records for Altitude . . . Wonderful Feats Never Before Attempted in History of World

So ran the headlines in New York's ebullient press during the last week in October 1910. In a program patterned on the *Grande Semaine* at Rheims, an all-star cast of birdmen from France, Great Britain, and the United States was drawing huge crowds to the famous racetrack on Long Island for a first-hand view of that extraordinary new invention, the heavier-than-air flying machine. The most ambitious affair of its kind yet held on American soil, the tournament was to culminate in the second contest for the now well-publicized Gordon Bennett Cup on Saturday, 29 October—about as late a date in the season that good flying weather could be hoped for.

The meet nearly didn't take place at all. Members of the French team had denounced the course as "suicidal" and staged a last-minute 'revolt' that was quelled only with tact and diplomacy by the officials. As it was, the Gordon Bennett would be run under field conditions very different from those prevailing at Rheims the year before.

In the fourteen months since Glenn Curtiss had flung down the gauntlet, France had virtually usurped the role which America had assumed in giving birth to the airplane. Flying meets and exhibitions had been organized in every part of the country; records of all kinds had been regularly broken; experiments, sound and unsound, had proliferated; further lucrative rewards had been offered for derring-do in the air. The United States may have been the cradle of aviation, but France had become the proving ground. Enthusiasm for all things aeronautical seemed to rise in proportion to the tremendous progress made by Frenchmen in powered flight. It was as if, stung to the quick by failure to capture the blue ribbon of the air on their home grounds, the French were bent on proving a natural aptitude not only as pilots but as builders of successful aircraft and motors. Nothing could have provided more incentive to achievement than the spirit of competition fostered by the first Gordon Bennett at Rheims.

By contrast, the United States was lagging. Few new constructors had appeared on the scene, and those already established clung to the conventional pusher biplane typified by the Curtiss and Wright schools. Europeans meanwhile were refining the monoplane and toying with another concept—the tractor biplane. The increased tempo in France was especially noteworthy in the company directed by Blériot. Since falling onto a housetop at Constantinople and breaking a number of ribs in December 1909, the runner-up at Rheims had concentrated on the manufacture of the versatile monoplane that bore his name. Though he had curtailed his activities as a pilot, the Type Onze was literally in the ascendant everywhere. With a Blériot, altitudes of several thousand feet were reached in the summer of 1910—a breathtaking leap from the 508 feet achieved by Latham only a year earlier. A Blériot had figured prominently in the prize money at Cannes, Nice, Rouen, Rheims, Caen, Nantes, and Bordeaux, as well as at Wolverhampton, Bournemouth, Blackpool, Lanark, and Brussels—winning first place in such varied categories as distance, duration, speed, altitude, and passenger carrying. A Blériot was the only plane to finish in the Circuit de l'Est, the first competition held across open country, taking both first and second place. A Blériot was the choice of fliers who exported their skills to foreign lands. Nobody could have been surprised that Blériots, characteristically equipped with the new rotary Gnôme motors, should be the mainstay not only of the French but of the British team that arrived at Belmont Park intent on bringing the cup back to Europe.

When the meet opened on 22 October, France could boast of a reservoir of more than a hundred licensed aviators from which it had drawn its team for the Gordon Bennett. (Elimination trials had been held at Rheims in the course of another great tournament from 3 to 10 July.) No such wealth of experience existed in the United States, the defending nation. Archaic regulations published early in 1910 stipulated that all candidates for a pilot's license "shall satisfy the officials of the Aero Club of America of their ability to fly at least five hundred yards, and of their capability of making a gliding descent with the engine stopped, before their applications can be entertained." Only twenty-five applicants had so qualified and won their licenses, fewer than Germany with thirty-seven certified airmen and about the same number as Great Britain with twenty-two and Italy with twenty-one. Not that it was essential to have a license in order to fly. Curtiss had won the trophy at Rheims before the Aero Club had officially issued him a certificate. Significantly, however, none of the American team had gained a license to fly earlier than three or four months before the Belmont meet.

America's true love was the automobile, not the airplane. The popularity of the horseless carriage was growing at an unprecedented rate. A seven-passenger Locomobile—"ideal for family use"—was selling for 4,500 dollars. The waltz song "In My Merry Oldsmobile" was a favorite of the man in the street, indirectly boosting the country's first mass-produced car. And the ubiquitous Model T Ford was becoming as deep-rooted a part of American folklore as the cowboy. Arguments abounded over the relative merits of steam, gasoline, and electricity as motive power. A White Steamer, such as the one owned by former President Theodore Roosevelt and produced by the thousand in 1910, was far more appealing than a flying machine whose future seemed unpredictable. Maxwell, Marmon, Peerless, Packard, Pierce Arrow, Pope–

Hartford: manufacturers advertised their models profusely. The public had only to choose among a host of competing claims as to comfort, quality, and performance.

Moreover, the airplane had yet to prove itself as fast as the automobile. The Vanderbilt Cup race was for Americans the epitome of speed. Offered for competition to the Automobile Association of America by William K. Vanderbilt, himself an accomplished driver, the 2,500-dollar cup with its lavish decoration occupied such a warm place in people's affections that a play of the same title, starring Elsie Janis, had become a smash hit. Night after night it had packed a Broadway theater. Popularized by road companies, the play would run for two years, spreading the word about motorcars far and wide. The name Vanderbilt held the same magic for racing devotees in America as Gordon Bennett had for international competition in Europe. Belmont Park, however, would introduce the thrilling new sport of racing in the air; and it would inspire another Broadway hit. *The Aviator*, with Wallace Eddinger in the title role, told of a contest like the Gordon Bennett, a real Blériot taking off from the stage with the aid of pulleys and wires.

In any case, the world was entering an age of speed. Trains like the *Twentieth Century Limited* were annihilating distance; four-funneled transatlantic liners like the *Mauretania* were promoting express trips to Europe; wireless telegraphy and the elementary use of radio were stepping up communications. "The world's splendor has been enriched by a new beauty, the beauty of speed," proclaimed the *Futurist Manifesto* of the Italian Filippo Marinetti. "A racing motor car, its frame adorned with great pipes, like snakes with explosive breaths . . . which looks as though running on shrapnel, is more beautiful than the Victory of Samothrace." The Futurists glorified dynamic action and danger. "We shall sing of the . . . gliding flight of aeroplanes, the sound of whose propellor is like the flapping of flags and the applause of enthusiastic crowds." Gordon Bennett might not have subscribed wholeheartedly to the Futurist creed, which had in it the makings of Fascism, but he certainly would have agreed with the president of the Indianapolis motor speedway, that speed and competition were what counted. Besides auto

56

races, the Hoosier magnate had said shortly after it was built in 1909, "I want to see a flock of airships fighting for first place" in the infield.

While Belmont Park's oval dirt track with its white guard rail was never intended to serve as a flying field, much less as the site for an international air race, it had advantages that resulted in its being chosen instead of other possible localities. For one thing, it was situated in flat country easily accessible from the city of New York, the center of population and wealth in America, which guaranteed a high attendance and therefore financial viability. In addition to a capacious grandstand, Belmont had a clubhouse and executive quarters, a ready-made scoreboard and judges' stand, ample restaurant facilities and rest rooms, a siding almost at the gates for special trains of the Long Island Rail Road, and a convenient Auto Parking Entrance for the swells who motored out from Manhattan in their open touring cars and spanking new limousines. Facing the grandstand a quarter of a mile to the north was a row of twenty wooden sheds and two mammoth tents, hastily erected to house the winged steeds that for one memorable week would displace the world's finest thoroughbreds customarily seen there in action.

Two courses had been staked off by red and white painted pylons: a short, hexagonal course 2.5 kilometers (about 1.5 mi) in length, and a long, tight course—especially designed for the Gordon Bennett race—of 5 kilometers (about 3.1 mi). Eleven carefully spaced pylons marked the long course. The 1910 contest for the cup was to be twenty times around the 5-kilometer circuit for a total distance of 100 kilometers (62.1 mi)—five times as long as the year before and a striking measure of the progress that aviation had made in the interval.

Contestants in the Gordon Bennett would be permitted to start at any time during a period of 7 hours on the day of the race, provided that the starting line was crossed at least 1½ hours before sunset. Any number of landings could be made during the contest; there was no minimum time in which the distance of 100 kilometers was to be covered, but time spent on the ground would be counted against a competitor. As before, the winner would receive a prize of 5,000 dollars in cash and the trophy would go to the recognized club of the victorious nation.

Adequate as the arrangements may have appeared to the organizing committee, they provoked a furor that threatened to stop the show before it began. "The international course as it has been laid out by the Aero Club of America is a death trap," protested Alfred Leblanc, captain of the French team. "It goes over houses, trees, telegraph wires and railroad tracks with scarcely a patch 300 feet wide where an aeroplane can land." The veteran Hubert Latham was even more outspoken, calling it an obstacle course—an invitation to suicide. "Raze the villages over which we must fly," he urged, "cutdown the forest, destroy the farmhouses directly in our path and curve the deep corner at the grandstand." At that particular point a mere 100 feet separated pylon from grandstand. Dubbed "Dead Man's Corner" by the press, it formed such a sharp angle that any attempt to "drive a monoplane around it would end in disaster, if not a collision with the grandstand." James Radley of the British team, after inspecting the field, agreed it would be impossible to make the turn at the current speed of an airplane; Augustus M. Herring, Glenn Curtiss's partner, condemned the course as dangerous; insurance companies refused to insure the spectators, except in the case of Lloyds', which issued a comprehensive policy for half a million dollars. Charging that the layout was inconsistent with the rules of the Fédération Aéronautique Internationale, a number of Frenchmen stayed out of the early events pending receipt of instructions from the Aéro Club de France as to whether or not they should compete.

There were other complaints. The effect of the wind on the various structures near the grandstand, so it was claimed, was to create eddies and crosscurrents: anemometers at ground level might register a velocity of only ten miles an hour, when it was obvious from flags on the pylons or from the behavior of machines in the air that the wind was actually much stronger. To make matters worse, the management had put up high canvas strips to keep out those who were disinclined to pay for admission. These billowed and swayed grotesquely in the breeze; allegations would be made that a gap in the screen on the third day of the meet had let in a gust of air that tipped over John J. Frisbie's biplane and caused it to crash from a height of 50 feet. As the host country,

The crowd at Belmont Park, scene of the 1910 contest. Courtesy National Air and Space Museum.

America took its responsibilities seriously, but little could be done to bring about changes except to remove a few minor bones of contention. In the end, alarm subsided and the temperamental flyers who had balked decided to brave the hazards of the course rather than hold up the schedule like dogs in a manger.

The crowds that streamed through the turnstiles at the track were united in a burning curiosity about men who could fly and motor-driven vehicles that could navigate the air; they came from every walk in life, paying one dollar for standing room in the general enclosure or two dollars for an unreserved seat in the jam-packed, two-tiered grandstand. The more opulent among the men wore watch chains across their vests and smoked cigars, their high stiff collars concealing the tie knots, their feet encased in two-toned high-button shoes. The women wore tailor-made suits or long, full dresses under coats of caracul or broadcloth trimmed with fur, their enormous hats embellished with clusters of fruit, flowers, feathers, or ribbons. Many were habitues of the Vanderbilt Cup race or other fashionable events, like the annual horse show at Madison Square Garden. For society leaders it was a must to be seen at the week's parade of "airships": esconsed in five-dollar box seats could be glimpsed luminaries such as millionaire Thomas Fortune Ryan, chief contributor to the 74,800 dollars in prizes for the meet; Clarence Mackay, president of Postal Telegraph; Harold F. McCormick of the International Harvester dynasty; Lt. Gov. Timothy L. Woodruff of New York and his socially inclined wife; Mrs. August P. Belmont, widow of the financier who had lent his name to the race course; Miss Eleanora Sears of Boston, noted sportswoman in an era when women didn't go in for sports; assorted Whitneys, Goulds, Hitchcocks, Havemeyers, and Harrimans; and, of course, Cortlandt Field Bishop, president of the Aero Club of America. James Gordon Bennett, whose trophy was the principal drawing card, was not present; if not at a Paris café, he could no doubt have been found at one of his favorite haunts on the French Riviera.

Leading the "foreign invasion" of American shores by "European monoplanes and European-trained monoplanists," as the newspapers had it, was France's dark-haired, mustachioed, forty-one-year-old Alfred Leblanc, right-hand man of Louis Blériot and according to one American authority, Albert F. Zahm, "the boldest, sturdiest and most dexterous pilot in a nation of renowned aviators." It was Leblanc who had awakened Blériot at 2:30 on the historic morning of 25 June 1909 with the news he had been waiting for: there was no wind, the stars were out, and a dead calm lay over the English Channel—a propitious moment to start the perilous crossing. After Blériot's resounding success, Leblanc resolved to become a pilot himself. He took his license, No. 17, at Pau on 16 December 1909, having gone to England in October for a meeting at Blackpool that was plagued by bad weather and flown briefly there on an Anzani-powered Blériot XI.

The oldest competitor in any of the Gordon Bennett races, Alfred Leblanc was born on 13 April 1869 at Paris, where his sporting instincts led him into ballooning in 1904. Soon he was an expert in the lighter-than-air field, making frequent trips of a thousand kilometers or more, taking part in the main competitions and winning numerous prizes. But in 1909 his interest switched to mechanical flight; as a close friend and disciple of Blériot he was not only the tireless helper who handled preparations for the Channel flight, standing vigil nightly over the weather, but also the efficient administrator of business details in organizing the embryo Blériot firm. Leblanc himself was catapulted into the headlines in August 1910 when, as a pilot in his own right, he won the Circuit de l'Est, the most stringent test yet devised for flying beyond the confines of an airfield. Sponsored by the circulation-conscious *Le Matin*, more of a ten-day reliability tour with controlled stops on fixed dates than an outright race, it attracted eight starters—only two of whom were able to complete the 860 kilometers from Issy-les-Moulineaux to Troyes, Nancy, Mézières, Douai, Amiens, and back to Issy.

On the first lap, Leblanc beat the express train from Paris to Troyes by a quarter of an hour; at the end of the second stage he was one of three contenders left; on the third, he won a sensational battle against the elements. Within minutes of takeoff he had lost his goggles to the wind. Blinded by rain, buffeted by one violent gust after another, he subsequently told the aviation writer Jacques Mortane "I never thought I would make it. Good luck pulled me through." More likely, it was an intimate knowledge of French topography, gained through countless hours in a balloon, that was responsible. While others went astray Leblanc flew unerringly to his destination. Riding the crest of a wave of popularity, Leblanc then participated in meetings at Rouen and Deauville. In the course of a meeting at Rheims from 3 to 10 July, he won a special race to choose France's contender in the Gordon Bennett, covering 100 kilometers in 1 hour 19 minutes $13\frac{3}{5}$ seconds. He took with him to Belmont the latest model Blériot XI, powered by a new fourteen-cylinder, 100-horsepower Gnôme engine fully expected to bring him victory.

Piloting another Blériot almost wing tip to wing tip with Leblanc in the Circuit de l'Est, Eugène-Emile Aubrun had been the only other contestant to finish, less than half an hour slower than the winner's total flying time of 12 hours 1 minute 1 second. He too was beset by tempestuous winds; flying through a hailstorm he lost his map. An inveterate prize-winner, Aubrun was a natural selection as the second member of France's Gordon Bennett team. Conspicuous for his bushy, elongated moustache, by profession a chemical engineer and by choice a many-sided sportsman, he was born at Brunoy in the department of Seine-et-Oise on 25 August 1881. After only six lessons on a Blériot he took license No. 21 of the Aéro Club de France on 6 January 1910. South America beckoned at that time as virgin territory for an aviator and Aubrun made his first exhibition flight in Buenos Aires, where on 20 April he was awarded the Aero Club of Argentina's license No. 1. Although his countryman Henri Brégi, at the controls of a Voisin, had flown several weeks earlier in the Argentine, Aubrun was a favorite with the public, collecting prize after prize—for speed, for altitude, and for quick takeoff—spreading the gospel of French proficiency in the air and strenghthening cultural and sporting ties between the two nations.

In June 1910 Aubrun returned to France and took part in a week's aviation meeting at Angers in Rochefort-sur-Loire. At the Rheims meeting in July he broke the record for distance with one passenger by flying 137 kilometers nonstop. He was the winner of a prize offered by the *Daily Mail* for the greatest distance flown between 14 August 1909 and 14 August 1910. He consistently won prizes at meetings in the Bay of the River Seine, at Bordeaux, and at Milan. During the first few days at Belmont Park, he captured prizes for speed and cross-country flying. Throughout this period his mount was the reliable 50-horsepower Gnôme-motored Blériot XI.

When Hubert Latham arrived in New York as the third member of the French team, he was promptly idolized as a perfect example of the new breed of "man birds." "I am a citizen of the world," he had replied

Latham at the controls of the Antoinette in which he finished fourth at Belmont in 1910. Courtesy National Air and Space Museum.

suavely to President Fallières when asked what else he did besides fly, and that response seemed to embody the universality of flight. People vividly remembered his two Channel attempts, as well as the fact that he had flown in the Gordon Bennett the year before. With his finely chiseled features, his insouciance, his slight stoop, and his inevitable cigarette holder, he was a romantic figure, the darling of the Sunday supplements; add his reputation as chief pilot of the Antoinette and he made irresistible copy. Hailed as "The Storm King" at Rheims in 1909, Latham had carved out a niche for himself at the Blackpool meeting shortly after by daring to fly when no one else cared to leave the ground. Ugly gusts were blowing in from the sea at 40 miles per hour. "With death at his elbow," as an impressionable scribe declared, Latham fought the wind literally to a standstill, completing only 4 miles in 11 minutes. With the wind at his back, it was estimated, he would have traveled at 90 miles per hour. "Come down, you splendid fool!" vainly shouted a friend. And when he did descend, he told the journalists who surrounded him that he deserved no credit: "All of it is due to Monsieur Levavaseur, the engineer who designed my wonderful Antoinette."

Indeed, the Antoinette was larger, more substantially built, and more stable than any monoplane then in existence; its weight, the wide spread of its wings, and the fine adjustments that could be made in its control mechanism enabled it to live in a tempest where other machines could not survive.

In the spring of 1910 Latham joined a band of other fliers giving exhibitions on the French Riviera. "Aviation Week" at Nice was high-lighted by a race on 24 April across the water to Antibes and return. While rounding the lighthouse, the Antoinette's motor failed again, and once more the pilot had to be rescued from his floating plane. Neverthe-less, Latham was in second place when the prize money was distributed, collecting the equivalent of 12,110 dollars. He also took part in the sec-ond Rheims meeting, trying especially for altitude. But Latham was not interested in monetary reward; he flew for the sake of flying—for the adventure, which he found mostly in private flights around the country-side. It was a different matter when his country's prestige was at stake. Even though his machine was not particularly noted for speed, he rel-ished the thought of again flying for France in the Gordon Bennett, this time with a new motor of 100 horsepower, a motor that reinforced his abiding faith in the Antoinette.

Two reserve fliers were listed by the French—René Barrier and René Simon—both Blériot pilots, both in their twenties, both using the stan-dard Model XI with a 50-horsepower Gnôme motor. Barrier, born at Chataudun on 23 May 1884, had become involved with the growing automobile industry at the age of twenty; intrigued by the possibilities of the internal combustion engine as applied to flight, he turned into a camp follower of Blériot in 1908 and before long decided to become an airman too. Enrolling in the Blériot school at Pau under the tutelage of Alfred Leblanc, he showed an unusual aptitude for flying; he received his license, No. 64, on 2 May 1910. Barrier then departed on an exhibition tour that took him to Seville, Barcelona, and Cordova in Spain, to Mondorff-les-Bains and Mulhouse in France, then to Warsaw, back to Mulhouse, and into Italy at Pescara on the Adriatic.

Simon, too, had followed Blériot's experiments from an early date; born at Paris on 8 December 1885, he obtained his license, No. 177, on a Blériot on 9 August 1910. While he lacked the experience of Barrier at the time of Belmont, his ability as a pilot was indisputable. In the days to come, he, Barrier, and Roland Garros would become known as "The Three Musketeers," giving spine-tingling performances that were the forerunner of latter-day aerial acrobatics.

No elimination trials were held by Great Britain and the Royal Aero Club did not name its principal entrant in the Gordon Bennett until a little more than three weeks before the event. In August the nation's leading aviator, Claude Grahame-White, accompanied by three mechanics, had sailed for the United States with a Blériot and a Farman—each powered by a 50-horsepower Gnôme motor—to take part in a meet from 3 to 13 September organized by the Harvard Aeronautical Society at Squantum, Massachusetts. Handsome, clean-shaven, gracious, and magnetic, unquestionably the favorite of the crowds, Grahame-White extended his stay in order to attend the tournament at Belmont Park. During the first week in October, while giving exhibition flights at the Brockton (Massachusetts) State Fair, he heard that he had been chosen to represent his country in the Bennett speed classic. He immediately cabled an order to the Blériot factory for the latest version of the Model XI, specifying that it be equipped with a 100-horsepower motor—for he knew that neither of his two 50-horsepower machines would be fast enough to win the cup. No guarantee could be given that the new plane would reach New York in time, but the factory promised to do its best.

Claude Grahame-White, born at Southhampton on 31 August 1879 and educated at Bedford Grammar School, had been a yachtsman, a motoring enthusiast, and a dealer in automobiles before he was converted to aviation at the Rheims meeting in 1909. Forthwith, he had ordered a duplicate of Blériot's ill-fated Model XII; and to become

65

acquainted with its construction he enrolled as a worker in the Blériot establishment at Neuilly-sur-Seine. He could hardly restrain his impatience. On the morning he was to take delivery at Issy-les-Moulineaux, Grahame-White found that the mechanics who were to give him instructions had not yet arrived. Impulsively he got into the machine and began practicing short hops. He then shipped the plane to Pau, where Leblanc was his instructor; and on 4 January 1910 he received the first French license—No. 30—to be awarded to a Briton. (Under date of 26 April he would be granted British license No. 6 for having qualified as a pilot at Pau.)

The Model XII, however, had only a brief career. A miscalculation on landing one day, with Blériot himself at the controls, resulted in the two-seater monoplane being wrecked; it was the last of its kind. Grahame-White returned to London and began the development of a great flying center at Hendon, on what was then a vacant, weed-covered lot. At the same time he entered the Henry Farman school at Châlons, learning to fly the biplane with which he would become famous for a dramatic dash in the dark of the night, racing Louis Paulhan for a 10,000-pound prize offered by the *Daily Mail*. The course from London to Manchester—a distance of 183 miles—had to be covered within 24 hours.

Defeated by the wind on a first try for the prize, Grahame-White discovered late in the evening on 28 April that his French rival had taken off, also in a Farman. Hurriedly getting into the air, he reached the town of Roade, 60 miles on the way, before he was compelled to come down and ask for directions. To cut Paulhan's lead, he resolved on a desperate ploy—to fly in the dark. At three o'clock in the morning on 29 April—without compass, altimeter, or fuel gauge—he was airborne again, guided by the headlights of an automobile and a freight train moving in the same direction. It was a vain though valiant attempt. Engine trouble and a rising wind brought him down at Polesworth, 107 miles out of London, leaving Paulhan the victor. But Grahame-White "became the hero of the day . . . the first Englishman to represent" the United Kingdom "worthily in any great aerial contest," according to Harry Harper, the writer on aeronautics. "His heroic flight through the night, a feat that would have appalled any airman, won him the admiration of the public. From being a little-known flyer, and in fact a novice, he became, in a bound, one of the best-known men in the world of aviation."

Grahame-White enhanced his standing in the summer of 1910 at a number of landmark meetings: at Wolverhampton he won 1000 pounds for the highest score; at Bournemouth he took the distance prize; he flew at Blackpool and gave numerous exhibitions in the vicinity of London. At Squantum he dominated the meet, garnering a total of 22,100 dollars in prize money, including 10,000 dollars put up by the Boston *Globe* for a 33-mile race around Boston Light, which he won without trouble in 34 minutes 11 $\frac{1}{5}$ seconds. He was in second place for the speed contest; he led all others in accuracy of landing and quick getaway; he was the high scorer in a bombing competition, for which a mock battleship was set up in front of the grandstand with the funnels serving as bull's-eyes. He capped these exploits by paying his respects to the government in Washington, nonchalantly landing his Farman and then taking off from West Executive Avenue, a narrow thoroughfare between the White House and the State, War and Navy Building. He was equally at home on a Farman or a Blériot, so much so that a more adroit flyer could hardly have been found to head the British challengers.

Second and third places, respectively, on the team were allotted to Alec Ogilvie, manager of the Wright company in England, and James Radley, a fresh-faced twenty-three-year-old who flew a Blériot for sport. With the smallest contingent at Belmont, the British could afford only one reserve—William E. McArdle, another Blériot pilot, who had been born at Cawnpore, India, on 24 January 1875 and was the holder of French license No. 72, obtained at Pau on 19 April 1910. All three had participated in a record-making tourney held at Lanark in Scotland from 6 to 13 August. Tall, well-built, even-tempered, Ogilvie had been issued license No. 7 by the Royal Aero Club at Camber Sands near Rye on 24 May 1910, flying a standard Model A Wright built under franchise by the Short brothers at their Eastchurch factory and proving grounds on the Isle of Sheppey, Kent. The firm had been authorized in 1909 to manufacture six machines of this type, the first of which, made for Charles S. Rolls, the automobile pioneer, flew in October of that year. These British copies of the familiar American biplane were fitted with wheels as well as skids; powered by a 36-horsepower Wright engine they were regarded as a robust, popular, and successful product. Ogilvie (who was later credited with having invented the first air speed indicator) was soon master of the machine. As one of a dozen fliers at Lanark, in the rolling hills near Glasgow, he gave a smooth if unspectacular performance, demonstrating the practical qualities of the biplane in a variety of events. The appearance at Belmont of this cousin from overseas—known as the Model C—was treated with no little interest and respect by domestic Wright flyers.

Radley had practiced assiduously with a Blériot at the Brooklands motor racing track near Weybridge, which a wealthy couple named Locke-King had given to the nation in 1907; the possibilities of the site for aerial experimentation were beginning to be realized. On 14 June 1910, he qualified for British pilot's license No. 12. Later in the month, though an early version of the Dunne biplane was generally believed to have been the first aircraft to get off the ground in that region, Radley made the first public flights in Scotland. After gaining experience at several English meets, he set up the first world's record over a 1-mile and 1-kilometer straight course at Lanark on 13 August, registering 77.67 miles per hour over 1 kilometer, 75.95 miles per hour for the flying mile, and 58.32 miles per hour over five laps of a 1.75-mile course. For some reason, Radley seemed able to extract more miles per hour from his monoplane than was usual in the case of 50-horsepower Blériots, which undoubtedly contributed to the decision to name him as Britain's third representative in the Gordon Bennett. On 25 October at Belmont he won the cross-country race—a venturesome trip of 20 miles to a tethered balloon and back—confirming British expectations he would do well in the cup contest.

Charles Rolls could well have been another member of the British team for the Gordon Bennett had he lived another three months.

Founder of the Royal Aero Club, Rolls had taken the second license to be issued by the club and was the outstanding Wright pilot in England. Tragically he lost his life on 12 July during the Bournemouth meet, the first British victim of a crash.

The make-up of the American team had been left almost to the last minute, and the question of who was to represent the United States would not be fully answered until the morning of the race itself. Organizers of the Belmont meet had set aside Wednesday, 26 October, as the date on which the best of the nation's aviators would compete for a place on the defending team, and the event was expected to draw a large crowd instead of what otherwise might have been a slack middle of the week attendance. But no one had reckoned with the weather. All that day a brisk wind blew out of the northwest, whipping a dark blue flag standing straight and stiff from its pole at the judges' stand: Flight Impossible. As the hours passed, people vainly brandished pennants emblazoned with a Wright biplane on a crimson background, while a brass band from the Seventh Regiment Armory offered distraction with operatic airs; field glasses for rent found few customers. By the time the wind started to die down and flying could be resumed, it was too late. Not enough daylight remained. The disappointed throng heard over a megaphone (the loudspeaker had yet to be invented) that the elimination trials had been cancelled.

With time rapidly running out—the rules required that a team be named at least thirty-six hours before the race—the governors of the Aero Club of America met behind closed doors to assess the situation. In a debate that lasted until the early hours of 29 October, the club arbitrarily picked its team on the basis of past performance and reputation. Among the pilots at Belmont who, presumably, might have been contenders in the trails were such stars from the Wright constellation as Walter Brookins, Ralph Johnstone, Arch Hoxsey, J. Clifford Turpin, and Phil O. Parmelee; a rival Curtiss contingent that included J. A. D. McCurdy, Eugene Ely, J. C. Mars, Charles F. Willard, and Clifford B. Harmon; John B. Moisant and J. Armstrong Drexel, flying Blériots; Charles K. Hamilton with a Hamiltonian, or modified Curtiss; and

Tod Shriver, Curtiss's mechanic at Rheims, now the pilot of a Howard–Dietz biplane. A sizable segment of the public had taken it for granted that Glenn Curtiss, the fêted winner of the year before, would look to his laurels and attempt to score another triumph. In fact, the Belmont committee had seen fit to print in the program that as the holder of the trophy, Curtiss had been offered the honor of heading any team that might be formed, without having to take part in qualifying trials. Actually, a different story was going the rounds: that the Aero Club had declined to sponsor Curtiss because of his insistence on exhibition flying—a practice disapproved of by the club but dictated by its advertising value if not by financial necessity. Whatever the case, Curtiss—his 1909 biplane already outmoded as a racing model—seems to have had no intention of competing against the fast new machines developed abroad. Returning from a summer visit to Europe, he gave a sarcastic answer to queries from the press: "I don't call it sport to send a man up to make a monkey of himself."

Nevertheless, in apparent lip service to the trend toward monoplane construction, Curtiss had brought to Belmont a single-wing machine with what may have been a vague hope that someone could be found to fly it in the Gordon Bennett. It was one of the few pusher monoplanes ever constructed. With a wing span of 26 feet 3 inches and a length of 25 feet, it displayed unmistakable Curtiss characteristics, such as a forward elevator, an exposed pilot's seat, and tricycle undergear; the addition of a short supportive airfoil above the center of the wing was a novelty. Powered by a Curtiss V–8 engine of 51.2 horsepower, it weighed 600 pounds empty. It had been built for Charles F. Willard, the first Curtiss exhibition flier, but so flimsy was it in appearance that Willard refused to take a chance as pilot; nor would anyone else. Eugene Ely, who would shortly become the first to take off from a battleship, posed at the controls for photographs. With the reported exception of a few short hops, however, there is no record of the machine ever having made a flight.

The airplane thought most likely to retain the international trophy for America was a small, compact biplane built by the Wrights known

Orville Wright about to make a test flight in the Baby Wright. Courtesy National Air and Space Museum.

as the Baby Grand. The company that year had begun production of its Model B, or "headless" Wright, without a frontal elevator and with a four-wheeled undercarriage—an important advance that did away with the need for a derrick, what was jokingly referred to as the guillotine launching effect. The rudder was enclosed in a frame of four longitudinal spars joined at the tail by tall uprights and short horizontals, while two triangular blinkers were added to the forward skids to increase the keel area. It was placed in the top rank of all flying machines by the *Scientific American* not only for its "exceptional climbing ability" but for its "excellence of construction and ease of manipulation." A variant of this model was the single-seater Roadster or Baby Wright, a smaller version of which was baptized the Baby Grand. Built of ash and spruce, the wings covered with bleached cotton, the Baby Grand had a span of only 19 feet 6 inches (6.53 m) and a wing area of 145 square feet (13.47

Walter R. Brookins, chief pilot of the Wright brothers. Courtesy National Air and Space Museum.

m^2). Just 6 feet 10 inches in height, it was hardly more than a framework for its large specially manufactured Wright V–8 engine, composed of two standard four-cylinder units and variously rated at 50 or 60 horsepower. Takeoff weight was 860 pounds (390 k). The propeller was of yellow pine. The Baby Grand had been flown by Orville Wright at better than 70 miles per hour and was considered to be far faster than any craft conceivably to be encountered in the Gordon Bennett contest.

The flier entrusted by the Wrights with this potential paragon of speed was their senior pilot, twenty-two-year-old Walter Richard Brookins, a native of Dayton who since the age of four had been a particular pet of Orville's. Slight, dark-eyed "Brookie" had been taught at school by the Wrights' sister Katherine and had been promised a plane of his own when he was old enough. He was one of the elite group whom the Wrights trained to be exhibition fliers and had the distinction of being the first to whom Orville gave lessons. In the winter of 1910 Brookins accompanied Orville to a field near Montgomery, Alabama (now Maxwell Field), where the climate was more conducive to flying than at the Wrights' Huffman Prairie, outside of Dayton. He was an apt pupil, soloing after two and a half hours of instruction and becoming an instructor himself when Orville went home. That summer Brookins took part in exhibitions at Indianapolis and Chicago, making a specialty of high flying; at the former city on 14 June he set a world altitude mark of 4,380 feet. Brookins had a few other tricks up his sleeve. On 7 July Wilbur Wright wrote to Charlie Rolls about Brookins's "record of a complete circle in $6\frac{2}{5}$ seconds . . . I do not expect to be beaten soon. It was the most hairlifting performance I have ever seen. The circle was not over a hundred feet in diameter, measured at the middle of the machine, and about eighty-five at the inside edge. The centrifugal force was nearly double the weight of the machine, and the strain of the machine was about two and a half times the normal strain. It was a beautifully executed feat, but the strains are too great to make such things safe for everyday work." At Atlantic City, New Jersey, a few weeks later, before an estimated crowd of 150,000, Brookins raised the world altitude record to 6,259 feet. On 30 September he made a notable flight of 187 miles from Chicago to Springfield, Illinois, with two stops; on one of them, after coming down in a cornfield, he had to persuade the farmer to cut a wide strip of his crop so the plane could take off again. At Squantum he won the altitude contest at 4,732 feet. Brookins qualified for the Aero Club's license No. 19 on 18 October, barely eleven days before the Gordon Bennett. He had no experience in speed contests, but the brand-new, much-touted machine he was to fly— even though it had not yet been fully tested—made him a natural choice as the chief American representative.

Second place went to a flier with a very different background from Bookins. J. Armstrong Drexel was an aristocratic Philadelphia expatriate with a well-cultivated moustache who made his home in Cavendish Square in London. Member of a distinguished banking family that at one time was allied financially to J. Pierpont Morgan in New York, he was a great-grandson of Francis M. Drexel, an Austrian portrait painter who emigrated to the United States and in 1838 founded the firm of Drexel & Co. in Philadelphia. A society favorite, Drexel had started flying a Blériot at Pau early in 1910 as a pupil of Grahame-White, who had himself received a license at Issy only weeks before. Air-minded sportsmen from England naturally gravitated toward Grahame-White as their instructor and when he moved his rudimentary school to Beaulieu in the New Forest district of Hampshire, Drexel continued his lessons there. He was awarded certificate No. 14 of the Royal Aero Club on 21 June, later gaining American license No. 8. In cooperation with McArdle, also a pupil of Grahame-White, he then financed his own flying school, earning at Beaulieu recognition as a skilled and careful pilot.

Drexel took part in the meeting at Bournemouth in July where the featured event, won by Léon Morane of France in 25 minutes $12\frac{2}{5}$ seconds, was an oversea race of twenty-one miles across the Solent, around the lighthouse at the Needles—a white rock formation jutting out at the western tip of the Isle of Wight—and return. Drexel completed the course in 25 minutes 28 seconds. He next joined the gathering at Lanark, where on 11 August he broke Brookins's altitude record by ris-

74

ing to 6,605 feet. To fly higher than anyone else was still a cherished goal of aviators, one most likely to impress their friends. On 24 October, the third day of the Belmont Park meeting, Drexel established a new American record of 7,185 feet—"more than a mile and a third in the air!" as an enraptured journalist exclaimed. Though he had less than ten months experience with his Blériot, such credentials could not be ignored. His style of flying was outstanding; besides, a monoplane like the Blériot was certain to make a good showing.

It must have been a perplexing task to choose the third member of the team, as well as the three alternates, with past performance and reputation as the main guidelines, for the papers in 1910 were filled with the exploits of aspiring American aviators. But few would have disputed the qualifications of Charles Keeney Hamilton, a swashbuckling, red-haired exhibition flier who on 13 June had become a national hero by flying from New York to Philadelphia and back on the same day. Hamilton had left Governor's Island in New York harbor at 7:43 A.M. using the same biplane with which Curtiss had won at Rheims, and, escorted by a special train, had covered the 86 miles to Philadelphia in 1 hour 43 minutes, landing on an empty lot at Front Street and Erie Avenue. As a precaution against falling into the water he wore three bicycle inner tubes. After lunch he had flown back, stopping only to change spark plugs at South Amboy, New Jersey, where he damaged his propeller; a telephone call to New York brought him a new one by automobile, enabling him to complete the round trip—a total distance of 149.54 miles—in 3 hours 27 minutes flying time. He thus won a prize of 10,000 dollars offered by the *New York Times* and the *Philadelphia Ledger*, taking over the headlines from Glenn Curtiss, who in a flight from Albany to New York two weeks earlier, had gained the *Scientific American* trophy for the third time.

Hamilton had begun his aerial career as a boy by jumping out the window with an umbrella. At the age of eighteen he left home to become a parachutist at county fairs and carnivals, leaping from a hot-air balloon with five chutes and discarding one after another until the last brought him to the ground. After experimenting with gliders, he

75

turned to dirigibles in 1906 and was for a time associated with the lighter-than-air pioneer Roy Knabenshue; in 1909 he took a dirigible to Japan for a series of exhibitions. Inspired by Blériot's Channel feat and the events at Rheims, he made his way to Hammondsport that fall to see if Curtiss would teach him to fly; in the absence of the latter one day, so the story goes, he appropriated a plane and managed a flight without a word of instruction. At first angered by this escapade, Curtiss was so impressed that he took Hamilton on as a pupil and engaged him to give exhibitions. Daredevil antics in the air, such as high glides, aerial dives, and, at Nashville, Tennessee, night flights, soon made him famous. A confirmed fatalist, Hamilton was reported to have said at Belmont, after watching the spectators' reaction to Frisbie's fall on 24 October, "I really believe that this game has gotten to the stage where they are disappointed if someone isn't injured or killed. We shall all be killed if we stay in this business," he added. He had obtained his license, the Aero Club's No. 12, on 26 August.

A tubercular cigarette fiend, twenty-five-year-old Hamilton had arrived at Belmont, according to one account, "limping, scarred and speaking with an impediment" because of an injury to his jaw incurred in an accident at Sacramento during the California state fair. He had brought with him a biplane—the Hamiltonian—copied directly from the product of Curtiss, with whom he had had a falling-out over money. It was powered by a monster 110-horsepower engine designed by the motorcar engineer Walter Christie, and Hamilton made fast time with it in a test on 24 October; wary of the tight turns around some of the pylons, he did not use full power. On the twenty-sixth, however, after the elimination trials were cancelled, Hamilton waited until dusk and then, said the *Scientific American*'s correspondent, "rushed around the track in a way that left no doubt of his chances for the Gordon Bennett trophy." That display probably clinched his nomination as the third member of the team. After all, if a Curtiss machine had won at Rheims, why shouldn't a late derivative of that model do equally well in the United States?

There remained the question of alternates, or reserves. First to be selected was James C. ("Bud") Mars, another early pilot trained by Curtiss. Adventurous, cool-headed, and reliable, he accompanied or followed the leader on tours throughout the country, helping to bring the name of the company before countless thousands of spectators and, at San Francisco, teaching the future stuntman Lincoln Beachey how to fly. Mars had come to Hammondsport in 1909 after being associated for several years with Capt. Thomas S. Baldwin, from whom he learned about balloons and parachutes and whom he had assisted in dirigible construction in 1903. He had made his first balloon ascent and parachute leap at Baldwin Park, Quincy, Illinois, on the Fourth of July 1892, a few months after his sixteenth birthday.

Born at Grand Haven, Michigan, on 8 March 1876, the son of Capt. Thomas D. McBride, a ship's master in the Great Lakes service, he adopted the name Mars when he joined a circus at the age of fifteen and became an acrobat. Proving that he had a head for heights, Mars moved up to the high trapeze, then replaced a high diver who had been killed in a 100-foot plunge into a five-foot tank. He had the change in name made legal by court order a few years later. From 1901 to 1902 he carried out a world tour featuring balloon and parachute exhibitions in Hawaii, China, Japan, Sumatra, Siam, and India—an itinerary he would repeat after the Belmont meeting, using a Curtiss biplane in his demonstrations. On 26 August 1910—the same date on which Hamilton received his—Mars was granted pilot's license No. 11. Two days later he found his picture in the papers when the United Press reported from New York that he had "leaped from his falling aeroplane at a height of 300 yards into the sea near Sandy Hook" after his motor failed. Ascending near the Atlantic Yacht Club at Sheepshead Bay and flying across Coney Island, he had been driven out over the ocean by the wind. "Mars was swimming slowly when rescued," said the report. "He had sustained no injuries."

Mars made more headlines on 1 October with another "miraculous" escape, this time at Helena, Montana. Trying for a prize offered by

77

John Ringling, the circus impresario, for a flight across the main range of the Rocky Mountains, he essayed a glide from 7,500 feet when, again, his motor stopped. His machine struck the side of a mountain, but, as so often was the case when airplanes were made of wood and canvas, the pilot survived without a scratch. As if nothing had happened, Mars left that night to fill an engagement at Spokane, Washington, before joining the Curtiss camp at Belmont Park.

A notable achievement that brought him international acclaim undoubtedly played a part in the choice of John B. Moisant as second alternate. On 17 August he had become the first aviator to cross the English Channel with a passenger and the first to complete a journey from Paris to London by air. Still in the limelight, Moisant found that his picture adorned the pages of the press everywhere, as did those of his mechanic Albert Fileux and their highly publicized mascot, a zebra-striped kitten named Mademoiselle Paree. From an unknown amateur, Moisant had, like Grahame-White, "in a bound" become one of the best-known airmen. He was regarded as a bold, exceptionally gifted flier who promised to more than hold his own against any competition.

John B. Moisant—nobody knew what the "B" stood for—was a short, alert man with a round, nearly bald head, a tanned, clean-shaven face, and scintillating black eyes. He had an ageless look but was thought to be approaching forty at the time of Belmont. He spoke French and Spanish fluently and sported a diamond stickpin as well as a diamond ring. Claiming Chicago as a birthplace, of French-Canadian origin, he was a quixotic figure, a soldier of fortune who had become wealthy through banking and sugar speculation in Central America and an import-export business in New York. An aura of Latin American intrigue floated about him: with his brothers George and Alfred he was reputed to have been involved in several revolutions, something he never took the trouble to deny. When his brothers were jailed for plotting against El Salvador's dictatorial regime, John was said to have twice led seaborne raids from the neighboring Nicaragua of President José Santos Zelaya to free them. One attempt failed when his band after landing was fired upon and dispersed by government forces, another when

78

Moisant's patched-together flotilla was threatened by a U. S. Navy cruiser patrolling the area. Eventually George and Alfred were released and John went to Paris, where in the winter of 1909–10 he took up the challenge of powered flight.

Moisant joined a group of novices who had settled in the Clement–Bayard dirigible hangar at Issy and experimented unsuccessfully with monoplanes of his own design. One, a curved wing concoction painted black, which he called *Le Corbeau* (The Crow), had a perverse tendency to turn turtle. Next was a machine with neither wood nor canvas in its construction—a high-wing model of corrugated aluminum with a fuselage and two horizontal stabilizers, one on each side, of aluminum and steel. It was an idea whose time had not yet come. Finally, he purchased—supposedly for the account of Nicaragua's President Zelaya—a Blériot XI-bis, a fan-tailed two-seater, gave it a tryout, and took his license at Etampes in July. On his third flight Moisant pulled off a grandstand play, swooping down to a landing at Issy with Roland Garros as passenger a few minutes before the starting gun of the Circuit de l'Est. After that, he was ready to fly to London in pursuit of a *Daily Mail* prize of 5,000 pounds for the first flight connecting the two capitals.

The trip was an epic of its kind. Competing with Moisant was Hubert Latham and his Antoinette; both started from Issy on 16 August and flew as far as Amiens without incident; there Latham damaged his undercarriage and dropped out. The following day, despite adverse weather, Moisant and his mechanic crossed the Channel from Calais to Tilmanstone, seven miles from Dover—"one of the most daring feats in the history of aviation," according to the Associated Press. It was all the more astounding because he had learned to fly only a month before and had never been to England; he had nothing but a pocket compass to guide him. That it took the fliers an additional nineteen days of forced landings, repairs, and refueling to reach their destination—three weeks altogether—in no way detracted from the applause.

Third place as alternate was allotted to twenty-six-year-old Arch Hoxsey of the Wright exhibition team, who had been taught to fly by Brookins in the spring of 1910. Hoxsey was introduced to aviation by

79

his friend, Roy Knabenshue, at the first air meet in America, held at Dominguez Field near Los Angeles in January of that year. He had been tinkering with machinery in Pasadena since boyhood, having left grammar school to work in a bicycle shop, then in a garage, and for a time as chauffeur to well-to-do families in the area; his knowledge of engines, gentlemanly manners, and good appearance won him friends and patrons, among them Charles Gates, son of multimillionaire John W. Gates. Hoxsey was a quick convert to flying and at the instigation of Knabenshue, who had been hired by the Wrights to organize an exhibition troupe like that of the Curtiss Flyers, he soon gave up his job as mechanic to enter the Wright school at Dayton.

Hoxsey soloed from the field at Kinloch Park, eighteen miles west of St. Louis, Missouri, on 11 June and two days later was making flights over Indianapolis, Indiana. He was a spectacular success from the start. Impulsive, happy-go-lucky, he captured his audience with wild dips and curves, low-level "roller coaster" and "toboggan" rides, and a chilling "Dive of Death"—often to the consternation of the Wrights. At Asbury Park, New Jersey, his steeplechasing over imaginary hurdles caused pandemonium among spectators, who gave him a standing ovation. But similar capers at Detroit brought a reprimand from Wilbur Wright for having "swooped and corkscrewed" all over the place: "I am very much in earnest when I say that I want no stunts and . . . frills." Hoxsey and his inseparable companion Ralph Johnstone, a former trick bicycle rider and vaudeville performer, were masters of the spiral glide and their sensational duels for altitude earned them the nickname of the "Heavenly Twins." Hoxsey was also known as something of a dandy; wearing pince-nez glasses, white flannel trousers, dark blue jacket, and checked cap turned backwards, he was frequently headlined as the Beau Brummel of the air.

On 8 October Hoxsey was in the news with a record nonstop flight from Springfield, Illinois, to the vicinity of St. Louis, where he spent a frustrating hour trying to locate Kinloch Field. But what thrust him into the public eye more than anything else was giving Teddy Roosevelt a ride of 3 minutes 20 seconds on 11 October at the St. Louis Aero

Club meet. PUTS T. R. UP IN AIR read the caption on one of the pictures illustrating the event. CROWD GASPS AS EX-PRESIDENT WAVES: CHEERS HIS SAFE DESCENT. Back from hunting big game in Africa, the former chief executive did not hesitate to accept the invitation to yet another adventure and called the flight the finest experience he had ever had. Hoxsey was granted his license, No. 21, on 18 October, four days before the meet opened at Belmont. There he was one of the stars, vying with Johnstone for altitude and braving winds that kept others on the ground. Two days before the race, he and Johnstone went up in a near-gale that was greater than the speed of their machines. "A howling wester," the AP correspondent described it, "that slammed down the benches on the grandstand, ripped out the canvas screens, and sent such a skirmish line of dust dancing around the track that the lamps had to be lighted outside the hangars for the mechanics to find their way about." It blew the two airmen backward until just before nightfall Hoxsey managed to land in a field near Brentwood, 25 miles away, and Johnstone came down at Holtsville, 55 miles from the aviation grounds. A popular performer and a natural flier, Hoxsey, it was felt, would ably represent America in the Gordon Bennett.

Of the fifteen airmen whose names appeared on the entry list (table 3), the majority were pilots of the Blériot, the rest (with one exception) of the Wright, Curtiss, or Curtiss-type biplane. A diverse and exceptional lot they were, these aspirants to the highest honor in the air— sophisticated sportsman, acrobat, adventurer, garage mechanic, motor-car salesman. All realized that the eyes of three nations were upon them.

New York awaited the second great international speed contest with mounting impatience, conscious as never before of stirring developments in aircraft. In the newspapers, two lighter-than-air sagas were competing for attention with the airplanes at Belmont Park. Walter Wellman's fat cigar-shaped dirigible *America* had lifted off from Atlantic City, New Jersey, bound for Europe on 15 October: seventy-two hours later, disabled and adrift after a voyage of a thousand miles, its crew was rescued by the Royal Mail steamer *Trent*—an operation in which wireless

81

Table 3
1910 • Entry List

Country	Pilot	Machine	Motor
United States	Walter Brookins	Wright biplane	50–60-hp Wright
	J. Armstrong Drexel	Blériot monoplane	50-hp Gnôme
	Charles K. Hamilton	Hamiltonian biplane	110-hp Christie
		alternates	
	James C. Mars	Curtiss biplane	50-hp Curtiss
	John B. Moisant	Blériot monoplane	50-hp Gnôme
	Arch Hoxsey	Wright biplane	35-hp Wright
France	Alfred Leblanc	Blériot monoplane	100-hp Gnôme
	Emile Aubrun	Blériot monoplane	50-hp Gnôme
	Hubert Latham	Antoinette monoplane	100-hp Antoinette
		alternates	
	René Barrier	Blériot monoplane	50-hp Gnôme
	René Simon	Blériot monoplane	50-hp Gnôme
Great Britain	Claude Grahame-White	Blériot monoplane	100-hp Gnôme
	Alec Ogilvie	Wright biplane	36-hp Wright
	James Radley	Blériot monoplane	50-hp Gnôme
		alternate	
	William McArdle	Blériot monoplane	50-hp Gnôme

telegraphy played an unprecedented part. On 17 October the fifth
Gordon Bennett balloon race had begun at St. Louis with ten starters.
Alan R. Hawley and Augustus Post of the Aero Club of America in the
America II had vanished into the Canadian wilderness, leaving the
world in suspense for a week while they made their way out on foot.
Aeronautics had pride of place in the news.

What else, actually, was there to write about? Nothing much to concern the average citizen. The King of Siam was dead. Portugal had
become a republic. Mark Twain had left an estate valued at 600,000
dollars. Not even the advent of Halley's Comet, that once-in-a-lifetime
visitor from outer space, could disturb the even tenor of people's ways.
For America and Americans it was an admirable era, a time of satisfac-

tion with the present, of high hope for the future. Taxes were minimal, trade was brisk.

Saturday, 29 October, dawned crisp and clear, the air deceptively calm. It would be a day long remembered by New Yorkers—a day of disaster, thrills, chagrin, and sustained excitement. At first light, Grahame-White wheeled out his brand new Blériot for a trial. The vessel on which it was shipped had docked with thirty-six hours to spare, and the mechanics, working by night as well as by day, had assembled it and tuned up its gleaming, fourteen-cylinder Gnôme motor just in time. A half-dozen circuits and Grahame-White brought the plane down, well pleased with its performance. As the sun rose in a cloudless sky, Brookins took the Baby Grand up for a three-minute spin. "There's nothing she can't do," was the verdict. "The Blériots aren't in it with her!"

Punctually at 8:30 a smoke bomb proclaimed the race open and all eyes turned toward the hangars where the national flags of France, Great Britain, and the United States were beginning to stir in a cautionary morning breeze. Strict instructions had been issued by J. C. McCoy, chairman of Belmont's Aviation Committee, to field officers acting as observers: "The correctness of the records and the integrity of the meet require from every official that he shall not leave the pylon or station to which he is designated for any cause whatever during the hour of flight, unless relieved." For the Gordon Bennett, the pylons were to be manned not later than 8:00 A.M. and arrangements had been made to relieve the field officers every two or three hours. Telephones connecting with the judges' stand were located in all but three of the pylons. The instructions were elaborated as follows:

> Each officer should have his watch correctly set, whereby the entering of time of a passage may be approximated, and all records uniform.
>
> Two men of the Signal Corps of the Army will be detailed at each pylon—under the direction of the observers—under orders of Major Samuel Reber, U. S. A., of the Aviation Committee.
>
> No one will be allowed on the course or field other than the Field Officers, the Signal Corps men and the Aviation Committee.
>
> Should a machine land at any point near the pylon (note Code 5,

page 31), observers MUST note and record the fact, but not leave the pylon. Service will be rendered from the hangars.

Each machine will carry numbers which should be easily read. The Signal Corps men are equipped with field glasses should they be required.

The duties of the Field Officers should be divided, whereby one should observe and the other to record flights; specifically the duties are as follows:

The observer to call the number of each machine, and the minute of passing the pylon to the recording officer.

To record the number, and moment of passing on the forms provided for that purpose, and if the passage has been outside the pylon, or, if high in the air outside the line it is a "Good" passage and should be so indicated on the form by the letter "G." A "Bad" passage would be made if the machine touched the pylon, or if high in the air passed over or inside the pinnacle of the pylon.

If a "Bad" passage is made (see Rule XI, page 25) the observer must instantaneously say "flag" to the Signal Corps men, who will immediately signal the other Signal Corps man who is stationed beyond with a red flag, to "flag" the aviator to return and make a "good" passage.

Observers should be constantly alert to note the approach and not the retreat of machines; after one has passed your pylon it is "up" to the officials of the next pylon, except where a "bad" passage is made.

All incidents, such as landings, apparent fouls or infringements of the regulations or code, should be noted on your records, together with the time, and whether on the approach or retreating stretch. These may prove most important should any questions arise or protest occur. (Refer to the Code of the Air.)

Taking no chances on a change in the weather, Grahame-White began his bid for the cup at 8:42 A.M. and was followed into the air by his teammate Alec Ogilvie at 9:08. Flying at 150 feet, Grahame-White finished the first of the required twenty circuits in 3 minutes 15 seconds. Rounding "Dead Man's Corner," the fuselage of his Blériot fairly shuddering with its 100-horsepower engine, he was carried by momentum over the grandstand, exactly as the protesting French had foreseen. At 9:20, to a roar from the crowd, Leblanc was off, his Blériot identical in every respect to the Englishman's save for a slightly shorter wing span and a more sharply pitched propeller, made by Régy Frères instead of Chauvière. Like angry hornets, the two yellow-winged monoplanes chased one another around the course, the slower Wright biplane of Ogilvie following overhead. Leblanc flew so low that spectators instinctively ducked as he sped past and at such a pace they could hardly believe he had completed one lap in 2 minutes $45^{63}/_{100}$ seconds. At the end of his fourth lap he was 1 minute 20 seconds ahead of Grahame-White.

The Gordon Bennett race, declared the New York *Herald*, was "a spectacle spectacularly modern, a spectacle as perfectly typical of the young century as ever a chariot-smashing, horse-slaughtering dash around the Colosseum in the most splendid days of Rome." A majority of those who gaped at the spectacle would agree—though to a few there was something blasphemous about the thundering, man-made mechanical contraptions driven through the air at the limit of their speed. "If God had meant us to fly," they said, "He would have given us wings."

On his seventeenth lap, Grahame-White was overtaken by the Frenchman and at that critical moment he was half-blinded by acrid smoke pouring from an overheated motor. It was now touch and go; but he held his course and completed the last three circuits, landing safely 1 hour 1 minute 4.47 seconds after takeoff—his average speed 61.3 miles per hour. When the figures were run up on the scoreboard thunderous applause burst from the stands. Incredible! Faster than a mile a minute! Nearly as fast, in fact, as an automobile—Harry Grant, averaging 65 miles per hour, had just won the Vanderbilt Cup race with the American Locomotive Company's 60-horsepower Alco—and proof indeed that the airplane was catching up.

Meanwhile Ogilvie, on his thirteenth lap, had been brought down by fouled spark plugs. In accordance with the rules a stop of 54 minutes while mechanics worked feverishly on the motor was counted against him. At 10:50 he was off again, methodically grinding out the remaining laps for a total elapsed time of 2 hours 6 minutes 36.6 seconds. His speed averaged 29.4 miles per hour, enough to win him third place in the final results. (If the stop had not been counted he would have averaged 51.8 miles per hour—a remarkable performance for the Wright biplane, fitted with an ordinary 36-horsepower engine).

But the real drama was about to be enacted. Leblanc had been clocked on one lap at 67.5 miles per hour—a world record—and finished the nineteenth lap just 52 minutes $49\frac{3}{5}$ seconds after starting for the electrifying average of 66.6 miles per hour. In the eyes of French fans led by Ambassador Jules Jusserand, who with his wife had come up from Washington to watch, Leblanc seemed all but certain to avenge Blériot's defeat of the preceding year and restore a sense of air supremacy to his nation. Bitter disappointment lay around the corner.

Streaking down the backstretch, with only one lap to go, Leblanc encountered the pilot's nightmare. Suddenly, his motor stopped. Reports would be circulated that the gas line broke or that the mechanics had failed to fill the tank, but the probable cause was that Leblanc himself, trying to save weight, had underestimated the amount of fuel a fourteen-cyclinder Gnôme—the largest aero engine so far built—would require to cover the 100-kilometer course. Tense with excitement, the crowd rose to its feet as the monoplane swerved and crashed head on into a telegraph pole—ironically, one of the hazards its pilot had complained about—knocking an eight-foot section out of the middle and leaving the upper part dangling from the wires. Fortunately for Leblanc, he was thrown clear by the impact, sustaining only minor injuries. Cuts about his right eye were dressed at the field hospital and he was able to limp past a cheering grandstand, jauntily waving his hand. Extra editions that afternoon gave New York a flutter with pictures of the shattered Blériot, its tough, complex motor still intact under the cowling. But buried in the wreckage was France's best chance of bringing back the cup that year.

A freshening wind that sent autumn leaves swirling underfoot now began to rise. Brookins, preparing to start when Leblanc's accident took place, impulsively decided to fly the Baby Grand down the field first to see what had happened and help if he could. Settling into the skimpy seat on the leading edge of the lower wing, grasping the levers on either side, the American entrant abruptly became the focus of attention.

The Baby Wright in flight, main hope of the 1910 American team. Courtesy National Air and Space Museum.

There had hardly been a chance for the public to make the acquaintance of this dark horse, though on one occasion when Brookins had taken the Wright speeder around the track the stands "were delighted to see him lap his rivals repeatedly." Pinned to its unusually designed engine were America's hopes of beating all comers.

Swinging the two chain-driven propellers, mechanics stepped nimbly aside as the blades turned into shining, blurred discs. The white-winged craft darted forward like a startled bird escaping from its cage and quickly reached an altitude of 100 feet. Turning downwind and straightening out smoothly, Brookins all at once was in trouble: without warning, a connecting rod had broken. With a dead motor and the wind at his back adding appreciably to its speed, he tried to set the machine down as gently and lightly as possible. As so frequently happens when an accident occurs, witnesses could not agree on the details of what followed, but it seemed that the Baby Grand's undercarriage was not equal to the shock of an unexpectedly fast landing. The pint-sized biplane tumbled head over tail as it touched down; when the dust settled, there was nothing left but to pick up the pieces. To the amazement of those who saw the crash, Brookins was unhurt: only his heart, as he said afterwards, was broken. And that spoke for countless of his fellow citizens who had confidently looked to the Wright brothers for an airplane that would keep the Gordon Bennett Cup at home. Although no one knew it at the time, it was the beginning of the end of the Wright biplane in competitive aeronautics; others would soon forge far ahead of the pioneer company in construction and design.

One minute to eleven o'clock and the Antoinette was airborne. "Latham now flying for France!" bellowed the announcer through his megaphone. A majestic eagle among lesser fowl, slower than the Blériots and taking wider turns than usual as gusts tore at its wing tips, the magnificent French creation was to steal the show, win or lose, as far as the crowd was concerned. Crouched high on the narrow fuselage, silk scarf streaming from his neck, cigarette holder clamped between his teeth, Latham was every inch the heroic birdman. But the Antoinette's 100-horsepower engine was no more reliable than its predecessor. Altogether, four precious hours were consumed on the ground in adjustments and repairs. It was not Latham's day. Caught by the wind at the end of his fifteenth lap as he rounded a pylon near the clubhouse enclosure, he almost hit the judges' stand. A total of 5 hours 48 minutes 53 seconds was chalked up against him; his average speed came to a meager 17.8 miles per hour.

French supporters waited with growing dismay for Aubrun, or Simon, or Barrier to take up the challenge, unaware of the reason behind their failure to start. To ensure the participation of French airmen in the meet, Belmont's managers had induced them to cross the Atlantic with a cash guarantee that would make it worthwhile to give up other engagements. Apparently, however, that payment was conditional on their not taking part in the Gordon Bennett race itself, for which, it was presumed, another team would be supplied. Whatever the basis for the mix-up or misunderstanding, Aubrun and Simon were notified early in the morning on the day of the race that if they flew in the international event they would not only forfeit the guarantee but be called on to refund advances already made. Neither one was prepared to give up cash in hand for the possible but by no means certain glory of winning the trophy. It was not clear whether Barrier, the second alternate, was included in the deal, but he too was a nonstarter. A frustrating finish for a team already shaken by its captain's unfortunate mishap.

With the Baby Wright eliminated, America's team remained on the sidelines until afternoon, when, it was thought, the wind might abate. On the contrary, conditions grew worse. Drexel delayed his departure until the last moment, while Hamilton wrestled with a cantankerous engine. Mars, the first alternate, had bowed out and was reported to have left for Connecticut to give an exhibition. Not expecting to be called upon, Moisant was leisurely topping off lunch in his hangar with a piece of pie when a message arrived from the Aero Club's president, Cortlandt Field Bishop, that he was to start. Though his 50-horsepower Blériot was no match for Grahame-White's 100-horsepower machine, Moisant was game. He took off in the teeth of the wind and fought a battle that was followed anxiously from the grandstand. On the sixth

89

A Blériot participating in the 1910 race at Belmont Park. Courtesy National Air and Space Museum.

lap he was carried over the heads of spectators massed below, regaining control with difficulty. Nevertheless, despite motor trouble that forced him down more than once, he kept on with dogged determination for the full twenty laps. His average speed, because of these delays, was 31.5 miles per hour, but it was enough to put him in the money.

Drexel had waited too long for the wind to drop; he crossed the starting line only seconds before the final gun was fired at 3:32 P.M. As everyone could see, it was hard going. The eighth time around, plagued by boisterous gusts and a faltering engine, he was compelled to give up. By the time Hamilton got away, the deadline had passed and he was flagged down disqualified. So, too, was Radley of the British team, who started a fraction over 35 seconds too late.

Nobody had come near beating Grahame-White's record, as the final score showed (table 4). Great Britain had taken first and third place, the United States second and France fourth.

90

Table 4
1910 • Results

Place	Pilot	Country	Machine	Motor	Speed
1	Grahame-White	Great Britain	Blériot monoplane	100–hp Gnôme	61.3 m/hr
2	Moisant	United States	Blériot monoplane	50–hp Gnôme	31.5 m/hr
3	Ogilvie	Great Britain	Wright biplane	36–hp Wright	29.4 m/hr
4	Latham	France	Antoinette monoplane	100–hp Antoinette	17.8 m/hr

It was the first British victory in a flying race and Britons in the crowd showed their joy as the Union Jack was run up and the band played "God Save the King." The next morning's press went overboard in its praise, echoing the admiration of the spectators for the foreign-made machines that had dominated the contest, as well as for the dash and verve of the winner. "In the decades that lie hidden in the future," rhapsodized a *Herald* reporter, "there may be possibilities that may make appear slight and trivial the incidents of yesterday, but to those who are now witnessing the events of aviation pioneering, the day on which the international trophy was won for England by Mr. Claude Grahame-White must be regarded as writing upon the pages of history an advance in science such as never before has been recorded."

America might have lost one cup: nevertheless, it could celebrate the taking of another. The cheers for England had scarcely subsided when Hawley and Post, who had captured the Gordon Bennett Cup for balloons with a record-breaking flight of 1,171.13 miles, arrived in New York with the wilds of Quebec. Rushed from the train to the St. Regis Hotel, they were fêted with a late supper party and impromptu reception. The name of James Gordon Bennett was everywhere linked with what many writers referred to as "the dawn of the aerial age." For a week, people talked of little else.

Grahame-White was acclaimed by New York as if he had won the race for America instead of for his own country. Modest, straightforward, unaffected by fame, the photogenic thirty-one-year-old aviator

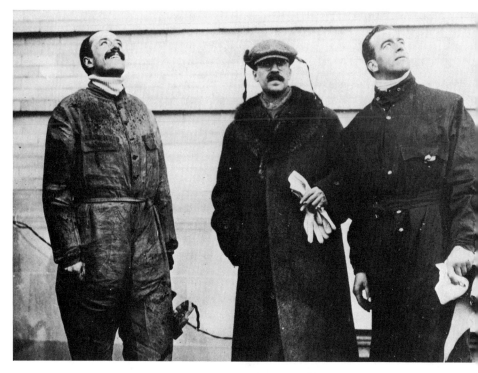

Count Jacques DeLesseps of France (left) and Claude Grahame-White of England (right) with an unidentified friend watching the contestants at Belmont Park. Courtesy National Air and Space Museum.

was besieged by reporters, lionized by society, and showered with passes to the theater by Broadway producers. Even a rumor that he might attend a play resulted in a full house; once inside, he would be invited to make a speech. Gossip columns dwelt on his romance with a showgirl, Pauline Chase, who was appearing as "The Pink Pajama Girl" in *The Liberty Belles*; from the stage of the Knickerbocker Theatre, Charles Frohman, her manager, announced that the two were engaged to be married. Polly sailed with Grahame-White on the *Mauretania* on 30 November to play the part of Peter Pan in London, but their relationship did not last: a year later they had drifted apart.

Back home, his countrymen gave Grahame-White an ovation for his performance, described by *Flight* as "the splendid victory which has assured to the United Kingdom the holding of the world's most important aerial race next year." A dinner and reception was organized by the Royal Aero Club, at which Field Marshall Lord Roberts, the earl of Kandahar, presented the flier with the gold medal of the Aerial League of the British Empire. Britain had at last made up her mind, *Flight* informed its readers, "to forge ahead in the new science of aviation . . . now there is the Gordon Bennett Race to be fought out on a British course. The pick of the world's flying men will come over to compete . . . there is the British title to defend. It may be confidently trusted that . . . there will not only be the men but the machines to ensure all-British victories."

Mixed with the eulogies was regret that in order to win, Grahame-White had used a French machine and a French motor. Though Britain had pilots equally skillful and daring as those of any other land, she lagged behind in construction. Holding the race in England, however, would change all that. The Gordon Bennett could have only a positive effect on development of the native industry. It remained to be seen whether this optimism was to be justified.

Louis Blériot was elated at the performance of his monoplane. Reflecting on the red letter year 1910, he said, prophetically, "The aeroplane as it exists today really stands upon the threshold of the most amazing, sporting and commercial possibilities . . . there is absolutely nothing to prevent flight becoming one of the greatest developments in the world's history . . . the possibilities of the future are just beginning to unfold themselves. We see already . . . that flying is to open a new page."

No one doubted that the next Gordon Bennett would contribute substantially toward that end.

Chapter 4 EASTCHURCH · 1911

England, so long the mistress of the sea,
Where wind and waves confess her sovereignty,
Her ancient triumphs yet on high shall bear,
And reign, the sovereign of the conquered air.

Grahame-White's brilliant victory at Belmont Park had brought the Gordon Bennett Cup to the British Isles, and to a nation joyously celebrating the coronation of a king in 1911 the prophecy in Thomas Gray's poem *Luna Habitabilis* might have seemed on the verge of fulfillment. Britannia indisputably ruled the waves; now the blue ribbon of the air also belonged—at least temporarily—to her. Edward VII, whose name was destined to identify an era, had died the year before; his son George V, with Queen Mary, the former Princess of Teck, had succeeded to the throne on 22 June. What could be a more fitting climax to the festivities than for Great Britain to win the great international speed contest again on 1 July and claim once and for all to be "sovereign of the conquered air"?

The pomp and circumstance of the coronation, with flares and fireworks setting London ablaze at night and the fleet at Spithead illuminated for a review, was still fresh in everybody's mind. Britain was at the zenith of her power and glory, ruling over an empire of more than thirteen million square miles with a combined population of more than four hundred million, on which "the sun never set." Yet the date had ominous overtones, too. The Moroccan crisis had boiled up anew and Count Metternich, Germany's ambassador to the Court of St. James, had chosen 1 July to announce that the gunboat *Panther* had been despatched to the port of Agadir for the protection of German lives and property. More than ever, the threat of war was in the air, for France regarded the move as a direct challenge to her position in that part of the globe. Prime Minister Herbert H. Asquith and his ministry would stoutly support the French, in the spirit of the Entente Cordiale. In a few weeks, the tension would increase as Italy joined the "new imperialism" with an attack on Turkish territories in North Africa, using airplanes for the first time in warfare.

Over in France, uneasiness prevailed about Morocco, but the chatter that season centered on fashionable Deauville, the feat of William Burgess in swimming the Channel in 23 hours, and the stupefying theft of Leonardo da Vinci's Mona Lisa from the Louvre.

The clouds on the political horizon were matched by those over the isolated airfield at Eastchurch on the isle of Sheppey, where the foremost champions of the air would meet in a third encounter to see which nation had the fastest airplane in the world. Even though it was midsummer the British climate was proving uncooperative. The sky was dull and threatening, with a wind that came in puffs and a drenching rainstorm that sent spectators scurrying into the refreshment stands for shelter. From a scheduled 11:30 in the morning, the start had to be postponed until the afternoon. Later in the day the sun would break through—much to the relief of thousands who had made the long journey to the flying field from London.

Several lessons had been learned from the previous races. At Rheims, the backstretch had been so far from the spectators that it was difficult to follow the machines without field glasses. Belmont had demonstrated the folly of a restricted course with tight turns and potentially dangerous obstacles. On the basis of his own experience, Grahame-White had

96

offered some advice in conjunction with a book he had written with Harry Harper: "Owing to the very high speeds which will, without doubt, be attained, a 3-mile course will be imperative. . . . Not only must the aerodome . . . chosen be quite unencumbered by trees but there must be at all points of the course a perfectly smooth landing place should a machine descend owing to engine trouble." Above all, the risks of wind and weather encountered in an autumn meeting would have to be avoided and the racecourse would, of course, have to be accessible to Londoners.

It had been no simple matter for the Royal Aero Club to select a site that met these conditions. The rival airfields of Hendon—frequently used for sporting events—and Brooklands—principally a testing ground for the designer—were obvious possibilities. *The Car Illustrated*, always interested in flying, had favored Portholme Aerodrome in Huntingdonshire, run by James Radley. But the choice finally fell upon Eastchurch, considered by many to be the true nursery of British aviation. The terrain was unobstructed, and a kite-shaped course marked by the usual pylons was laid out, 3.76 miles in length, which competitors would have to cover twenty-five times for a total of 94 miles (150 km). Stepped up from the 62 miles (100 km) of the year before, the increase in distance was fully commensurate with the spectacular advances in aviation since 1910.

Eastchurch had a history as one of the earliest flying centers in Britain. It had its roots in Mussel Manor on Leysdown, Kent, which in February 1909 was converted into a clubhouse with sheds for flying machines. Subsequently the members moved to Eastchurch, where the facilities became primarily a mecca for wealthy amateurs. It was also the home of an infant aircraft industry. There the Short brothers had taken up construction at an early date, becoming agents for the Wrights in 1909, building biplanes and monoplanes to specifications, and producing their own first machine in 1910. There, too, under the stimulus of the Royal Aero Club, the investigation of accidents had originated and a crude form of technical report and study started.

On two occasions in the recent past, Eastchurch had been in the public eye; first on 18 December 1910 as the takeoff point for Thomas Sopwith's winning flight of 169 miles to Thirimont, Belgium, in competition for the Baron De Forest Prize of 4,000 pounds for the greatest distance flown from England into the continent; second, on 2 March 1911 when four British naval officers began a course in flying with Valkyrie monoplanes under the tutelage of George B. Cockburn, Britain's unsuccessful entrant in the first Gordon Bennett. Later in the year it would see the establishment of a naval flying station, where fledgling pilots would live a Spartan existence in the bleak and often wind-swept surroundings.

Whatever its merits, however, Eastchurch was roundly criticized by *The Aeroplane*: "The course was the wrong shape, was in the wrong place and had a shocking surface except along the starting and finishing straight." There was no pretense of a grandstand. Forty-five miles from London in an estuary of the Thames, the field was not easily reached, either by rail or road. Special express trains of the Chatham and Dover Railway took more than two hours to arrive at the scene, and the line had the greatest difficulty in coping with the estimated ten thousand passengers who besieged it for transportation. Another thousand perhaps drove down in their Daimlers, Napiers, Wolseleys, Rolls Royces, or lesser marques in about the same amount of time it took the train. Half a dozen horse-drawn vehicles were counted. Two or three of the more adventurous came by air. Some two hundred glittering motorcars, many equipped with elaborate picnic hampers, were parked at the rear of the various enclosures, furnishing, as one correspondent wrote, "an imposing and splendid background to the keenly enthusiastic crowd."

The gathering did indeed make up in enthusiasm for what it lacked in sheer numbers. Compared to the hundred thousand or more who had been lured by the tournaments at Rheims and Belmont Park, the attendance was relatively small. One of the reasons for this, aside from the problem of transportation, may have been that the novelty of watching an air race had begun to wear off. On the other hand, the turnout was impressive considering the circumstances; it was a national event of the first magnitude, attracting not only dedicated fans of the flying machine but their ladies, prettily decked in summer clothes, who with their escorts occupied half a mile of garden seats along one side of the course. Many of them were moved by the same sporting instincts that drew spectators to a horse race—Ascot, the Derby, or the Grand National. *Pour le sport* any effort was worthwhile; it was not only the latest, most diverting thing to do but a patriotic obligation—to encourage the British defenders in their attempt to retain the cup.

By all standards, the crowd was well positioned to observe the race. Directly in front of the press enclosure was the starting line at the opposite end of which, between the scoring boards and the public announcements, was the judges' box. Across the field stood the hangars in full view of all, while for those willing to make the climb an especially fine panorama of the entire flying area could be obtained from nearby Standford Hill, a natural vantage point. Catering arrangements had been entrusted to the Army and Navy Stores, though in contrast to the *Grande Semaine de la Champagne* and the ample buffets at Belmont, they left much to be desired. "I have seen worse," was the acid comment of C. G. Grey, editor of *The Aeroplane*, "but I cannot recall when."

Conspicuous in the Royal Aero Club's enclosure were well-known pioneers and supporters of aviation such as Louis Blériot and the Seguin brothers, makers of the highly regarded rotary Gnôme engine; among the officials were Mervyn O'Gorman, Roger Wallace, K. C. and Mortimer Singer: under the auspices of the club's secretary, Harold E. Perrin, a committee took over all arrangements, assisted by a corps of stewards, starters, and timekeepers who ensured everything would go off without trouble. Among others from abroad came Cortlandt Field Bishop, representing the Aero Club of America, and Henri Deutsch de la Meurthe of the Aéro Club de France. James Gordon Bennett was not present. He had returned to his villa at sunny Beaulieu on 25 June after a cruise to Ceylon and Indonesia lasting five months and did not elect to extend his travels further for the occasion. Aligned from the start with the proponents of flight, his reputation widespread as a firm advocate of sports, he was content to let the Coupe d'Aviation speak for itself and indulge his interest in aeronautics nearer home. A young native of

Villefranche named Auguste Maicon, buzzing up and down the Mediterranean coast in a small Caudron *hydro-avion*, fascinated Bennett, providing him and his friends with all the aerial entertainment they wished in the picturesque seaside setting.

Although the cash bonus of 5,000 dollars previously awarded to the winner had been halved, this in no way lessened the allure of the cup. The Gordon Bennett was still the most prestigious event of the year in aviation. But for the first time the public was being treated to rival air spectaculars, in which speed was not the only requirement. Daring cross-country races transcending international frontiers filled the front pages of European dailies with graphic, play-by-play accounts of the action. Grueling courses with hundreds of thousands of francs at stake in cash prizes claimed readers' attention: a thousand kilometers from Paris to Madrid, sponsored by *Le Petit Parisien*, and from Paris to Rome, backed by the *Parisien*'s competitor *Le Petit Journal*, in May; a grandiose Circuit of Europe, organized jointly by the *Journal* and the London *Standard* tested the stamina of pilots and the quality of their machines as never before. Popular enthusiasm spurred the fliers on: an estimated 300,000 Parisians watched the predawn start for Madrid, 500,000 saw the airmen off for Rome, 700,000 viewed the beginning of the European Circuit.

No invention had ever made such enormous strides in so short a time. Only three years had elapsed since Wilbur Wright's spectacular demonstrations in the sky above Le Mans; it seemed incredible that after centuries of baffled effort, as editorial writers liked to remind the reading public, "the secret of keeping a machine in the air without help from a balloon had at last been wrested from nature." By comparison, lighter-than-air vehicles were "mere playthings." Man truly found his wings, it was said, in the summer of 1911; along with the German menace and the naval race, aviation was a main topic of conversation.

Anything seemed possible for an airplane provided it had the right pilot; anything was possible for a pilot provided he had the right airplane. The question was whether the goals were not too high for the state of the art, for the toll these contests exacted in needless accidents—

due chiefly to structural failure or inexperience of the pilot—underscored the belief that flying was too dangerous for the average mortal. Fliers of eleven different nationalities—French, British, American, Italian, German, Belgian, Spanish, Russian, Dutch, Hungarian, and Peruvian—had perished in crashes. "I must marry an aviator," macabre humor had a young fräulein say in Germany, "I look so well in black."

No one had yet been killed in the Gordon Bennett, but the contestants shared the homage and praise given to aviators everywhere. Aviators were exalted to the skies, as it were, in prose and poetry because of the risks they ran. Grandiloquently paying tribute to the airmen of France, "the country of sad-eyed mothers" whose "martyred sons were the noblest of heroes," a widely circulated ode by Edmond Rostand glorified "those who had to die for those about to be born." As danger was reputed to increase with speed, the possibility of a crash was ever present.

When the curtain went up on the morning of 1 July, a new cast of characters—with four exceptions—was on the program. As in the first race at Rheims, America was represented by a single entry; but Great Britain and France had again nominated three fliers each, with three reserves. Ogilvie and Radley of the British team, Leblanc and Aubrun of the French, were veterans of Belmont; the others were fast-rising stars in the aviation firmament, bringing added luster to the cup race overnight. And as the earlier record holders in altitude, distance, and duration had yielded to newcomers, so were the first airplanes being superceded by more efficient, more reliable machines.

Thus, Henry Farman was not heard from for the first time since aviation began in Europe, though his biplane was still a best seller among those learning to fly. The Blériot and the Wright would be inscribed for the last time in a Gordon Bennett race. The Voisin and the Antoinette were becoming obsolete, edged out by an array of new monoplanes like the Morane–Saulnier, the Deperdussin, the R.E.P., the Hanriot, and the Nieuport. Moisant and Hoxsey had been killed; Brookins, Mars and Hamilton were exhibition flying; Grahame-White was busy developing Hendon. Latham was out of the running, absorbed in experiments with an Antoinette aerodynamically far ahead of its time. If successful, it might have outsped any challenger: a monoplane fully encased in alumi-num cloth, its landing gear of ten wheels enclosed in "pants." The pilot entered from below, and the mechanic could move about the motor dur-ing flight. (Its 100-horsepower Antoinette motor was inadequate for the machine's weight of 1,870 pounds empty.)

Britain's best bet to win, it was agreed, was young Gustav Hamel, born at London on 25 June 1889, the son of a naturalized German doctor. Quiet-spoken, modest, with dark curly hair, educated at Westminster and Cambridge, Hamel had begun a meteoric career as an aviator when he was twenty-one. Hamel's one idea was to fly and to fly continuously; in this he showed astonishing aptitude and soon developed such exceptional skill that within a month of taking his pilot's license at Hendon on a Blériot he won the inaugural race between Hendon and Brooklands, his first cross-country venture. One of the first British pilots of the French machine, Hamel obtained his license, No. 64, on 14 February 1911; earlier, on 3 February, he had taken French license No. 358 as well. It was not long before he replaced Paul Prier as chief instructor at the Blériot school that the Frenchman had come over to England to open at Hendon in 1910. (Prier made the first nonstop flight from London to Paris on 12 April 1911.)

Hamel's name had been frequently in the news; in the spring of 1911 he was prominently reported for having flown over the Oxford–Cambridge boat race at Henley in the company of Prier and C. S. Greswell on other Blériots, Grahame-White and Charles Hubert on Farmans, and another dashing young adept, Douglas Graham-Gilmour, on a Bristol biplane. While the crowds were vastly entertained by their display of low-level flying, race officials were not amused—particularly when Graham-Gilmour repeatedly zoomed over the crews, cutting his engine and gliding down again until forced to land on a nearby cricket field for lack of fuel. In May, Hamel had participated in a noteworthy flying exhibition arranged at Hendon for the Parliamentary Aerial Defense Committee. He was also the winner of a race from Brooklands to Brighton, which again brought him to the attention of the public. Thereafter he crossed the Channel and entered the Circuit of Europe,

Gustav Hamel, Great Britain's hope to win the 1911 Gordon Bennett, who crashed on the first lap. Courtesy National Air and Space Museum.

from which, however, he was forced to retire because of mechanical trouble shortly after the start. His place in history, aside from serving as Britain's main entry in that year's Gordon Bennett, would be assured by subsequent exploits for which his popularity would almost equal that of Grahame-White.

Unfortunately, from the British point of view, few domestic manufacturers equalled their French counterparts in developing machines that could qualify as entrants in the blue ribbon Gordon Bennett. One could hardly make a comparison. Colonel Samuel F. Cody from Texas, newly naturalized as an Englishman, was attracting notice with his *Flying Cathedral*, a cumbersome biplane of his own design and construction; the Bristol biplane, inaccurately called the Boxkite, was a commercial success and the company's monoplane was well regarded. The Short brothers were introducing an innovative, twin-engined biplane. But these were all too slow when speeds already attained on the continent were taken into account. "We are lagging behind France in a deplorable and utterly inexcusable manner. Why?" remonstrated *The Aero*. The answer, said the magazine, was because there were no great patrons of the art like Archdeacon and de la Meurthe to offer prizes, because of a lack of money in the industry, because of an unprogressive War Office and Admiralty, and so on. A handful of experimenters were moving away from slavish imitations of other machines and striking out on original lines: Robert Blackburn, inspired by the Antoinette; L. Howard-Flanders, a pioneer not yet in production; the firm of Martin and Handasyde, also influenced by the Antoinette's success. These were beginning to show promise, but progress was painfully slow. Even Grahame-White had turned impatiently to a foreign firm, the Burgess Company of Marblehead, Massachusetts, to build him a Baby Grahame-White pusher biplane, incorporating features of the Farman and Curtiss, of which he made effective use.

In this situation it was no surprise that Hamel should turn to France for a machine that would bring him victory. The Blériot he had chosen was a specially designed racing model that the company had begun to market in response to the demand for ever-faster craft. First tested by

Alec Ogilvie, pilot of the British Wright biplane in both the Belmont Park and Eastchurch races. Courtesy Science Museum, London.

the practiced Blériot pilot Léon Morane at Rheims, where it attained record speeds for 5, 10, and 20 kilometers, Type XXIII had a slim, tapering, fabric-covered fuselage, a wing area of not much more than 100 square feet, and a flaring tail. It was 24 feet 8 inches in length and its normal wing span of 29 feet 4 inches was greatly reduced for the Gordon Bennett. With a 70-horsepower Gnôme motor it was believed capable of 120 kilometers per hour, but in light of the competition it would face, even this, might not be enough to keep the cup in England. In preparation for the race a fourteen-cylinder Gnôme of 100 horse-power weighing 220 pounds was installed, and to obtain more speed Blériot himself clipped an additional eighteen inches from each wing tip—a highly dubious procedure because it cut off part of the warping mechanism and so was certain to sacrifice some stability, control, and

105

lift. It gave the monoplane a spindly appearance, making it look, in the words of *The Aeroplane*'s caustic editor, "more like the latter half of a dogfish with a couple of visiting cards stuck on it than anything else."

Second place on the British team was allotted to Alec Ogilvie, whose experience in placing third at Belmont Park was counted a strong factor in his favor. He had followed up this accomplishment on 28 December 1910 by remaining in the air 3 hours 55 minutes at Camber, near Rye, while competing for the Michelin distance cup. With Ogilvie at the controls the Wright biplane had always been a dependable performer. For the 1911 Gordon Bennett his machine had been fitted with a 50-horsepower water-cooled motor manufactured by the New Engine Company of London, makers of the N.E.C. motorcar. It had been planned to use a new V–4 two-stroke engine, but owing to a mishap incurred by Ogilvie a few days before the race, in which the shaft was damaged, a more conventional four-stroke V–8 unit was substituted. The Wright machine was not noted for speed; but on the principle of the tortoise and the hare it was thought to have a chance in the event an accident befell the faster machines—a not unreasonable premise, given the uncertainties of the day.

The third British entrant was Graham-Gilmour. Born at Dartford in Kent on 7 March 1885, he had commenced his training in December 1909 at Pau on a Blériot powered by a J.A.P. air-cooled engine. On 19 April 1910 he received the French Aéro Club's license No. 75. He took part in the meetings at Lanark and Wolverhampton, specializing in cross-country events, then made Brooklands his base with a Gnôme-powered Blériot; using a two-seater machine of the same type he there engaged in passenger carrying. On 13 September 1910 Gilmour was in the news with a 45-mile flight from Brooklands to Hampton Court. His natural talent as a flier brought him into contact with the Bristol and Colonial Aeroplane Company, which had been formed in 1910 and manufactured to their own designs a wide range of flying machines, using Salisbury Plain at Brooklands as a testing ground. In February 1911 Graham-Gilmour joined the firm as pilot. Noted as an audacious, if not brash, pilot, he was soon in trouble with the authorities for flying over London; the case was dismissed, but his antics over the Henley regatta resulted in his certificate being suspended, with subsequent litigation. He won second prize in the Brooklands–Brighton race in May and was then assigned to pilot the latest Bristol product in the Gordon Bennett—an 80-horsepower Gnôme-equipped monoplane whose box section fuselage was convex on the bottom to minimize resistance. Mounted on two wheels and two skids, with two smaller wheels attached at the forward end, it was sturdily built and potentially capable of more than 70 miles per hour. It was, in fact, the only British craft then in existence that seemed likely to stand up against the competition from abroad.

A second Bristol, with a 70-horsepower motor, was to round out British representation. At the controls was Oscar C. Morison, who had won a race between two Bristol Boxkites on 13 May. He had obtained license No. 46 with a Blériot at Brooklands on 17 January 1911 and later became a Morane pilot. Morison was listed as the first of the British reserves. The second alternate was Radley, with his Blériot and its reliable 70-horsepower Gnôme. The third was James ("Jimmie") Valentine, licensed No. 47 on the same day as Morison with a biplane built by Robert Macfie. Valentine had since acquired one of the fast, slim-bodied Deperdussins beginning to make a name for themselves in France, and perhaps for that reason he was considered a good choice by the Royal Aero Club.

Although satisfaction was voiced that England had produced enough pilots qualified to compete in the world's premier speed contest, sharp comments were made about their equipment. "One would have thought," exclaimed one of the more vocal critics, "that the moment had come when an effort should have been made to select a team in which not only the pilots but the machines and motors should all be British." Instead, Hamel and Radley were flying French Blériots, Ogilvie's Wright had originated in America, Valentine was using a new French plane; five of the six machines listed for the team were powered by Gnôme, not British, motors. However desirable it may have been that the race should pit the products of one country against those of another—

Alfred Leblanc, chief pilot for the Blériot company and caption of the French team in the 1910 and 1911 races. Courtesy National Air and Space Museum.

not merely the skills of individual aviators—it was an accurate reflection of the state of affairs that Britain's defense of the cup would rest mainly on foreign airplanes and engines.

"Whoever will be master of the sky will be master of the world," the pioneer experimenter Clément Ader had said. More determined than ever to give effect to the first part of that prediction, the French were again led by Alfred Leblanc, intent on making up for the mishap that had cost France the cup at Belmont in 1910. The intervening months had done nothing to diminish the reputation of this veteran: forty-two years of age, he was considered the most sagacious and experienced of Blériot professionals. Leblanc had been supplied with a Model XXIII identical to that of Hamel, including its 100-horsepower Gnôme motor; as in the case of Hamel's machine, Blériot had personally reduced the wing span by sawing off half a meter from the main spars at either end. Although the machine responded well in tests before the race, the altered balance stemming from abbreviated, square-cut wings and the installation of a heavy new motor made for a potentially dangerous situation. Two truncated Blériots, evenly matched with speed the only consideration—one flying for France, the other for England—suggested a duel like Leblanc's effort to beat Grahame-White at Belmont Park. The public expected a thrilling contest. The experts anticipated tremendous speed—or else a serious accident.

The French team, chosen on the basis of speed tests conducted at different airfields during June, could not have been stronger. Leblanc was backed by two pilots from the Nieuport school, each flying one of the latest and most original aircraft to come out of the skies of continental Europe. A small, compact monoplane, it was the brainchild of Edouard Nieuport (originally the name was de Nieport), engineer, sportsman, constructor, a man of intellect and of action, a likable person with a sense of humor, whose black moustache sported a twist at each end and who affected white turtleneck sweaters worn beneath his flying togs. Nieuport had pioneered the concept of a fully covered fuselage that left only the head of the pilot exposed; the pilot entered the cockpit by a small door under the left wing. In designing his airplane Nieuport had shown an early grasp of streamlining. In addition, he had discovered and incorporated in the wing an important principle of aerodynamics: the flatter the camber (curvature) the greater the speed. Powered by a modest 20-horsepower Darracq motor, the machine had attained a speed of 72 kilometers per hour (45 m/hr), drawing favorable comment.

The son of a colonel in the French army, Nieuport was born at Blida in Northern Algeria on 24 August 1875 and in accordance with the wishes of his father prepared for the examinations of the Ecole Polytechnique at Paris. At the Ecole Supérieure d'Electricité in that city he was regarded as one of the best pupils, endowed with unusual intelligence. But to the scandalized surprise of his friends, and in the face of strong parental disapproval, he suddenly abandoned his studies to take up bicycle racing. There was method in his seeming madness, however, Nieuport had become intrigued by aerodynamics and the problems of mechanical propulsion, to which the bicycle served as a useful introduction. His choice was the British Rudge–Whitworth, whose thin, extended frame seemed to offer less resistance to forward motion. He won a dozen races in 1895 at the Paris Vélodrome d'Hiver; in 1897 he won the Zimmerman Prize for riding tandem 1 kilometer and in 1898 finished third in the championship of France.

In 1902, bemused by ignition difficulties encountered with the early internal combustion engine, Nieuport invented an accumulator, a spark plug, and a magneto—all of which, bearing his name, were part of the first automobile to attain a speed of 200 kilometers per hour (a Darracq) and of the power plants used by Santos-Dumont and Henry Farman in their early flights. Nieuport was at first a pessimist about the practical aspects of flying. In November of the same year, commenting on the glider experiments of Ferdinand Ferber, he published an article on aerial navigation in the magazine *La Locomotion*: "This will become a game and a sport, nothing more. . . . We shall never see the sky traversed by air machines or frontiers abolished by the high-flying vehicles described by poets . . . or as forecast by inventors. The laws of gravity, above all of geometry, which will never be altered . . . will forever be opposed."

Four years later, in 1908, Nieuport would give the lie to his own words by building a monoplane that flew briefly at Issy-les-Moulineaux on its first trial, an unheard of accomplishment at the time. He went on to experiment with various models of his own creation, qualifying for a license, No. 105, with one of them on 10 June 1910. To the second Rheims meeting, from 4 to 10 July, he brought three machines, choosing as his teammates two erstwhile Voisin pilots: Albert Niel, who had received a license the same day as Nieuport, and Maurice Noguès, a captain in the French army, certified eleven days later. (Nieuport himself had been flying a Voisin on 18 April when it caught fire in the air, but he had escaped injury.) Rated by most observers as the best competing aircraft, the Nieuport was next seen at a meeting at Maubeuge in Sep-

The Nieuport monoplane, supreme in all contests for speed in 1911, including the Gordon Bennett race at Eastchurch. It took top honors in the French military trials as well. Courtesy Musée de l'Air.

tember, where its designer gained further experience and sought to perfect his ideas. It was enough for him to proceed with the establishment of a factory on the banks of the Seine at Suresnes in suburban Paris, where he was assisted during 1911 by the up-and-coming young designer Alfred Pagny.

At Mourmelon on 6 March 1911, using a refined version of his monoplane powered by a two-cylinder 28-horsepower motor—another of his inventions—Nieuport broke the record for one hour's flight with passenger, traveling at the rate of 101.25 kilometers per hour; on 9 March he flew with two passengers at a speed of 102.855 kilometers per hour and alone at 109 kilometers per hour. Then on 11 May he set a whole series of world records from 10 to 100 kilometers, at one time attaining a speed of 119.68 kilometers per hour (74.37 m/hr). It was convincing proof that Nieuport had a product hard to beat and that France had good reason to select him as a contender for the world speed championship.

111

The Nieuport racer was 8 meters (26½ ft) in length and had a wing span of 8.7 meters (28½ ft). Its rectilinear fuselage, carefully contoured so that it had what has been described as a deep-chested appearance, was of ash reinforced by steel tubing; behind a semicircular tail plane, affixed to the rear of the fuselage for stability, was a one-piece elevator carrying twin rudders. The chassis was entirely of metal; there was no tail skid, but a single long wooden runner between the two front wheels helped support the machine when at rest. Empty, the plane weighed 240 kilograms (529 lbs). With rounded nose effectively reducing drag, the Nieuport—save for the undercarriage and a tripod with its guy wires between the wings—offered a minimum of resistence to the wind. The experts, said L'Aérophile admiringly, "never ceased to be amazed" at the little monoplane's neat appearance, its potential for speed, and its remarkable cornering ability.

Considerable discussion went into the matter of reserves, with Emile Aubrun—no longer piloting a Blériot but an Anzani-powered Deperdussin—ending up as first choice. Roland Garros, an acclaimed second in the arduous race from Paris to Rome, was rumored to be next as an alternate, but the final list gave the place to Jules Védrines, who had been thrust into the forefront of European fliers by being the sole contestant to finish the Paris–Madrid race.

Védrines—Jules Charles Toussant Védrines to give him his full name, Julot, as he was nicknamed—was at the beginning of a career that would earn him a reputation as one of the greatest, if not the greatest, aviators of his day. A short, compact, dark-haired man with a fierce-looking moustache, he had risen from a humble job as mechanic to become the pilot of a new monoplane—the Morane–Saulnier—that rivaled the Nieuport in speed and simplicity of design. An avowed socialist (if not an anarchist at heart), truculent, profane in his language, easily roused to fury, by turns surly and good-natured, Védrines came from the working-class district of Saint-Denis, an industrial suburb of Paris, where he was born on 29 December 1881. Apprenticed as a mechanic at an early age, he acquired a thorough knowledge of the internal combustion engine, particularly as it applied to the coming age of the airplane. As an expert at the Gnôme factory in 1909, he was reputed to extract more power from a motor than anyone else, which led to his being hired away by British actor and aviator Robert Loraine, a convert to flying after Blériot's crossing of the Channel.

Determined to be a flier, Védrines moved on to the Blériot establishment, obtaining license No. 312 on 7 December. With no further training, he was named as test pilot of the world's first tractor biplane, a staggered-wing affair built by Ambroise Goupy, which he flew on 23 January 1911 from Juvisy to Etampes in 22 minutes and back in 19 minutes. Five days later he made flights for a total distance of 200 kilometers; so impressed were Gabriel Borel and the Morane brothers that they engaged him without further ado to fly their newly constructed monoplane. Védrines took the Prix de la Depêche linking Toulouse and Carcassonne on 11 March; the Paris–Pau Cup, offered by the Aéro Club de Béarn, covering 708 kilometers in three days; and, on 30 April, a Pommery Cup award of 7,500 francs for distance in a straight line, which he won by following the railway for 335 kilometers from Paris to Poitiers.

The Madrid race, which started in tragedy at Issy-les-Moulineaux on Sunday, 21 May, was the making of Védrines. He had aborted his take-off and capsized when a gust of wind threatened to carry him into the line of spectators. Borrowing another machine from Verrept, a Belgian colleague who had withdrawn, he had gotten away just before Emile Train's monoplane, its engine faltering, plunged into a group of high officials that chanced to walk across the airfield, killing Minister of War Berteaux on the spot and amputating the right arm of Prime Minister Monis. Driving his Morane monoplane as if possessed, Védrines reached the Spanish capital via the control points of Angoulême and San Sebastián in three days, with 14 hours 55 minutes 18 seconds actual flying time. Over the lofty Somosierra Pass in the Pyrenees, he was attacked by a ferocious eagle but warded it off with revolver shots— an incident that grew into a legend extolled in the illustrated magazines and by the artist L. Printemps with an evocative painting hung in the Paris Salon of 1912. On his arrival at Garafa, outside Madrid, where

113

100,000 cheering Spaniards had assembled to greet him, Védrines sat scowling and cursing at the imaginary injustices he had encountered on the trying flight. Fearing that his mind had become deranged, the welcoming committee sent for a doctor, which only increased his anger. Presented to King Alfonso XIII and his English-born Queen Ena, Védrines embarrassed everyone, according to the historian J. Castelnau, by talking of his poverty-stricken days, his 22-sous lunches, his horror of the British. "Give me a stick of dynamite and I'll blow up their whole fleet!" The king quickly changed the subject. A great deal more would be heard from this high-strung—"man of the people" in the days and months to come.

Louis Gibert, a robust, thick-set native of the small town of Albi in the department of Tarn-et-Garonne, was the third alternate named by the French. He had been born on 19 June 1885 and in 1908 began experimenting with a machine of his own construction. These initial attempts to fly were unsuccessful, whereupon he enrolled in the Blériot school at Pau and graduated with license No. 92 on 10 June 1910. Gibert took part in the meeting at Bordeaux three months later, thereafter being much in demand as an exhibition flier throughout central and southwest France because of his willingness to put up with the makeshift airfields provided by local organizers. A dexterous pilot, he was one of four able to make a clean getaway in the Paris–Madrid contest before the train disaster caused the start to be suspended. He was close behind Védrines over the Pyrenees and could have come in second had he not crashed his Blériot at Alsasua on the last leg of the trip. In the Circuit of Europe he finished fifth with a Sommer monoplane. For the Gordon Bennett, as announced by *L'Aérophile*, Gibert would be flying a 60-horsepower R.E.P. monoplane, which had been setting speed records at the hands of the company's test pilot, Pierre-Marie Bournique.

If Britain was hard pressed to compete with the French, so was the United States of America. Compared with the progress that aroused Europe to sudden and intense interest, flying was in a state of stagnation with little choice among aircraft beyond the conventional products of Wright and Curtiss, or copies of the Blériot monoplane. An inexplica-

ble apathy seemed to prevail toward the challenge of the Gordon
Bennett or toward aerial achievement in general: the public was more
interested in the first motor race on the Indianapolis speedway than in
the famed airplane contest across the Atlantic. "This should not be so,"
contended a pamphlet designed to attract pupils to the Moisant School
of Aviation at Hempstead Plains, Long Island, conducted by John B.'s
brother Alfred, "for we have in this country the finest material for great
pilots that can be found anywhere in the world. We have factories to
build aeroplanes and flight motors. As a people we have courage, ability,
common sense, everything aeronautical." Yet a survey of the scene
showed a dearth of candidates for a team that could hold its own in a
race that promised to be the fastest ever. The Aero Club of America
was forced to look abroad for suitable representation, and as at Rheims
in 1909 the nation's chances depended on one man and the quality of
his machine. Charles Terres Weymann, the son of an American sugar
planter in Haiti, whose sporting instincts had led him to take up flying
in France, was the club's sole nominee. The other two places on the
team were unfilled, nor were any reserves chosen.

Weymann had been born at Port-au-Prince on 2 August 1889 and
received his entire education in France. Unruffled and unassuming,
clean-shaven, round-faced, rather short of stature and dusky-skinned, he
was virtually unknown in America. Wearing pince-nez glasses, a loose-
fitting raincoat over a turtleneck sweater, with cap and goggles instead
of a crash helmet, he had the studious air of a country gentleman—
hardly the popular image of a dauntless, resolute airman who had
passed the tests for a French brevet on 6 June 1910 and had since built
up an enviable record of aerial activity. Taking advantage of elastic
rules in the charter of the Fédération Aéronautique Internationale, the
Aero Club of America had claimed the right to issue him its own license
No. 14 as of the same date, and with this document the Haitian-born
Weymann flew as an American pilot.

It was an anomalous situation to say the least. Weymann's ties with
France were far closer than those with America; he spoke English with
a French accent; the machine he was flying—a late-model Nieuport

with a 70-horsepower Gnôme engine—was strictly French; yet, he was entitled to American citizenship and therefore to represent America in the race. Had he not been available, there might have been no United States representation.

Once granted a license, Weymann lost no time in competing for honors. On 28 July, under the tutelage of Henry Farman, he tried out one of the latter's Gnôme-powered biplanes at Mourmelon and spent the next three days on extended test flights. He was at Issy-les-Moulineaux on 7 August for the start of the Circuit de l'Est and placed fifth in the first stage of that contest from Paris to Troyes. Prizes were offered for events at each stop and at Troyes Weymann won the cross-country prize and the prize for passenger carrying. On 12 August he flew the Troyes–Mézières leg, where he again entered the local competitions and captured a prize for carrying passengers, as well as one for total points scored. That evening, while trying to land and help a disabled fellow flier, he smashed his undercarriage, which put him out of the tourney. Nevertheless, at the conclusion of the circuit, he was given a prize for his share of local successes. With the confidence thus gained, he decided to tackle one of the most unusual and difficult flights imaginable, judged by many at the time as impossible of fulfillment.

Two and a half years earlier, on 7 March, 1908, the Michelin brothers Edouard and André, anxious to encourage French aviation in the midst of persistent rumors about the Wrights' progress in America, had offered the sum of 100,000 francs for the first aviator to alight with passenger on the summit of the Puy de Dôme, a forbidding, cone-shaped mountain 1,468 meters in height, approximately 360 kilometers from Paris near the town of Clermont-Ferrand in the province of Auvergne. Any number of stops were permitted en route, but the trip had to be completed within six hours. To most people, the idea of such a flight seemed unthinkable when Europe was still celebrating Farman's closed circuit of 1 kilometer. The press called the plan preposterous and opened a vigorous campaign against it; but the Michelins, bent on hastening the day when a flying machine should be capable of "traveling for several hundred kilometers at a speed of 60 km/hr or more," let the offer stand. No one had the temerity to try for such a prize until Weymann made the attempt on 7 September 1910. The only spot to land on the mountain was a boulder-strewn field at one end of which stood an observatory and the ruins of a temple to Mercury. Less than 150 square meters were available in which to put a plane down. On every side the mountain sloped away precipitously, as often as not shrouded in mist. With his friend Manuel Fay as passenger, Weymann took off from the airfield at Buc under a clear sky at 11:45 A.M. Slowed by frequent patches of fog he was obliged to make several stops for refueling, as well as for reconnoitering the approach. Luck was against him. In gathering darkness, he descended at Volvic, a few kilometers short of his goal. It was 7:00 P.M.—over the time limit. Although Weymann's bid was unsuccessful, it constituted a record for carrying a passenger across country in the period of one day, and it stamped him immediately as a courageous and cool-headed pilot. (Six months later the prize was won by Eugène Renaux in a Maurice Farman biplane.)

Weymann's next venture confirmed the impression that he was not averse to taking risks. As the opener for an international meeting to be held at Milan on 25 September, the organizers had announced a contest for the week of the eighteenth that made the postage-stamp landing on the Puy de Dôme look like child's play. It was nothing less than a *Traversa delle Alpi in Aeroplano*—crossing the Alps by airplane—an event, said the Società Italiana di Aviazione Milanese, that would "bring Italy into the first rank of nations concerned with flying . . . [and] would show more than anything" that Italy was the equal of the United States, France, and England in aeronautics. From the Swiss village of Brigue (elevation 678 m) contestants would have to fly over the Simplon Pass at an altitude of not less than 2,100 meters (nearly 7,000 ft) before coming down at Domodossola, the first control point on the Italian side. A purse of 70,000 lire and, of course, a hero's welcome, awaited the flier who made it to Milan—a total distance of 125 kilometers (75 mi)—within 24 hours.

The hazards of such a flight were self-evident. Even if a plane's motor should function perfectly in the cold, rarefied air, the pilot would

117

have to contend with capricious winds in the mountain passes; blinding clouds might form unpredictably; emergency landing spots were nonexistent. Public opinion in Italy, led by the aeronautical engineer Canovetti, was apprehensive. The Meteorological Observatory at Zürich issued a warning that from the Swiss point of view crossing of the Alps by air was not feasible. Yet thirteen aviators signed up for the perilous passage. Only five of these, however, were accepted by the committee in charge as experienced enough for the undertaking: America's Weymann, with his Farman biplane; Jorge Chavez, a high-flying Peruvian with a Blériot; Eugen Wiencziers, German pilot of an Antoinette; Bartolemeò Cattaneo, holder of license No. 2 in Italy, also with a Blériot; and the twenty-six-year-old Frenchman Marcel Paillette, who had qualified for a license in June on a Sommer biplane. When the last three changed their minds and one by one withdrew, the game became a match between Weymann and Chavez.

When the contest opened on 18 September, a Sunday, the weather was ideal—the tail end of a fine spell that marked the last days of summer. To the annoyance of the two remaining airmen, the opportunity was lost. In a ruling that seems needlessly rigid today, the Swiss authorities refused to permit even trial flights to break the Sabbath. Next day the weather changed. Clouds sprang up and with them icy gusts of wind. Despite the turbulence Weymann took off and tried in vain to rise above the cloud cover. Compelled at length to turn back, he spent the next two days waiting for conditions to improve. On the 22 September, in freezing temperatures, he made three more attempts at departure; but the Farman performed sluggishly, with ice forming on the carburetor, and visibility was obscured by snow flurries. Unable to gain altitude, he finally admitted defeat. Chavez made the crossing on the twenty-third, only to crash on landing at Domodossola and succumb to his injuries four days later.

In January 1911 Weymann again took up passenger carrying, setting new records for town-to-town flights; on the twenty-second he made the first cross-country trip with four aboard. By spring, however, he had discarded his Farman in favor of a Nieuport with a 70-horsepower Gnôme, with which he entered the Paris–Madrid race. Weymann was allotted the second position in the order of departure, five minutes after the 5:00 A.M. takeoff of Blériot pilot Le Lasseur de Ranzay. The schedule was not adhered to because of faulty organization, and Weymann had not yet left the ground when the fatal accident involving Train's machine put a stop to further departures until the following morning, 22 May. Instead, he entered the Paris–Rome contest a week later. Again dogged by bad weather, he left Troyes under heavily overcast skies and a steady drizzle on the second day. Weymann came down hard at Cellé-sur-Ouese, damaging his undercarriage so severely that it took him out of the competition.

Ahead was the demanding Circuit of Europe, due to get under way on 18 June, from Paris through Belgium and Holland, across the Channel to London, and back to Paris in nine orderly stages. Practically every type of airplane in Europe was represented, although, as in the other great races, not a single American machine took part. Weymann placed third in the first stage, from Paris to Liège, and by the time Utrecht was reached on the third stage he was fourth in the general classification, the winner of nearly 6,000 francs in prize money so far. Once again, no one had made allowance for the weather. On 24 and 25 June all contestants were grounded by wind, rain, and hail, and the crucial leg from Calais to London was rescheduled for 2 July, overlapping the Gordon Bennett on 1 July. As soon as the delay became apparent Weymann dropped out: he could not afford to jeopardize his engagement to represent the United States at Eastchurch. If he had continued, he might well have forced into the lead, for his Nieuport was outperforming many others. He was on the Isle of Sheppey tuning up the day before the Gordon Bennett and in the air early on 1 July putting the Nieuport through a number of flight tests.

For a time it was thought that other nations would compete. Austria-Hungary was reported to be sending two Etrichs and a Farman; Germany was preparing to take part and had planned to hold elimination trials at Cologne in May. But the incident that excluded Germany from the European Circuit probably was responsible as well for the absence of German fliers in the Gordon Bennett—then and later.

Not that there was a scarcity of German airmen in 1911 nor a lack of machines from which a team could have been made up. Outstanding among the pilots were Helmuth Hirth, winner of the Upper Rhine Circuit and the Kathreiner Prize, and Hans Vollmöller, shortly to win the Circuit of Würtemberg and the 25,000-mark Count Zeppelin Prize, both of whom flew the Etrich–Rumpler monoplane; Martin König, the star of the year for taking first place in the Circuit of Germany with his Albatros biplane; Bruno Büchner and Emile Jeannin, each using the 100-horsepower Argus driven Aviatik biplane; and Felix Laitsch, winner of the Circuit of Saxony, also with an Albatros. At least a score of other able fliers were active, based for the most part at the Johannistahl airfield outside Berlin. While a growing emphasis on military training may have displaced some interest in aviation as a sport, the Deutschen Luftfahrer-Verbandes had by 1 July issued a total of ninety civilian licenses. It was in keeping with Germany's new awareness of the airplane, as opposed to the dirigible, that when plans were announced for a grand circuit of Europe it was decided to send two emissaries to Paris to discuss German participation.

Leader of the delegation was Major von Parseval, constructor of a nonrigid type of dirigible noted for its unequalled portability when deflated. At the instigation of the kaiser, the Motorluftschiff Studien Gesellschaft had been formed in 1908 to acquire an experimental airship of the most promising design, and Parseval's product was selected. By 1911 at least half a dozen of his dirigibles had been built. Parseval was accompanied on his mission to Paris by a Major von Tschudi, and they brought with them the suggestion that the Preis der Lüfte offered by the *Berliner Zeitung* could be added to the prizes offered for the circuit by the French. The German envoys, however, met a cool reception. In a chauvinistic mood, the French let it be known that German participation would not be welcome, one newspaper going so far as to put the rhetorical question to its readers whether they should have anything to

120

Table 5
1911 • Entry List

Country	Pilot	Machine	Motor
Great Britain	Gustav Hamel	Blériot monoplane	100-hp Gnôme
	Alec Ogilvie	Wright biplane	50-hp N.E.C.
	Douglas Graham-Gilmour	Bristol monoplane	80-hp Gnôme
		alternates	
	O. C. Morison	Bristol monoplane	70-hp Gnôme
	James Radley	Blériot monoplane	70-hp Gnôme
	James Valentine	Deperdussin monoplane	70-hp Gnôme
France	Alfred Leblanc	Blériot monoplane	100-hp Gnôme
	Edouard Nieuport	Nieuport monoplane	70-hp Gnôme
	Louis Chevalier	Nieuport monoplane	28-hp Nieuport
		alternates	
	Emile Aubrun	Deperdussin monoplane	80-hp Anzani
	Jules Védrines	Morane-Saulnier monoplane	70-hp Gnôme
	Louis Gibert	R.E.P. monoplane	60-hp R.E.P.
United States	Charles T. Weymann	Nieuport monoplane	100-hp Gnôme

do with the visitors from over the Rhine. It was a foretaste of the sentiment prevailing in Paris before the war. The affronted Germans dropped the subject and returned home, where a Circuit of Germany was organized for German pilots under the auspices of the Berlin newspaper. After that experience, it was hardly surprising that Germany was not represented in the Gordon Bennett.

Of the thirteen entrants (table 5), six were actual starters: three Nieuports, two Blériots, and one Wright. Four were to finish the course. Védrines and Gibert were still involved in the Circuit of Europe and could not drop out to act as reserves; so was Valentine, though he left the stalled circuit for a day to watch the race at Eastchurch. Graham-Gilmour's Bristol was not ready and the other British alternate pilots proved to be unavailable. In the end, the United Kingdom's team was reduced to two machines, one of which could not be expected to exceed a speed of a mile a minute.

As in the previous races, competitors were allowed to pick their own time of departure. The crowd was kept on edge by glimpses of the machines through half-opened hangar doors, by the occasional roar of a motor being tested, by the tantalizing haze of blue exhaust smoke, and by the odor of burnt castor oil drifting across the field. Hamel, whose Blériot bore the number 4, was the first to get away. It was 2:50 P.M. He had eaten nothing since an early breakfast and had shown signs of nervousness when trying out the clipped-wing monoplane in the morning. But the rain squall had passed, and he was anxious to make his attempt before the 20 mile per hour wind should increase. Flying low and fast, Britain's main hope got off to an impressive start.

What happened next was high drama. Hamel swept past the first mark tower (a "scattering pylon" placed outside the course to space the racers), turning at too sharp an angle. Trying to get back to the racecourse proper, he was unable to recover from his steep bank. To the alarm of the onlookers, among them his mother and two sisters, he sideslipped, dived, and made a frantic effort to pull up. Too late. Perhaps a wind gust hit the right wing of the Blériot. In any case, the left wing struck the ground and the machine collapsed in pieces 150 feet beyond the pylon with such force and at such speed that the engine, still revolving, bounded along for another 60 feet, carrying the wreckage with it. Hamel was wearing no seat belt—it was not yet the custom to do so; he was thrown clear, rolling over and over "like a shot rabbit" as an eyewitness had it, only stopping several yards beyond his machine. There was evidence to show that the craft had traveled more than 100 feet from where it first hit to where it crumpled up and the pilot was flung out. Experts thought it possible that Hamel had almost succeeded in leveling off and was actually running along the ground when the chassis collapsed. Had he been flying at sufficient altitude, it was conjectured, and had the warping system not been interfered with, he might have avoided a crash altogether.

The airman lay dazed until help reached him, then managed to gain his feet and before being carried off to wave to the crowd. Doctors who examined him could find no broken bones or internal injuries, though he was bruised and badly shaken. That he escaped being seriously hurt seemed to everyone nothing short of a miracle.

The other representative of the Nieuport was Louis Chevalier, born 12 July 1883 at Nantes. He had developed into one of the firm's most proficient pilots since taking his license (No. 333, with a Nieuport) on 23 December 1910 and was highly regarded as a specialist in speed. At three o'clock Chevalier was in the air for France, his Nieuport displaying the number 12, flying well, banking steeply on the turns, the two cylinders of his 28-horsepower Nieuport engine making appreciably less noise than the powerful Gnôme. For five laps—30 kilometers—everything went smoothly, then a disturbing knock was heard from the motor. The Frenchman kept going for eleven full rounds, completed in 50 minutes $53\,^3\!/_5$ seconds; but on the twelfth lap he was forced down in rough pasture among a flock of sheep, breaking his undercarriage. Not to be deterred, he started again with the same type of machine, a procedure permitted by the rules, though the delay counted against flying time. The cards, however, were stacked against him. While flying over the disabled No. 12, so as to go on from where he had left off, his motor failed again and by a freakish coincidence let him down within a few hundred yards of where he had landed before. It was too much. To begin anew would be too costly in time, and Chevalier abandoned the race—a jolt to the house of Nieuport, which had prided itself on the reliability of its engines.

Meanwhile Weymann on his Nieuport, painted number 2, had crossed the starting line at 3:45 P.M. at a pace that made the multitude gasp. Heeling over viciously at the pylons "like a bird of prey about to knock you off the face of the earth," as one of the observers said, he sped around the course in a rising wind at close to 80 miles per hour, probably reaching 100 miles per hour with the wind at his back on the long straight stretch to the pylon at the eastern edge of the field. Round after round the fourteen cylinders of his Gnôme functioned without a hitch. Weymann made a magnificent, faultless flight, for which the host country was quick to give him credit. He finished the 94 miles in 1 hour 11 minutes $36\,^1\!/_5$ seconds. After flying on for several more laps he landed gracefully at 5:05 P.M. in a series of narrowing circles, his average speed computed at a record 78 miles per hour.

Ogilvie, all the odds against him, got off at 4:47 and began a relatively slow but steady circling of the course, his Wright lapped repeatedly by Weymann's Nieuport. The peculiar, penetrating sound of his New Engine Company motor, due partly to its unusually long exhaust pipes, and the fact that the Wright was the only biplane in the race provided added interest for the crowd. At the end of his twentieth lap Ogilvie stopped to refuel, losing 4 minutes, but he finished without incident in 1 hour 49 minutes $10\frac{3}{5}$ seconds for an average speed of 51.31 miles per hour. It was 26.69 miles per hour slower than the Nieuport's time; but the home team found consolation in that the Wright was the only plane equipped with a British engine. Prolonged cheers greeted Ogilvie for his sportsmanlike attempt.

To the French camp it was all too apparent that Leblanc's clipped Blériot would have to beat Weymann's mark if France was to win the cup. But Leblanc was not feeling well. He had been ill with influenza, and Aubrun, first of the French reserves, was standing by to replace him with the Deperdussin. Despite his being indisposed, Leblanc nevertheless decided that with Hamel's Blériot smashed and out of the contest he would fly anyway, not only for his country but for the sake of the firm's reputation.

Waiting until the wind had nearly died down, first Nieuport—with the number 1—then Leblanc—his machine numbered 5—took off.

Table 6
1911 • Results

Place	Pilot	Country	Machine	Motor	Speed
1	Weymann	United States	Nieuport	100-hp Gnôme	78 m/hr
2	Leblanc	France	Blériot	100-hp Gnôme	75.83 m/hr
3	Nieuport	France	Nieuport	70-hp Gnôme	75.07 m/hr
4	Ogilvie	Great Britain	Wright	50-hp N.E.C.	51.31 m/hr

Charles T. Weymann, winner of the 1911 Gordon Bennett for the United States. In the background is Edouard Nieuport, designer and builder of the machine that brought him victory. Courtesy National Air and Space Museum.

Ogilvie was still in the air, creating the unusual spectacle of three airplanes racing at the same time. It was soon clear that Nieuport, with only a 70-horsepower engine, would not be able to better the record set by Weymann, even though he was doing more than 75 miles per hour. While Leblanc flew in superb style, with Hamel's crash still freshly in mind he took no undue risks and made his turns slowly and cautiously. It was nearly seven o'clock when Leblanc descended, with a time of 1 hour 13 minutes $40\frac{1}{5}$ seconds and an average of 75.83 miles per hour—two minutes slower than America's entry. Close behind was Nieuport; his time was 1 hour 14 minutes $37\frac{1}{5}$ seconds, and his average speed was 75.07 miles per hour. So keenly contested was the race that the times of the three fastest were within three minutes of one another (see table 6). At last the airplane had proven faster than the automobile. To win the Vanderbilt Cup race in 1911 Ralph Mulford on a Lozier averaged 74.07 miles per hour.

America had captured the cup for the second time. Weymann was hailed with one round of cheering after another as Cortlandt Field Bishop draped his shoulders with the Stars and Stripes—the same flag that had decorated Glenn Curtiss's hangar at Rheims in 1909 and was on display at Belmont in 1910. For the French, it was Leblanc's "fatigue" that was to blame for losing the cup. His American opponent's picture would head the "Champions of 1911" published in a color-illustrated supplement to *La Vie au Grand Air* at the end of the year.

The Royal Aero Club entertained at a gala dinner for one hundred persons that evening in a specially erected marquee. The competitors were guests of honor. The Coupe Internationale d'Aviation in all its symbolic glory was presented to the victor, toasts were drunk, speeches were made, and international sportsmanship was celebrated. Weymann acknowledged the congratulations heaped upon him in two words of French—*Merci bien!*—which some thought passing strange for a representative of the polyglot United States. No matter. He had returned the cup to America, and to laughter and applause Cortlandt Field Bishop expressed the hope that England would win next year "so that America could win it back again."

Angry commentary followed in British aeronautical circles. With America taking first place and France second and third, the consensus was that England got what "she thoroughly deserved." One writer echoed the complaint of the Moisant School, "We have plenty of fine flyers if only someone would go the right way to provide machines for them. Where are all our mounted sportsmen who find the money for English teams to go abroad for international athletic meetings, yacht races, polo matches, and so forth?" It was resolved then and there that a much greater effort would have to be made to prevent the cup "from remaining on the other side of the Atlantic."

On the other hand pride and joy reigned among the advocates of aviation in the United States. The *Scientific American* best summarized the triumph with its lead article: THE WINNING OF THE INTERNATIONAL AVIATION TROPHY. HOW WEYMANN UPHELD OUR COLORS SINGLE-HANDED AND WON THE WORLD'S GREATEST SPEED EVENT. Without detracting from the skill of the aviator, many American writers conveniently ignored the obvious—that the race had been won with a French, not American, machine and motor, that the clean design and careful attention to detail of the Nieuport had shown the plane's superiority over anything the United States could have produced. Americans cheerfully took it for granted that somehow, one way or another, their country would win again. The birthplace of aviation could achieve no less.

Such confidence was scarcely justified. The French knew their airplanes were more advanced than those of any other nation and their airmen would make every effort to prove it. They would have their chance the following year.

127

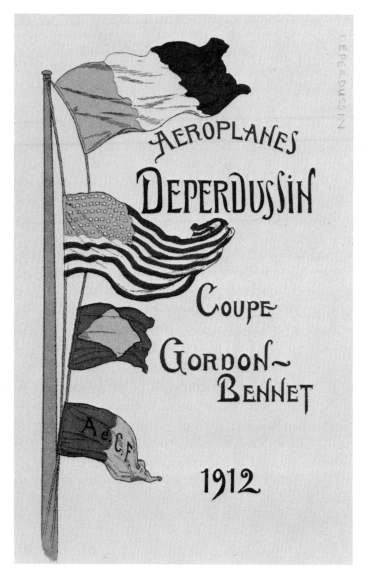

AEROPLANES DEPERDUSSIN COUPE GORDON-BENNET 1912

The French flag flies supreme over the other nations competing in the Gordon Bennett. Courtesy The Royal Aeronautical Society.

128

Chapter 5 CHICAGO · 1912

Early in 1912 a flurry of activity began on both sides of the Atlantic in preparation for that year's Gordon Bennett. The Fédération Aéronautique Internationale, after conferences held in Vienna and Rome, announced that the next race would be over a minimum circuit of 5 kilometers (3.1 mi)—essentially the same as the two previous years—but that the total distance to be flown would be increased from 150 to 200 kilometers (124.28 mi). It was a measure of the dramatic progress in man's ability to fly that the course proposed was ten times the length of the initial race only three years earlier at Rheims.

As usual, it was left to the holder of the cup to select the time and place for the contest, and the Aero Club of America named Chicago as the site, with all local arrangements for what the newspapers glowingly described as "the blue ribbon of international aviation" delegated to the Aero Club of Illinois. The date would depend "upon the best weather conditions, to be based on the calculations of the United States Weather Bureau." As it happened, when 15 August was chosen, widespread protests that this allowed insufficient time to get ready caused a postponement to 9 September.

Chicago, the Windy City, bustling hub of an expanding Middle West, was not to be outdone by cosmopolitan New York in organizing an

129

international air meet. Already, in 1911, it had successfully staged a tournament at Grant Park fronting Lake Michigan. Now a three-day program of events along lines made familiar by Rheims and Belmont was promised in conjunction with the speed classic. "The world is looking to Chicago for whatever of great significance is achieved in demonstrating the advance of aviation," boasted a brochure issued by the Illinois club over the names of its president, Harold F. McCormick, and secretary, Harold W. Robbins. "Here is outlined a plan by which it is proposed to meet this expectancy and at the same time return greatest credit and permanent benefit to Chicago, make sure the city's premier place in the world of progress and give to Chicago first, the greatest things in this newest scientific attainment—subjugation of the air."

Just why Chicago was looked upon to lead the world in aviation that year was explained in a burst of civic bombast addressed to "those to whom there appeals the advancement of Chicago's reputation and standing in all that promotes human achievement and comfort, to whom world-wide preferment of Chicago in any field of betterment is of interest, and to whom promulgation of clean, broad public support appears desirable." The plan included two major events: the "remarkable Gordon Bennett contest, emblematic of the world's championship in the art of flying," and an American Grand Circuit race of 1,800 miles—two "Classics Unrivaled in Previous Human Endeavor." Emphasizing the importance of the Bennett contest in developing the flying machine, the pamphlet noted, "Speed alone has been the determining factor, yet it has gone far to complete the mastery of mechanical flight since speed has demanded of designers more and more knowledge of the effect upon flight of each constructional detail." In other words, the Gordon Bennett Cup made an invaluable contribution to progress because it enforced higher and higher standards every year. "Three times previously," the reader was reminded, "air racers have swooped around circular courses, straining man and machine for victory. Twice of those three times a single American entry has wrapped the flag of the United States around the trophy and brought it home." That Chicago should be the scene of another American triumph was the heart's desire of the promoters, openly encouraged by the millionaire harvester manufacturer McCormick, whose abiding interest in aviation had been fueled by the Belmont Park meet in 1910.

Patriotic Chicagoans were asked to lend their moral and financial support to the extent of 100,000 dollars—a tidy sum made necessary "largely because of the expense of the Gordon Bennett race," to which no admission would be charged. Chicago, the city, was compared to an individual who needed a respite from business cares and activity. "No such opportunity to provide a city holiday on a scope as comprehensive as this and at a figure so insignificant in proportion to the returns in entertainment and prestige, ever has presented itself to an American city before," was the sweeping claim. Students of aeronautics might also have mentioned that Chicago was the home of the late Octave Chanute, renowned Paris-born engineer who had retired in 1889 to study the art of gliding and whose experiments, carried out over sand dunes along Lake Michigan, helped significantly to launch the Wright brothers on their careers.

Fortunately, the promoters' high-flown rhetoric contained an escape clause: in allotting cash for the different events, it was "proposed to limit the scope of the undertaking to only those events as sufficient funds to warrant" were raised. The Gordon Bennett, as the prime attraction, was assured of support. But the Grand Circuit, modeled on the long-distance European races, would remain an American dream, the victim of inadequate financing, public indifference, and the absence of professional organization. The tragic death of two fliers at the start of the general meet further discouraged such a project. America's destiny, it seemed, was more likely to be linked to the land and to the sea than to extended flights through the air.

Each club affiliated with the Fédération Aéronautique was, of course, entitled to challenge the holder of the cup: the challenge had to be sent in before 1 March. At first it was feared that no aircraft from overseas would take part because of the possibility that the Wright brothers, then engaged in acrimonious litigation with foreign as well as domestic airplane manufacturers, would institute court action. A short time before, the brothers had obtained an injunction against Claude Grahame-White for patent infringement, forbidding him to use his plane in the United States, and for a while it looked as though the race might be ruined because of legal complications. But the Wrights magnanimously decided to dispel such doubts. In a statement to the press they announced:

> With reference to the contest for the Gordon Bennett Aviation Cup, which will take place in Chicago this year, the Wright Company, through the Aero Club of America, have given the following guarantee regarding aeroplanes taking part in the race:—In the interest of good sport, the Wright company will permit representatives of foreign nations to participate in the 1912 race for the Gordon-Bennett Cup, regardless of any questions as to whether their aeroplanes do or do not infringe patents owned by this company. The Wright Company will not bring suit against representatives of foreign clubs because of participation in the contest for the Gordon-Bennett Cup.

Wilbur Wright could hardly have done less. The Wright name was closely identified with the cup. The trophy itself was adorned by a model of a Wright biplane, permanent symbol of leadership in the early days of flight. Wright biplanes had flown in every Gordon Bennett race so far. In addition, the brothers had many friends among foreign fliers whom they had no desire to offend by barring them from the competition. It was an irony of fate that, after making this conciliatory gesture, Wilbur Wright would not live to see that year's contest. The fifth person in the United States to receive a pilot's license, he died from typhoid fever on 30 May at the age of forty-five, shocking the aviation community and evoking eloquent tributes from all over the world. Among the most heartfelt messages was one from England, where at Eastchurch the previous summer he had helped Alec Ogilvie prepare his machine for the 1911 contest, setting for the mechanics an example of hard work and relishing the outdoor life and the campfire meals cooked by amateurs at the Royal Aero Club's shed. "Everyone interested in aeronautics must feel the irreparable loss caused by the death of this pioneer," wrote Griffith Brewer of the Royal Aero Club summing up the prevailing sentiment in *Flight*. "Before those brothers set out to solve the problem which had baffled scientists for centuries, the people of this earth could travel either by land or sea, but on restricted lines only. Now one may travel by air in any direction, regardless of whether the earth below is wet or dry, and thus a third and still more useful means of locomotion is at the service of mankind."

The question was raised in later years whether Wilbur Wright, had he lived, would have adopted a more farsighted policy than that followed by Orville, his junior by four years, in building airplanes that would have kept up with the ever-higher standard set by the Gordon Bennett. But the company, its initiative sapped by venomous litigation, would adhere to the outmoded twin-propellered pusher until after the beginning of World War I.

The Royal Aero Club was not entirely satisfied with the Wright assurances and cabled the Aero Club of America asking for a guarantee that the company would take no action against British aviators or their airplanes for a period of three months from the date of arrival, should they enter the Gordon Bennett contest. In reply, the Wright company said it would guarantee nothing beyond the statement already given. "They will never get many aviators to go to America as things are," commented Harold E. Perrin, the Royal Aero Club's secretary.

Nevertheless, with the specter of lawsuits at least temporarily laid to rest, entries began coming in. So widespread was the interest, so deeply was national honor involved, that at one point it appeared as many as nine countries would be represented. In addition to the United States, which entered a team of three, France, Britain, and Belgium promptly signified their intention to compete. From London came word of Grahame-White's "desire to uphold the prestige of Great Britain" in person, probably with a racer of his own design modeled on the Nieuport and with the same 100-horsepower Gnôme motor that had brought him victory at Belmont in 1910. The choice of Gustav Hamel as the second member of the British team was announced by Perrin. Later it was made known that George M. Dyott, who had been licensed on a Blériot at Hendon on 17 August 1911 would be the third man and that he had been negotiating in Paris for a machine of undisclosed make capable of attaining 100 miles per hour.

Henry Wynmalen, well-known pilot of a Farman biplane and holder of his country's license No. 6, entered the contest for Holland. His racing monoplane was specially built by the German firm of Max Oertz and somewhat resembled the Etrich Taube; it had made its initial flight in 1911 at Schrevesdingen on the Lüneburger Heide and was expected to reach a speed of 94 miles per hour. Wynmalen had won the Automobile Club de France's prize for a flight from Paris to Brussels and back with a passenger on 16 and 17 October 1910 in a flying time of about 15 hours for the 380 miles. Edmond Audemars, pilot of the Demoiselle and the Blériot, signed up for Switzerland in an unexpected move to join the ranks of fast flyers.

In the thought that Germany, Austria-Hungary, and Russia, where substantial progress had been made in flying, might also be induced to take part, the closing date for entries was extended to 12 March. But the applications failed to materialize—Germany's, perhaps, because of the rebuff to participation in the Circuit of Europe, and Russia's because that country took no part in sports beyond its territorial boundaries. The number of contestants was then listed as six; three each from the United States, France, and Great Britain, one apiece from Holland, Belgium, and Switzerland.

Mingled with elation at having the cup back, to be competed for on American soil, was a sober realization among United States experts that another American victory would not be easy. In their plush headquarters at 297 Madison Avenue, a stone's throw from Grand Central Station in the heart of New York, officials of the Aero Club of America weighed the prospects of retaining the trophy and debated ways and means of fielding a winning entry. The handsome building that housed the organization was a converted four-story town house on the corner of Forty-first Street, from the second floor balcony of which floated the club's distinctive pennant—a red, white, and blue shield of stars and bars against a triangular crimson background. Up the red carpeted staircase, in addition to the dining room, was the heavily paneled library with books and pictures along the walls; lounge chairs and a couple of writing desks were served by a long, magazine-strewn table. It was a meeting ground for members, a board room, and a place for formal or informal discussion, a quiet sanctuary for a small, congenial scientific and social body. The club was the aeronautical nerve center of the nation, the birthplace of ideas, the source of all licenses to fly, and a modest mecca for out-of-town airmen.

The club represented the Fédération Aéronautique Internationale in the United States, and affiliated with it were twenty-four local aero clubs in different parts of the country. Its president in 1912 was Robert J. Collier, publisher of *Collier's Weekly,* Cortlandt Field Bishop having retired to become chairman of one of the club's numerous committees, that on dirigible balloons. There were four vice-presidents: Maj. Samuel Reber of the U.S. Army, Henry A. Wise Wood, James A. Blair, Jr., and Harold F. McCormick. Collier stood almost alone in the United States as a patron of aeronautics. A wealthy sportsman and devotee of over-water flight, he had inaugurated early in January a trophy bearing his name "for the greatest achievement in aviation in America" during the preceding year. The bronze group by Ernest Wise Keyser of New York portrayed the triumph of man over gravity and other forces of nature. Won the first time by Glenn Curtiss for his work in developing the hydro-airplane, it is still awarded annually for excellence in aviation. Of the more important committees, Major Reber headed the contest committee, Blair was in charge of the Gordon Bennett Cup committee, and Wood—easily recognizable by his ruddy complexion and long, waxed moustaches—served as chairman of the club's committee on foreign relations and as nominal editor of its house organ, the *Aero Club of America Bulletin.*

Just off the ground-floor lobby with its cigar counter and telephone switchboard was a green baize door behind which most of the club's business was conducted, as were the editorial activities of the *Bulletin* and its parent publication, the illustrated magazine *Flying.* The man who held the threads in this tight little world of aeronautics was a

135

remarkable individual named Henry Woodhouse, unquestioned eminence grise of club policy and politics, the dynamic manager of both *Bulletin* and *Flying,* a prolific writer, and a recognized authority on American aviation and its tireless promoter. A self-made patriot of Italian origin with a dubious past, Woodhouse was a short, stocky, swarthy figure with a head as round as a melon, penetrating black eyes, and an ingratiating smile. Henry Casalegno had come to America in 1904 as a cook at the age of twenty-three. Soon thereafter he stabbed a man to death during an altercation. Tried and convicted by the county court in Troy, New York, for first-degree manslaughter, he was sentenced to four years and two months at hard labor in Clinton Prison. After his release he translated his surname literally into Woodhouse and started a new life, the momentary aberration buried in the absorbing subject of aeronautics. Foreseeing the age of the airplane, he began to write articles on flight and in 1911, with Robert Collier and Henry A. Wise Wood, founded the magazine *Flying.*

As one who made the wheels go round in the Aero Club, nobody knew better than Woodhouse the situation that confronted the United States in defending the cup. American constructors were as much as two years behind the Europeans, seemingly oblivious to innovative designs, holding to obsolescent types, and copying old models instead of experimenting with new ones. Little attempt was made to popularize aviation, to encourage research, or to engage in systematic studies. The public, unconvinced that the airplane had a practical future, still looked on flying as a stunt or carnival sideshow and on aviators as acrobats or circus performers. To those who understood the tremendous possibilities of travel through the air, it was a puzzle why this was the case. But the reasons are not hard to understand today. Foremost among them was the debilitating involvement of American manufacturers in legal arguments with the Wrights, which deterred independent thought and enterprise. Another was the lack of financial incentive, either from angels of the art or from corporate interests. A third was the absence of government support. Congress was deaf to the army's plea for appropriations to enlarge its minuscule air force, blind to the military potential of aircraft.

France, on the other hand, uninhibited by patent suits, had several machines capable of surpassing Weymann's 78 miles per hour of the year before; nor was there any lack of experienced pilots to fly them. World records continued to fall to the French in all categories of flying. France, still smarting from having twice lost the cup to foreigners piloting French aircraft, was certain this time to make an all-out attempt to win. The easiest defense from an American viewpoint was to bring over Weymann with the newest of the Nieuports in the hope he would repeat his 1911 performance, and at the instigation of Woodhouse and others 40,000 dollars was raised for this purpose. If the Nieuport had won once, it could win again. But for reasons that were never satisfactorily explained, the plan did not work out.

If a foreign-made craft was not to represent America once more, there was no time to lose in finding a high-powered airplane that could challenge successfully what other countries would produce. Equally important was to select a pilot qualified to fly such a machine to victory. To stimulate domestic manufacturers, and persuade them to build a plane to keep the cup at home, the club set aside 10,000 dollars to finance the construction of a racer that would measure up to the best at Chicago. E. R. Armstrong, technical editor of *Aero,* published in the magazine's 24 February 1912 issue plans for an "International Aviation Cup Defender." A monoplane with exceptionally clean lines, it was designed to be capable of 110 miles per hour—a speed Armstrong predicted would be required to win the cup that year; two such entries would not only assure superiority but would open a lucrative market for the maker. While there is no evidence to show that Armstrong's ideas were adopted, they may have spurred the club to send out letters to the dozen or so aircraft firms in the country urgently inviting proposals. However, the terms of the club's offer were regarded as unrealistic, with all risks to be assumed by the builder, and the appeal met with a discouraging lack of response.

When New York's first Aero Show opened at the Grand Central Palace on 9 May, the event uppermost in most members' minds was the tragic destruction of the *Titanic* less than a month before. Like other organizations touched by the disaster, the Aero Club was profoundly affected and passed resolutions honoring members it had lost. The name of Edgar Meyer was inscribed beside the names of those who had "given their lives in furtherance of the science of aviation, and others no less esteemed for their manhood and example." Joseph F. Loring was cited for having given "his life for the women and children, for although he was not a swimmer, he refrained from any attempt to save himself through recourse to the lifeboats, and remained on the steamer to meet the fate he knew was inevitable." But the well-attended display of aircraft available in the United States again brought the question of American representation in the Gordon Bennett sharply to the fore.

Of the twelve biplanes, nine monoplanes, and one quadruplane on exhibit, there was little to suggest blue ribbon caliber. The Curtiss company showed five standard pushers, including the *Rheims Racer,* winner in 1909, and a small headless racing model reputedly intended for the 1912 competition. The Wrights showed a new Model C with a 30-horsepower Wright motor, embodying improvements suggested by soaring experiments lately conducted by Orville Wright at Kitty Hawk. Some structural details had been made stronger and simpler and the form and size of the blinkers had been altered; it was in no sense a racing craft. Evidence of an Aero Club stake in the impending contest was a two-seater, 50-horsepower Gnôme-motored Nieuport, vintage of 1911, which the club had imported as a practice machine and possible substitute entry for America.

The machine that made the most favorable impression was the Rex *Gordon Bennett Racer,* an airplane of more advanced design than usually seen in the United States, with streamlined fuselage and complete cowling for the engine. Built along Blériot and Nieuport lines by the Rex Monoplane Company of South Beach, Staten Island, New York, it had interchangeable wings, which made it possible "to enter SPEED, show or passenger contests during the same day. What other aeroplane

138

can do this?" asked a company brochure. "Remember we guarantee to fly the Rex before delivery at least 1,000 ft. high and ten miles across country." The price ranged from 1,200 to 4,800 dollars. The model at the show had been hastily assembled, without its four-cylinder, in-line Kirkham motor. Perhaps it did not come up to expectations, for despite the promise in its name nothing more would be heard of the Rex as a Gordon Bennett entry.

These machines were in marked contrast to their European contemporaries, such as those shown at the Paris *salon* in December 1911. Among the latter was a radical *Torpedo,* built by the aeronautical engineer Victor Tatin in collaboration with Louis Paulhan, which, as its name implied, was designed strictly for speed. The length and wing span of this projectile-like monoplane were identical—approximately 9 meters (28 ft); the total wing area was 12 meters (36 ft), and the tips of the wings curved upward in an unconventional bid for stability. At the rear was the propeller, driven through a long hollow shaft by a 50-horsepower Gnôme motor located directly behind the cockpit. Tested in a wind tunnel by the famous engineer Gustave Eiffel, it breached new frontiers in the quest for speed.

Along similar lines at the New York exposition was the Gallaudet *Bullet,* a fishlike, streamlined craft that reminded some people of a fat carp. It had a three-bladed propeller at the rear, also driven through a long shaft, with power supplied by a fourteen-cylinder 100-horsepower Gnôme. Mounted on a tubular spar, the wings had a span of 32 feet (9.75 m) and a total area of 200 square feet (18.5 m^2); they were equipped with a "secret" device that permitted change in the angle of incidence during flight. Alone among the machines at the show, its speed was estimated at 100 miles per hour, "sufficient to insure the retaining of the Gordon Bennett Cup in this country on the basis of foreign speeds." *Aero* magazine reported an expert opinion that "real brains" had been "put into every square inch"; it had "raised the hopes of many that the United States had at last turned out a monoplane that should be able to show her tail to the best of foreigners." The main object in the design, it was made clear, was "Speed, with a capital S."

Built by the Gallaudet Engineering Company of Norwich, Connecticut, the completely enclosed, low-slung fuselage allowed only the head of the pilot to protrude, as in the Nieuport. Its inventor, Edson F. Gallaudet, made the mistake, however, of sacrificing stability to tail surfaces that were totally inadequate. On a demonstration flight for the Aero Club on 14 July he took off too steeply. According to an eyewitness, the monoplane rose at breakneck speed at an angle of nearly 90 degrees, turned on its side, and plummeted to the ground from a height of 400 feet in full view of the horrified spectators. Although seriously injured, Gallaudet was undaunted. He vowed to rebuild the machine in time for the Gordon Bennett—a vow that unfortunately would not be fulfilled.

Summer had arrived with Aero Club activists looking frantically for a proper entry, their efforts fruitless so far. But there was one encouraging development. Two residents of Chicago who were determined that America should stand her ground in preserving the cup from foreign assault had formed a syndicate with the object of purchasing the best machine that money could buy and entering it in the contest. Charles Dickinson, a prominent businessman, headed the syndicate; its vice-president was blond, mustachioed Norman Prince, an energetic, likable, well-to-do young man who was fated to lose his life flying for France in World War I. Prince was the spark plug of the project. Born at Pride's Crossing, Massachusetts, on 31 August 1887, he was the grandson of Frederick O. Prince, a former mayor of Boston, and of George H. Norman, an eminent citizen of Newport, Rhode Island. He was educated by private tutors and at the Groton School, graduating from Harvard in 1908 and from the Harvard Law School three years later. The family's business affairs revolved in large part around railways and stockyards in Chicago, and Prince had started out in those surroundings as a practicing lawyer. He soon neglected his profession, however, for aviation, in which he developed an overwhelming interest not only as a sport but as a practical and scientific avocation. He had given rein to his bent in April 1910 by joining a small group under the leadership of another Harvard graduate, W. Starling Burgess, in trying out a skid-mounted pusher biplane christened the *Flying Fish* on the marshes of

Plum Island thirty miles north of Boston; here he was reported to have entertained the experimenters by jumping off the hangar roof in a glider. Prince's association with Burgess led to his qualifying for pilot's license No. 55 on 6 August 1911, using one of the twin-propellered biplanes that Burgess was then building under license from the Wright brothers.

Raising money for the syndicate was no problem. Prince was a popular figure in Chicago and his enthusiasm proved contagious. The crucial question was whether a suitable machine could be constructed in time for the September race. As a first step it was decided to order from France, at a cost of 8,500 dollars, the most powerful engine in existence—a fourteen-cylinder 160-horsepower Gnôme—around which a plane could be built. Because of their past relationship and the company's reputation for fine craftsmanship, it was only natural that Prince and his syndicate should next approach Burgess. The outcome of their request to construct a Gordon Bennett contender forms one of the most extraordinary chapters in the annals of American aviation.

William Starling Burgess, son of the famous yacht designer Edward Burgess, was born at Boston on Christmas Day 1878. He had taken a degree in architecture and naval engineering after an interruption in his college studies to serve as gunner's mate in the Spanish–American War, but in 1904 he opened a shipyard in Marblehead specializing in small boats and racing craft. In 1909 he formed a partnership with Augustus M. Herring, after the latter split with Glenn Curtiss, for the fabrication of airplanes. But the temperamental Herring was soon replaced by Greely S. Curtis (not to be confused with Curtiss the aviator). The recipient of an engineering degree at Cornell in 1896, Greely Curtis had lived abroad and had met such aeronautical pioneers as Hudson Maxim in England and Otto Lilienthal in Germany. A new company was formed: the W. Starling Burgess Company Ltd. became Burgess Company & Curtis, with a capital of 80,000 dollars, eventually simplified to the Burgess Company, which advertised "a guaranteed excellence in design and construction."

One of the first acts of the firm was to hire Alexander L. Pfitzner, a former artillery officer in the Hungarian army, who had been employed as a specialist in internal combustion engines by Buick Motors and then by the Curtiss company at Hammondsport. It was not a propitious start. The engine that had brought victory to Curtiss at Rheims in 1909 was largely Pfitzner's work, but he also had ideas about aircraft. He designed and built a monoplane that incorporated a novel principle of lateral control. Sliding panels or "equalizers" were installed in the wing tips, one to slide inward while the other slid outward to provide a variable wing surface, such as exercised by birds in flight. The increased extension of one tip caused greater lift on that side and hence a tendency to turn in the opposite direction. Pfitzner applied this principle to a Burgess pusher, but successive crashes left him in a state of deep depression. On 12 July 1910, carrying his aeronautical drawings in a suitcase, he rented a dory and rowed out into Marblehead harbor. Neither Pfitzner nor his drawings were ever seen again, but a pistol, recently fired, was found in the empty boat. With his disappearance, the sliding panels ceased to be a feature of Burgess biplanes.

A happier state of affairs followed. At the September 1910 Harvard–Boston Aero Meet, Burgess introduced a new model fitted with interplane ailerons and a triangle landing gear. It won immediate praise for its "fine workmanship and beautiful appearance" and it gained Burgess a 250-dollar cup as second prize for amateurs. He further received an order from Claude Grahame-White for construction of three baby biplanes, which the Englishman had designed. During the winter of 1910–11 Burgess negotiated with the Wrights an agreement that gave him permission to build copies of their machines. The Burgess–Wright biplane met with considerable success in 1911, notably in the hands of Harry N. Atwood, billed as the "King of the Air," who broke the American distance record by flying from St. Louis to New York in 28 hours 31 minutes air time, and of Lt. Thomas de Witt Milling, who set a world record for duration with two passengers—1 hour 54 minutes 43 seconds—at the Nassau Boulevard meet on Long Island near the end of September. Fitted with floats and tested by a talented twenty-year-old, Clifford L. Webster, the Burgess product performed well from the water too; while company fliers kept busy in Florida during the cold weather, Frank T. Coffyn demonstrated the versatile "hydro" in the ice-covered waters of the Hudson around New York.

Better credentials could not be found for construction of a cup defender. Reluctant at first to accept an order that called for delivery of the finished product in a matter of weeks, Burgess pointed out that a machine intended for speeds of 100 miles per hour or more should be planned with particular care and subjected to exhaustive tests. Yet the urgency was so great that the firm agreed to go ahead and do its best under the circumstances. Throughout the summer, work proceeded apace in the wooden buildings comprising the company plant at Marblehead. Starling Burgess himself did the original design work on all new models. He had finally found the time to qualify for a pilot's license—No. 136, bearing the date 15 June 1912—and now threw himself wholeheartedly into the creation of a high-speed monoplane, the first of its kind in America. At his side were Greely Curtis and Frank H. Russell, at one time general manager of the Wright company, and two draftsmen, Hashimoto and Agatsuma, both of Japanese origin.

The white-painted craft that emerged on 19 August was a source of pride to all concerned. Impressive in its strength of construction, care shown in design, and attention to detail, it left little doubt that American manufacturers could, if need be, keep fully abreast of Europe. As *Aerial Age* described it, the airplane was "a thing of beauty, designed on a combination of lines partaking [of] the best of all foreign makes." More than any other monoplane the Burgess racer resembled the Morane–Saulnier, with a certain similarity to the Nieuport and Hanriot as well; the wing section was related to the Paulhan–Tatin Torpedo. Its principal characteristics were as follows: wing span, 29 feet 3 inches; length, 24 feet 6 inches; area of main planes, 128 feet; chord, 5 feet; weight empty, 755 pounds; weight loaded, ready for flight, 1,135 pounds; Intégrale propeller, 8 feet 2½ inches in diameter; aluminum cowling over the motor; wings and fuselage, covered with Goodyear fabric, were of ash and spruce. The undercarriage was composed of two short skids slightly turned up in front and the standard Wright four-wheeled running gear. The stabilizing surface at the rear, about 10

The Burgess *Cup Defender,* especially built for the 1912 race by a syndicate of Chicago businessmen. It never left the ground. Courtesy National Air and Space Museum.

square feet in area, was semicircular in outline; just in front of it were twin rudders, the combined area of which was a scant 4 square feet; the elevator, semielliptical in shape, had an area of 12 square feet. There were two 12-gallon fuel tanks and two 6-gallon tanks for oil.

The Marblehead designers had in general followed Wright practice in the construction. But realizing their lack of experience with pylon racing, they had their own stress figures checked at the Massachusetts Institute of Technology, which assured them that the cup contender would stand any conceivable strain with a comfortable margin of safety. There was no time for a tryout, nor did the syndicate find this disturbing. Company officials were told that the syndicate had complete confidence in the small monoplane and that all trials could take place after it was brought to Chicago.

The machine arrived there on 24 August and Burgess followed on his own initiative and at his own expense to put himself at the disposal of the syndicate and, at its request, to supervise the assembly of the racer. He found the city with a good deal more to preoccupy it than prepara-

144

tions for the Gordon Bennett. It was a presidential election year and Chicago was engrossed in a noisy political campaign. The Republican Convention, meeting there in June, had nominated Taft for a second term; at a stormy convention in Baltimore the Democrats had nominated Woodrow Wilson on the forty-sixth ballot; and Theodore Roosevelt was the nominee of a hurriedly organized third party, the Progressive, or "Bull Moose," at a second Chicago convention.

In Washington the administration was embroiled in Latin America: Mexico was a restless neighbor, unhappy at foreign exploitation of its natural resources, fearing industrial dependency on the United States and concerned at the poverty of its people; led by Felix Diaz, a revolt against the Madero government had taken place. In his annual message to Congress, Taft concentrated on Central America, invoking the Monroe Doctrine in respect to Honduras and Nicaragua. To forestall foreign intervention in the "vital neighborhood of a Panama Canal [not yet built] and the zone of the Caribbean" when Nicaragua delayed payment on its European debts, the United States itself intervened. By presidential authority, not by congressional action, the Marines landed in that country on 14 August.

Few paid attention to the far-off Balkan wars that culminated in a treaty between Bulgaria and Serbia, or to the war in the Libyan desert that ended with the cession of Tripolitania by Turkey to Italy. Of more immediate interest to Americans were the new motor cars. It was the year that Harry Leland put the Kettering self-starter on a Cadillac, thereby doing away with that lethal appendage, the hand crank. The Ford, Reo, Maxwell, Chevrolet, and Hupmobile were all on the market at less than a thousand dollars; a Cadillac could be bought for not much more. To the strains of "Alexander's Ragtime Band" or "The Turkey Trot," "The Grizzly Bear" or "The Bunny Hug," a dance craze was sweeping the country. A full-course dinner at a leading restaurant cost one dollar and fifty cents.

To the dismay of Burgess, virtually every part of his beautiful airplane was immediately the target of criticism by self-styled authorities. A major question was that of controls. Burgess machines had always

145

been equipped with the Wright system of one stick operating the elevator, the other the warping and steering mechanism, but company experts had considered these unsuitable for high-speed flight. Frank Russell had pointed out that the Wright control required much wrist action, which on a long flight with many turns around pylons could produce a dangerous degree of pilot fatigue. Nevertheless Wright controls had been installed, only to be the subject of renewed controversy. Among other objections, said *Aerial Age* with heavy sarcasm, common comment was that the "rudder surface was too small or too large, one way or the other, and there should have been lots more guy wires to the wings." Thus far, it added, there "had been no suggestion that the craft, greased, would slide through the air easier, but outside of this, Mr. Burgess . . . has been offered every suggestion capable of being devised by the near-technical board. . . . Parts which they are skeptical of . . . will be altered so that nothing short of a cyclone or a few rods of stone fence will . . . cause the aircraft to do more than hesitate. Then, too, a gallon of pitch has been purchased to help the propeller, should this too meet the disapproval of the gallery experts." Only the magnificent 160-horsepower Gnôme motor escaped the critics' censure; it performed without a hitch on a block test.

Even more serious was the question of a pilot. Difficult as it is to believe, little thought seems to have been given to the matter when the Burgess racer was commissioned. The firm had hoped that a proficient flier would be named by the syndicate to live at Marblehead and follow the construction as it progressed. But no such assignment was made. At the beginning of 1912, only eighty-two aviators had been licensed by the Aero Club of America, of whom eight had so far been killed. The field, therefore, was not large from which to choose an airman with sufficient expertise to handle an untried machine specifically designed for speed. Curtiss claimed that he was too busy, and any possibility that the Wrights might supply a pilot had been quashed by a statement, repeated in *Aircraft* magazine, that they were "entirely out of the racing game" and were confining their "attention exclusively to the construction of the regulation machine."

146

Vainly, the nationwide hunt went on for alternate American entries. In July, with no pilot in sight, the Aero Club of Illinois issued a near-desperate appeal to all United States licensed aviators "willing to uphold American prestige and reputation by driving the club's new $15,000 racing aeroplane in defense of the Gordon Bennett international aviation trophy." Prospective candidates were offered the use of the two-seater Nieuport brought over by the Aero Club of America, along with the assistance of Marcel Tournier, factory representative of Nieuport in the United States, to familiarize themselves with the workings of a monoplane. Under the supervision of Max Lillie, proprietor of an aviation school and taxi-plane service at Cicero Field, Chicago's close-in airfield, two local Wright fliers—Andrew Drew and DeLloyd Thompson, both well known on the exhibition circuit—took advantage of the opportunity. Thompson had only just qualified for a license, having received No. 134 on 15 June. Drew, a field director at the Lillie school, had received his, No. 50, on 8 August 1911. They were joined in warm-up flights by Norman Prince, considered in some quarters to be the most likely pilot of the Burgess, and succeeded in getting the Nieuport up to 70 miles per hour—hardly enough to defend the trophy but useful in gaining experience. According to *Aero and Hydro,* Thompson in particular astonished his mentors "by the masterful way in which he handled the craft." Optimistically, the weekly predicted that "a plenitude of pilots" would be ready to compete for America come September.

But after they had had a chance to examine the advanced Burgess, both Thompson and Drew bowed out. Prince averred that he was "willing to take a crack at her," and Charles Dickinson backed him up, whereupon a virulent dispute broke out with the committee in charge of the race, which alleged that Prince did not have the necessary experience. The argument further delayed a decision; it was not until 27 August that the syndicate agreed to ask Glenn Luther Martin, who was then at the height of his fame as a barnstormer on the Pacific Coast, to take over the racer with Prince as alternate. At the same time, E. R. Armstrong was called in as "technical adviser."

Martin had learned to fly in 1909 on a Curtiss-type biplane of bamboo and varnished cotton cloth, powered by a secondhand 15-horsepower Ford engine. Born on 17 January 1886 at Macksburg, Iowa, he had spent his boyhood in Liberal, Kansas, where his father ran a hardware store, and in Salina, where he became a garage helper. In 1905 the family moved to California, where the elder Martin opened an automobile repair shop at Santa Ana. When Glenn Martin heard about the Wright brothers he decided to follow their example, building and practicing first with a glider then with his homemade flying machine. He began giving public demonstrations in 1910 and by the following year was much in demand at expositions and county fairs. He was awarded pilot's license No. 56 on 9 August 1911.

Martin had a flair for publicity, which in 1912 catapulted him into the news. On 20 January he took off with a sack of mail from the old Dominguez Field near Los Angeles and shortly thereafter dropped the bag into the outstretched arms of the postmaster at nearby Compton— "Pacific Aerial Delivery Route No. 1," as a front-page story described the feat the next day. On 10 May, after fitting his biplane with pontoons and carrying an inflated tire tube as a life preserver, he established a record by flying from Newport Bay to Catalina Island—a distance of 38 miles—and back again. He made more headlines by dropping a baseball into a catcher's mitt; by delivering the Fresno *Republican* by parachute; by chasing coyotes and hunting escaped criminals from the air; by releasing a blizzard of department store advertising on a goggle-eyed public. He claimed to be the first to take his mother aloft and the first to shoot movies from an airplane. Stern, shy and reserved by nature, wearing thick-lensed glasses that belied his daring in the skies, he would later play the romantic role of an aviator in a Hollywood film with Mary Pickford—*The Girl of Yesterday.*

Martin had registered for the Chicago meet and had indicated his intention of going out for an expert aviator's certificate, tests for which were to be given at Cicero Field on 12, 13, 14 and 15 September. He had never been up in a monoplane. Yet he had his own ideas about the *Cup Defender*'s design. Although the plane had still not been flown, he expressed the opinion that the wings were too large. While Burgess advised against it, new wing panels were hastily built to Martin's specifications and rushed to Chicago, together with large quantities of spare parts as insurance against further delays. Martin also voiced dissatisfaction with the Wright controls, and the syndicate had no choice but to let him install his own. Heated discussions about possible structural changes led nowhere while precious hours that might have been spent in trial flights ticked by inexorably.

Meanwhile another pilot was being considered as a member of the American team. Paul Peck, a twenty-two-year-old stunt flier from Charlestown, West Virginia, who like Weymann wore pince-nez glasses under his goggles, had obtained license No. 57 on a Rex–Smith monoplane equipped with a Gyro motor over the weekend of 29 and 30 July 1911 and was now in the limelight as a preeminent exponent of the Columbia biplane. Made by the Washington Aeroplane Company of Washington, D.C., the Columbia pusher featured a short torpedo-shaped nacelle protecting pilot and passenger, a 25-gallon fuel tank, and a 7-gallon tank for castor oil. Mounted on skids that were flexible, by means of a solid steel axle and rubber springs, were two sturdy wheels as undercarriage. Width of the plane was 30 feet, the chord 5 feet 9 inches, of which 2 feet were flexible; ailerons that took 4 feet of the end of each plane were interconnected so as to give movement of about 4 inches, which appeared to be sufficient. A tail plane with a surface of 27 square feet was also flexible; the rudder had 7 square feet of surface. The weight of the plane empty was 600 pounds. At an estimated 65 miles per hour it could remain five hours in the air.

Peck had broken the American duration with this type of machine on 24 May 1912 in a highly dramatic flight at Nassau Boulevard of 4 hours 23 minutes 15 seconds. Part of it was accomplished in a blinding rain and electrical storm, with wind gusts, according to the Weather Bureau, that reached 48 miles per hour. As dusk descended on New York City, black clouds so darkened the sky that the pilot could not see his watch or instruments, and before he could attempt a landing a fire had to be lighted to guide him into the field. Peck's record was regarded as a boost for the air-cooled, seven-cylinder, 50-horsepower Gyro motor—the only successful rotary engine, it was claimed, in America. It had proved itself two months earlier on a flight of 138 miles lasting 2 hours 18 minutes at the Army Aviation field near Augusta, Georgia, where on 27 March Peck had the Columbia climb 1,500 feet in 3 minutes. Made of nickel and vanadium steel throughout, it was a product of the Gyro Motor Company, also of Washington, D.C. While obviously not in the same class as a Gnôme of 100 or more horsepower, its performance compared favorably with that of any stationary engine of American manufacture. Offered in three models, according to an advertising brochure—three, five, and seven cylinders of 22, 35 and 50 horsepower respectively—it weighed only 3¼ pounds per horsepower.

Known for his unorthodox style of flying, Peck liked to call himself "Peck's Bad Boy of Aviation." He followed up his Nassau Boulevard success with a demonstration of mail carrying that brought him added publicity. Under the management of an organization called Berger Aviation, he staged a three-day aerial circus at Coney Island, an amusement park on the Ohio River near Cincinnati named after the similar establishment outside New York. For an extra attraction, Peck asked Cincinnati postmaster Elias A. Montfort for authorization to fly souvenir mail between Coney Island and the township of California on the eastern edge of the city. Permission was granted and, with the approval of United States Postmaster General Frank Hitchcock, the course was designated "Ohio Air Mail Route No. 631,003." A substation set up at Coney Island was stocked with picture postcards and a supply of one-cent stamps, and a special cachet "U.S. Official Aerial Mail" was applied to each piece of mail flown.

A week later Peck was drawing crowds at Middletown, Ohio, where from a ball park south of the city he filled a two-day engagement on 25 and 26 July, then extended the exhibition by another day. "Thousands and thousands of people," reported the Middletown *Journal,* watched him fly 5,000 feet above the grounds and "jump and glide and spiral to safety." On 17 August he carried passengers for the Merchants' Association at Brazil, Indiana, heading for Chicago with his eye on the

Paul Peck, American entrant in the 1912 Gordon Bennett, with his
Gyro-powered Columbia biplane. Peck was killed while testing the machine
a few days after the race. Photograph in author's collection.

Gordon Bennett and bringing with him two Gyro-powered Columbia aircraft, one a biplane the other a monoplane.

To compound its difficulties in finding the right combination of plane and pilot, the Aero Club of America had disqualified both Peck and Martin for violation of the rules during a meet at Boston; with their licenses suspended, neither was technically eligible to represent the club in an international contest. "All America has is brand new machines and no one to fly them," observed Glenn Curtiss sadly, predicting flatly that France would win. The club was in a quandary; 9 September was fast approaching and no other qualified pilots had come forth. Appeals were made for reinstating Peck and Martin in view of the national emergency, and at the eleventh hour club officials relented. The Burgess and Columbia pilots would be allowed to compete. Also at the last minute, Howard Gill, a Burgess-Wright exhibition flier, was added to the list of theoretical starters.

Across the Atlantic the French elimination trials, held in a series of three runs on 14 July over a 200 kilometer course at Rheims, had produced what appeared to be an invincible team. It was led by Jules Védrines, who since his victory in the Paris–Madrid race had added lavishly to his laurels. In the Circuit of Europe he had taken first place in the second stage and was fourth in the general classification; only motor trouble with his 70-horsepower Gnôme-driven Morane kept him from doing better. The grueling Circuit of Britain—one of the three great races of 1911—for a *Daily Mail* prize of 10,000 pounds had brought to the fore his remarkable qualities of physical endurance, iron nerve, and tenacity of purpose. In a thrilling duel with black-bearded Ensign Jean Conneau of the French navy, who flew under the pseudonym of André Beaumont, he put on a memorable performance but in his eagerness lost time by losing his way. Beaumont on the contrary made no mistakes in navigation and brought his Blériot home ahead of Védrines in the equally speedy Morane. Védrines's temper did not endear him to the caustic editor of *The Aeroplane*: "We can only be thankful that La Belle France sends us very few such specimens of her population. He went off very fast, and was soon out of sight—the best place for him."

Cruelly disappointed at losing the thousand-mile race, the Frenchman was given a consolation prize of 200 pounds by Lord Northcliffe's paper; later he received 2,000 pounds from a flying benefit in his honor arranged by Grahame-White at Hendon, where—despite his impolite behavior—50,000 people accorded him an ovation.

Back in France, Védrines continued to make one notable flight after another, including delivery of *Le Journal* on 12 August from Paris to seaside Trouville, 180 kilometers distant, in 1 hour 43 minutes. He participated brilliantly in military maneuvers that summer and in the *Concours Militaire* for airplanes in the fall. For covering a total distance of 2,334 kilometers, he received 2,500 francs in October as one-quarter of the Quentin–Bauchart Prize, and he was declared winner of the Pommery Cup on the basis of his Paris–Angoulême flight of 22 May, for which the Aéro Club de France awarded him its gold medal.

Widespread attention at this time was directed to the striking Deperdussin monoplane—capable of 90 kilometers per hour (56 m/hr) with a 50-horsepower Gnôme motor. No less than seven of these highly acclaimed machines had been entered in the Circuit of Europe, in which third place went to a Deperdussin with René Vidart at the controls. Védrines saw the possibilities of the slim-fuselaged, wheel-controlled craft, in which skids were part of the undercarriage and disc wheels optional from the start. He opened the year 1912 at Pau by breaking the world speed record on 12 January with a 100-horsepower version of the Deperdussin, reeling off 145.177 kilometers in one hour. On 2 February with a 140-horsepower engine he broke all records for 50, 100, 150, and 200 kilometers, reaching a speed of 161.290 kilometers per hour. It was the first time an airplane had attained the magic mark of one hundred miles an hour. On 1 March, surpassing his own records for speed, he drove the Deperdussin at a rate of 166.821 kilometers per hour, pushing this up on 2 March to 167.910 kilometers per hour (104.303 m/hr). "He driveth furiously," someone said, quoting the Old Testament.

Védrines was temporarily put out of action when, flying from Douai to Paris on 29 April, he struck a cluster of telegraph wires near his home district of Saint-Denis and crashed on the railway tracks. Picked up unconscious, he remained in a coma for two days. He was decorated in his hospital bed on 3 May as a chevalier of the Legion of Honor. By the middle of June he had recovered sufficiently to enter the Circuit of Anjou—the first contest designed to show to what extent the airplane could be depended upon in war—as a member of the Deperdussin team with Vidart and Marcel Prévost. At the start on 16 June a violent storm was raging, bending the poplar trees almost double. Still shaken, perhaps, by his accident, Védrines showed unusual caution. Standing atop a gasoline tin, he harangued his fellow fliers on the risks of taking off and, in good socialist style, called for a pilots' strike—a plea ignored by a dozen daring airmen, including Roland Garros, the eventual victor and the last to win a major race with a Blériot.

On 13 July, the day before the elimination trials at Rheims, Védrines had once more demolished his own records for distances between 10 and 200 kilometers with a fantastic 170.77 kilometers per hour. His best time in the trials themselves was a shade less—169.9 kilometers per hour—but that was enough to assure him of the leading place on the French team. These speeds were achieved with a revolutionary new Deperdussin of monocoque design, powered by a 140-horsepower Gnôme, the brainchild of Louis Béchereau, one of the greatest aeronautical engineers of the period. It was an outgrowth of the standard single-seater Type B Deperdussin, made of ash and spruce with an aluminum cowling extending to the cockpit, which in 1911 had been a favorite of both civil and military fliers in French and British aviation. The difference lay in the hollow, cigar-shaped shell that formed the fuselage of the monocoque—a word derived from the Greek *monos* (single) and the French *coque* (shell). It permitted speeds hitherto unattainable by craft offering more resistance to the wind.

It was the Swiss pilot-engineer Eugène Ruchonnet, shop foreman in Léon Levavaseur's factory for the Antoinette, who first introduced the concept of the monocoque, and Béchereau applied the principle to the construction of the Deperdussin fuselage. Thin strips of wood from the tulip tree—a tough species often used in cabinet work—were placed in

The record-breaking Deperdussin monocoque flown to first and second place for France in the 1912 contest at Chicago. Courtesy Roger-Viollet, Paris.

a mold, criss-crossing one another and glued together in three layers to a thickness of 4 millimeters, then covered inside and out with a glued and varnished fabric. The resulting product, requiring the most skilled and painstaking workmanship, carried all of the structural loads without internal bracing—as opposed to a framework left open like a cat's cradle or covered with cloth.

Thirty-two-year-old Béchereau was a graduate of the Ecole des Arts et Métiers at Angers and in his youth had been associated with Clément Ader. He had won a prize of 150 gold francs in a model competition organized by the newspaper *L'Auto.* After completing his military service, he joined the embryonic Société de Construction d'Appareils Aériens, founded by a nephew of Ader at Levallois, near Paris. In 1909 the firm was approached by Armand Deperdussin, an enterprising silk merchant, with an order for a flying machine to be hung in the Bon Marché, Paris's largest department store, during the Christmas shopping season. The outcome was a monoplane of the canard type, with a four-wheeled undercarriage and a four-bladed propeller, a wing span of 8 meters and a fuselage of the same length. Flight-tested in 1910 with a

155

40-horsepower Clerget motor, first at Laon and later at Rheims, it was the forerunner of all airplanes subsequently built by the Société Pour les Appareils Deperdussin, for which Béchereau was engaged as chief engineer and technical director.

An affable man with a large moustache and a lordly air, always elegantly dressed, Deperdussin had left Belgium in 1901 to seek his fortune in the silk business in Paris. Restless, brimming with energy, intelligent and ahead of his time, he prospered sufficiently to indulge a speculative bent; before fathering the airplane that would become a symbol of speed, he had opened an institute that specialized in hot-air therapy. His start in life was under more modest circumstances. On 28 December 1895, when the Lumière brothers gave the first of their novel Cinématographe shows in the basement of a Paris café, they hired young Armand as barker to draw in an audience from the sidewalk. Becoming wealthy, he spent generously, not only in the development of his popular machine but in lending a hand to friends in distress and supporting worthy causes. At the Circuit of Anjou he unveiled the plane to admiring throngs in a public relations display that took up an entire floor of the leading hotel. Acting on the advice of Emile Aubrun, his director of sport, he advanced half a million francs toward the purchase of the Bétheny airfield and its forty-two hangars to prevent the historic Rheims site from being acquired by foreign business interests.

Wisely, Deperdussin gave Béchereau a free rein in research and design. Védrines's sensational monocoque was 6.25 meters (20 ft 6 in) in length; it had a wing span of 7 meters (22 ft 11½ in) with a total wing area of only 10 square meters (107.64 ft²). Power was supplied by a two-row Gnôme motor of 100 horsepower, consisting of two standard 50-horsepower units on a common crankshaft bearing, protected by a semicircular cowling joined with the wings to form the nose. For the Gordon Bennett a 160-horsepower model was installed. The front of the motor was concealed by a circular cone that turned with the rotary motion of the cylinders—an innovation that proved very helpful in cutting down drag. Designed to withstand a high degree of stress, the wings were only slightly cambered and inversely tapered on the inboard trailing edge. Longitudinal spars were partly of hickory, partly of ash, and the ribs were of ash anchored in pine. The covering was of extra-strong linen doped with a preparation known as Emaillete. Wing warping was controlled by a steering wheel like an automobile's; steering itself was by foot bar. Sleek and streamlined, with a simple yet sturdy undercarriage to which large disc wheels and a central skid were fitted, the latest Deperdussin required skillful pilotage. Its *landing* speed was no less than 60 miles per hour—a rate that in the air had won the Gordon Bennett trophy for Grahame-White in 1910.

A similar machine was provided for Marcel Prévost, the second flier chosen to represent France, but it had a 100-horsepower motor. Prévost had turned in an average of 164.338 kilometers per hour in the elimination trials, and a week later he had shown what the monocoque could do in a meet at the grass-covered airfield of Juvisy, an hour or so from Paris, to the wild applause of an overflow audience in the small grandstand. A native of the city that had sponsored the first Gordon Bennett, he was born at Rheims on 11 April 1887 and educated at the Ecole Pratique de Commerce et d'Industrie. But instead of following a business career he became so imbued with the excitement of the early days of flying that he began to take lessons as soon as he had completed his military service. He received pilot's license No. 475 on 11 April 1911 and gave his first exhibition at Compiègne; with no further experience he entered the Circuit of Europe in June. In that race he got as far as Calais, where he withdrew because of mechanical difficulties. Prévost was brevetted as military pilot No. 38 in July and placed third in the *Concours Militaire* of October–November, where Weymann and his Nieuport were first and René Moineau with a Bréguet biplane was second. Prévost's 100-horsepower Deperdussin registered a speed of 89.5 kilometers per hour, enough to gain the substantial cash award of 218,000 francs. With the same monoplane at Rheims on 2 December, he broke the record for altitude with one passenger, climbing to 3,000 meters in 55 minutes, after which he embarked on a series of exhibition flights that took him to Compiègne, Nouzon, and Gaillac.

Prévost began the year 1912 with another record: on 3 January he ascended to 2,200 meters with two passengers. On 13 April he made the first flight with a passenger from Paris to London in a day, delivering a two-seater Deperdussin to the Royal Naval Air Station at Eastchurch. After several flights around France he tried for the Pommery Cup on 30 April, flying from Nancy to Les Sables-d'Olonne in one day and breaking the world record for cross-country flying with a passenger. In August he took part in the British military trials, where the Deperdussin won a 2,000-pound second prize. Strong-featured, chestnut-haired, with an incipient moustache, Prévost was chief instructor at the Société Deperdussin's school near Rheims when nominated to fly for his country at Chicago.

Third place on the French team was allotted to André Frey, who had registered an average of 142.800 kilometers per hour at the elimination trials; he had also broken the world record for speed with one passenger, covering 150 kilometers in 1 hour 7 minutes. Frey, a native of Tours, was born on 21 January 1886; he attended the Ecole des Arts et Métiers there and performed his military service in the balloon corps at Versailles. Good-looking, with black hair and a prominent moustache, he was quick to make friends because of his personable manner, his imperturbable demeanor, and his daring. He was drawn to powered flight from its inception, making his initial ascent on a Sommer biplane in 1909. He was one of the first hundred fliers in France to receive a license, taking the Aéro Club's No. 93 on 10 June 1910. Not to be confused with the German Alfred Frey, who was licensed in France at about the same time, he participated in most of the meetings which marked the beginning of European aviation—at Budapest, in Belgium, Holland, Germany, Italy, and at various French towns—piloting successively a Blériot, a Morane–Borel, a Savary biplane, Paulhan's Aéro-Torpille as well as his experimental biplane, and finally the Hanriot monoplane with which he scored his greatest success.

In the Paris–Rome race, flying a Morane monoplane, Frey placed third, after Beaumont, the winner, and Garros, "the eternal second." Only one other of the twelve starters finished the course. From Rome, promoters extended the race over the dangerous Apennines to Turin, and on this stretch Frey was the sole contestant. He had flown as far as Castiglione d'Orcia when he lost his way in a fog. Trying to land in the Cimini hills near Viterbo, he fell into a wood and was critically injured. At a hospital in the small town on Ronciglione, where surgeons operated on his legs, Frey became a local hero because of the exemplary fortitude he displayed over the weeks leading to his recovery. The authorities outdid themselves in providing the best of care, and when he departed the municipal council presented him with a testimonial in remembrance of his stay. Besides courage, Frey had a strong constitution. Still on crutches, he entered a Bologna–Venice–Rimini race and easily won. In the Circuit of Anjou he lost out to motor trouble, but starred in the meeting at Vienna that followed.

The Hanriot monoplane on which Frey qualified for the Gordon Bennett was, as in so many other cases, the outgrowth of its designer's experience in bicycle and motorcar racing. A dark-haired, strong-jawed figure with a bushy moustache who had started life as a champagne producer, René Hanriot began to compete in 1898 in the great road events that were a hallmark of the times, including the Paris–Vienna auto contest of 1902—"the race of races"—and the hectic, lethal Paris–Madrid race of 1903. Using various makes of vehicles—Darracq, Benz, Clément-Bayard—he drove not only in France but in Austria, Italy, Belgium, Sicily, and America: in 1904 he was world speed champion at 128 kilometers per hour. In 1907 thirty-one-year-old Hanriot settled in Châlons-sur-Marne, the better to pursue his training on the relatively good roads of the region. There his interest shifted to aviation, and after taking part in the Automobile Club's Grand Prix in 1908 he placed an order with Levavaseur for an Antoinette, to be delivered early in 1909. Impatient at successive delays, he decided to build a model that he had designed himself the previous year. He went into production at Rheims in 1910 with a light but well-built machine that had an open framework fuselage and a 50-horsepower Buchet motor, exhibiting it at the second aeronautical *salon* in Paris and opening a London branch, the

159

Hanriot Monoplane Company on Great Portland Street. He had sold twenty planes at the *salon* before trial flights were made at the Bétheny airfield.

The results were unimpressive, and Hanriot sought the collaboration and advice of Levavaseur's engineer Ruchonnet in working out a totally new design. Ruchonnet had at one time been a boat builder; it was not surprising that he should design a fuselage like a racing skiff, on the order of the Antoinette, whose robust frame, covered with mahogany plywood, required very little wire bracing. Powered by a 45-horsepower Clerget engine, with Ruchonnet at the controls, the first monoplane of this type was heavily damaged on landing; a smaller version, Darracq-powered, was used for instruction at a flying school that Hanriot established at Mourmelon in the spring of 1910. Later models were equipped with either a Gyp or E.N.V. engine.

Hanriot's young son Marcel had been a passionate follower of his father's career as a racing driver and took naturally to flying. He was not yet sixteen when on 10 June 1910 he was granted a license, No. 95, thus becoming a boy wonder; René Hanriot did not pass his pilot's test until 3 February 1911, when he obtained license No. 368. With Louis Wagner, a former driver of Darracq racing cars and chief pilot at the Hanriot school, Marcel Hanriot represented the company in many of the meetings in 1910 and 1911 both on the continent and in Great Britain. Wagner won all the first prizes at Budapest in June 1911, except the one for speed, for which he placed second, while at Lanark in 1911 Marcel Hanriot was second in speed and won the prize for altitude. The machine in production at that time was powered by an eight-cylinder, 35-horsepower, water-cooled E.N.V. engine mounted high on the nose of the mahogany-skinned fuselage. The frame was of ash, spruce, and steel tubing, the propeller was mahogany, and the wings and tail were covered with unbleached cotton. A machine of this type was taken to Tashkent in Turkestan by the Italian pilot Campo di Scipio for one of the first flights in Asia on 20 November 1911. Concurrently a two-seater model was entered in the French *Concours Militaire*, as a result

Table 7
1912 • French Team

Pilot	Machine	Motor	Propeller
Jules Védrines	Deperdussin monoplane	160-hp Gnôme	Chauvière
Marcel Prévost	Deperdussin monoplane	100-hp Gnôme	Chauvière
André Frey	Hanriot monoplane	100-hp Gnôme	Chauvière

of which four machines were ordered, to form a squadron under the command of army pilot Capt. E. Franezon.

A marked change in design occurred early in 1912. Alfred Pagny, who had become chief engineer of the Nieuport firm, was engaged by Hanriot to design a faster monoplane: the resulting product bore a close resemblance in its contours to the contemporary Nieuports. Two two-seater models took part in the British military trials that August, putting up the best speed and climbing performances, though attempts to promote the monoplane commercially in Britain were not successful. That did not prevent Frey from bringing to Chicago the 100-horse-power Gnôme-driven racing model with which he had done so well at the French elimination trials. It had a length of 21¾ feet (6.65 m), a wing span of 24 feet (7.30 m), a weight of 661 pounds (300 kg), and a total wing area of 91 square feet (8.50 m²). Its potential speed was considered to be 106 miles per hour (170 km/hr).

The composition of the French team is shown in table 7. Guillaume Busson, another Deperdussin pilot and holder of license No. 121 since 21 June 1910, and A. Liger, pilot of a Morane–Saulnier who had gained license No. 573 on a Vinet monoplane on 22 August 1911, had been named as alternates. But it was Emile Aubrun who would go to Chicago and stand by as substitute if needed. Altogether, six machines were sent to America. Arriving in New York on 1 September, Védrines was saluted by the press as "the world's foremost skymaster." With his companions he entrained at once for the scene of the contest.

No finer flying facility could be imagined than the 4.14 mile semielliptical course laid out during the summer months at Clearing, not far from the Illinois Aero Club's Cicero Field, which was judged too small for the race. The verdict was unanimous, said *Aircraft,* that the course with its six pylons and eight commodious hangars was "the very best ever arranged for a flying contest anywhere in the world," an opinion to be shared by Védrines after he had flown over it. In mid-March, when club officials had begun looking for a suitable circuit, it seemed that lakeside Winnetka, within twenty miles of commuting distance from the city would afford "the ideal place . . . as far as could be seen under a heavy blanket of snow." When the snow melted, this proved an illusion. Clearing offered many miles of wide open space: a small army of gardeners had worked assiduously to create a flat, grassy surface safe for landing at any speed and protected by six miles of wire fence from an expected crowd of 240,000. There were no grandstands. The judges' and press stands were located on the north stretch, on both sides of which were enclosed areas for club members and automobiles; to the east were the hangars.

From the public's standpoint, the course had one serious defect—inaccessibility. Those fortunate enough to come by automobile had a route mapped out for them, starting from Michigan Boulevard. Railroads were reported ready to handle up to 130,000 persons an hour. But the only practical way to reach the grounds was by streetcar, entailing a two-hour trip with a hot and dusty walk at the end. Coupled with the fact that 9 September fell on a Monday, a working day instead of a weekend, attendance was foredoomed to be sparse.

With mixed emotions the French discovered that whatever competition they had expected was fast fading. Charles Dickinson, confronted with allegations that the Burgess was unsafe and required modifications yet to be completed, and despairing of the pilot problem, had decided to withdraw the syndicate's *Cup Defender.* Paul Peck's Columbia was immobilized with a broken magneto part while he searched in vain for a replacement, well aware that "for want of a nail" the [kingdom] could be lost. Nothing had been heard from the other entrants. Grahame-White and Hamel were assumed to be sailing from England the last week in August, but neither had put in an appearance, nor had George Dyott, though already in the United States, brought his machine to Chicago. Holland had dropped out, so had Switzerland, and there was no word from Belgium.

Particularly disappointing was the defection of Britain's leading airmen who, without further explanation, were simply reported by *Flight* as "unable to go across the Atlantic." One reason may have been the expense, but there could have been another factor in the case of Grahame-White. He had celebrated his marriage that summer to Dorothy Taylor, daughter of Bertrand Leroy Taylor of New York. The ceremony at Widford Church near Chelmsford was a highlight of the social season and the first in which airplanes played a part. Most of the guests traveled from London by special train or motor, but the groom flew in on a Howard–Wright biplane, and his friends Pierre Verrier and B. C. Hucks came on a Maurice Farman and a Blériot. Hucks scattered confetti from the air, and then the three machines lined up on the lawn of Sir Daniel Gooch's residence "Hylands" for a festive reception. As the couple sped off in the latest creation of the motor industry, a Belgian Métallurgique, Grahame-White's gift to the bride, they were roundly cheered by well-wishers. The scene was hardly consonant with making plans to enter the Gordon Bennett in America.

Headed by Maj. Samuel Reber, the contest committee of the Aero Club of America arrived in Chicago on 7 September. Other members were George M. Myers, president of the Kansas City Aero Club, Capt. Charles deForest Chandler of the U.S. Army, W. Redmond Cross and Henry A. Wise Wood of New York, and Frank X. Mudd of Chicago. They were joined by Bernard Dufrèsne, official representative of the Fédération Aéronautique Internationale. While the French machines were lined up in a row, flight-tested and ready, an American team (table 8) was still the subject of wishful thinking.

Aerial Age was clutching wildly at straws. In a special bulletin issued on 8 September, it suggested that Lincoln Beachey, who had arrived in Chicago with his modified Curtiss stunt machine, might yet save the

Table 8
1912 • Potential U.S. Team

Pilot	Machine	Motor	Propeller
Glenn Martin	Burgess monoplane	160-hp Gnôme	Chauvière
Paul Peck	Columbia biplane	50-hp Gyro	Chauvière
DeLloyd Thompson	Nieuport monoplane	70-hp Gnôme	Chauvière
Howard Gill			

day for the United States should the race be affected by adverse weather. High speed monoplanes didn't do well when there was too much wind, but if one flier announced himself ready to race, the course would have to be opened. The other fliers could then either withdraw or take a chance and fly. Beachey, an adept at bad weather flying, could insist that the race be run and "walk away with the Cup."

An erratic cross-wind was blowing at 9:30 on the sizzling hot morning of 9 September when the race was declared open, but it was not enough to stop the monoplanes. At that time of year the winds were usually stronger at midday, and Védrines, who had drawn the first start, was wasting no time. At exactly 9:40, he was in the air, acclaimed by a thin crowd of shirt-sleeved, straw-hatted fans. The left side of the Deperdussin's sleek brown fuselage was emblazoned with a likeness of the stolen Mona Lisa—as if her enigmatic smile held the secret of victory. He made the first lap in 2 minutes 24 seconds, bettering that on the sixteenth by nearly 7 seconds. In rough air, flying at 100 feet or less, he rounded the pylons at a 60-degree angle and came thundering down the stretches at speeds up to an estimated 115 miles an hour. Masterfully, he completed the thirty laps in 1 hour 10 minutes 56 seconds, treating the spectators to what *Aircraft* would call "the greatest exhibition of speed flying ever seen in America." His average for the 124.28 miles was 105.5 miles per hour (170 km/hr), slightly below the mark he had set in the French elimination trials. After the customary extra

France's famous pilot Jules Védrines, winner of the 1912 Gordon Bennett.
Courtesy Roger-Viollet, Paris.

lap, Védrines landed near his hangar, where his compatriot Jacques
Schneider, member of the armaments family, ran out to meet him, to
kiss him on both cheeks and drape the French tricolor around his shoulders. In high good humor for once, the generally moody Védrines quiz-
zically fingered his cap: "*La force du vent m'a arrachée le bouton!*" he
remarked with a smile. The wind had blown off the small button from
his cap.

A mounting breeze from the south—without which the temperature
would have been unbearable—kept back Prévost and Frey until just
before the time limit for crossing the line expired at 4:40 p.m. To the
onlookers' delight, it seemed like a real race, Prévost flying as low as
20—never more than 50—feet from the ground, Frey 100 feet above

165

him. Then the superior speed of the Deperdussin began to tell and Prévost passed the Hanriot on the back stretch, finishing the circuit in 1 hour 12 minutes 55 seconds with the same clocklike precision displayed by Védrines—but to some, cutting the pylons and banking even better. His average time was calculated at 100.05 miles per hour. Frey abandoned the contest on the twenty-third round, citing a motor overheated in the broiling sun as the cause. For the 93.3 miles he had covered, his average speed was 93 miles per hour and his fastest lap was at 2 minutes 41 seconds.

In the course of the afternoon, not content with his morning's work, Védrines successfully attempted to lower the world's record for 20 kilometers (12.4 mi). While the band played *La Marseillaise,* he covered the distance in 6 minutes 56 seconds at a speed of 107 miles per hour.

To the acute embarrassment of the United States, no American machine, not even the club Nieuport, which might have made a token flight, had left the ground. So outclassed did the defenders of the cup feel that they did not deem it worthwhile even to make a try.

Feted at a banquet that evening, crowned by the press with the title "World's Champion Aviator," Védrines took occasion to praise the advantages of speed as opposed to aerial acrobatics: "Development does not consist in frightening or amusing crowds. It is getting the aeroplane to serve safely and efficiently. . . . Speed is security, for it drives one through airholes and bad air before they can harm you." This theme of speed was developed by Schneider, who spoke of the trophy he was about to present to the Aéro Club de France for a race over water. The Schneider Cup for seaplanes would become an annual event in 1913, eventually to succeed the Gordon Bennett as the blue ribbon of the air.

Védrines departed the next day, to sail for Europe on the S.S. *La Lorraine* 11 September. He left behind warm thanks for the treatment he had received in America. "It is superb," he told a correspondent. "When you come to France next year we will do our best to make the visit as pleasant for you as you have made this one for us." Over in Paris, Georges Besançon, secretary of the Aéro Club de France, described the jubilation of its members to Gordon Bennett's *Herald,* which gave the story a two-column front-page spread. "While we had come so near win-

Celebrating the triumph of the Deperdussin monoplane, which brought the
Gordon Bennett Cup to France in 1912. Around the table at the Aéro Club
de France are (in the foreground, left to right) Jules Védrines, Marcel Prévost,
Armand Deperdussin, and Comte Henri de la Vaulx, vice-president of the club.
From *L'Aérophile,* Fall 1912, courtesy National Air and Space Museum.

ning" the cup, he said, "every year since its creation, it had always
eluded us, as though fate were against us. We are particularly glad that
a Frenchman has won, because, as a result, the race . . . will take place
in France. It is certain that interest in the contest will be much keener
than ever before. Nations that did not care to send their champions as
far as America will enter in Europe, and we may safely predict that next
year's struggle . . . will be the occasion of a brilliant manifestation."

For Charles Dickinson, whose syndicate, said *Aero and Hydro* tartly,
now had an unused racing machine on its hands, there was nothing discouraging about the fiasco: "I think we will soon begin to prepare a
machine and pilot for next year's race, in France. Then, we hope to
win." But the unused racer would play no part. The 160-horsepower
Gnôme was shipped back to France, and the hapless *Cup Defender,* victim of too many cooks, was stored in a shed where Dickinson kept a collection of old automobiles. In 1935, the shed would be cleaned out and

167

the white-winged Burgess dismantled. Donald J. Lockwood, a Dickinson associate, would write the author in 1984: "I have many pieces of it here and there—including the shipping crates. Some parts were stolen." A photograph shows the disintegrating fuselage in a group of discarded vehicles—one more object on the ash heap of history. A pity, too, because Orville Wright, when asked by the editor of *Aircraft* what was the matter with the machine, had supplied the final irony. "Nothing at all," he replied, was "the matter with it."

On 18 October Védrines, Prévost and Deperdussin were guests of honor at an Aéro Club reception in Paris, where the Gordon Bennett Cup, having once more crossed the Atlantic, was proudly turned over by Schneider to the vice-president, Comte de la Vaulx. Congratulations filled the air. Cortlandt F. Bishop, on behalf of the Aero Club of America, diplomatically paid tribute to French constructors and pilots; toasts were proposed in champagne; and the club's gold medal was awarded to Deperdussin for the machine that had finally brought the trophy to France. Schneider expressed the ardent hope it would remain there permanently.

The score was America two, Great Britain and France one each. To keep the cup permanently, the public was again reminded, three straight victories were necessary.

Chapter 6 RETURN TO RHEIMS · 1913

After three unsuccessful bids to win the Gordon Bennett Cup, France in 1913 was basking in the admiration of the world for having taken the 1912 race hands down. No other country had dared to challenge the combination of French men, motors, and machines for supremacy of the air. National pride was restored. "It was a glorious victory," was the undisputed verdict rendered by *Aircraft* magazine, "although strange to relate there were no competitors." But competitors or not, the Frenchmen among themselves had staged "a marvelous performance . . . worth going around the entire globe to witness." In the spirit of true sportsmanship, the journal had given "All honor to France and a million thanks to her noble airmen for coming to the United States and showing Americans what real speed was like."

Louis Béchereau, chief engineer of the winning firm, could not conceal his satisfaction with the Deperdussin monocoque and sang its praises to a reporter for the Paris *Herald.*

> Frankly, we are not surprised at M. Védrines' success. A year ago we made up our minds to capture the Cup, and ever since have been working with that end in view. M. Deperdussin and his engineers have never ceased to study and experiment in designing a flying machine that should be the fastest in the world.

169

Before M. Védrines left for America we knew that we had succeeded. The record which he had established a few weeks previously assured us of this. It should be observed, too, that, apart from the extra high-powered motor, the aeroplane which M. Védrines piloted to victory is now an ordinary model, and can be sold to anyone for ordinary usage. That is to say, it is strong and sound in every respect. No essential part was sacrificed for lightness. For we hold that speed must always be secondary to security.

Simplicity, too, is one of our aims in building an aeroplane. Our latest model, of which M. Védrines' racer is the first of the series, has a fuselage built in one piece, instead of being composed of a number of different parts. Greater strength and security is the result. M. Védrines' speed during the race was slightly under that of his own record in France, but this was due to the smaller circuit at Chicago . . . with the more frequent turns.

But in aviation circles across the United States faultfinding and reproof were the rule. Americans charged themselves with being too cocky—"thinking that all they needed to do was to build a machine a few days before the event, select a pilot a few hours before the start and then—WIN." Now, it was hoped, one knew better. It was just as ridiculous to suppose that a man who had been flying a machine capable of doing 60 miles an hour, put suddenly into a machine designed for 110, could have operated the craft successfully "as to expect a cart driver to drive a spirited horse without any training. It could not have been done." The Burgess *Cup Defender* was a costly object lesson. Even if it had been decided that the machine was ready to fly, no one had been trained to pilot it. In the view of the experts, it was just as well for the reputation of American aviation that the foolhardy attempt had not been made.

In the wake of the humiliation suffered by the United States the cry taken up by those most concerned was that if the country seriously intended to win the cup back again the training of aviators would have to be started at once, as well as the building of not one, but several machines for the event. Setting an example, the Goodyear Tire and Rubber Company of Akron, Ohio, opened a publicity campaign to bring the cup back in 1913. Conscious of its position as a leading supplier of balloon and airplane equipment, and aghast at the implications of the failure at Chicago, the company tried to rally support for a new contender by taking out advertisements couched in patriotic terms: "You who are most advanced in aeronautics," it asked indignantly, "are we Americans going to continue trailing our European cousins in the most modern and fascinating of sports, or is Uncle Sam going to lead? Surely, we have the pluck, pride and inventive genius to accomplish the utmost in aerial navigation."

But as far as practical steps were concerned, these exhortations seemed to fall on ears receptive to any contemporary subject but aviation. New York, always the center for matters of current interest, held an auto show, a motorboat show, an electrical exposition, a travel show, a photography exhibition, and a first-run motion picture show of Scott's Antarctic Expedition in 1913 but no air show. Art loomed large in public consciousness. The exhibition at the Sixty-ninth Regiment Armory of cubist and expressionist paintings would have far-reaching effects on American artists. That year John D. Rockefeller gave a hundred thousand dollars to establish the Rockefeller Foundation. The dance craze was gaining momentum with syncopated rhythm made respectable by Irene and Vernon Castle, while in Hollywood Mack Sennett and Charlie Chaplin were beginning to turn out comedy shorts that would live long after the era of silent films had ended. More than ever, Americans were bemused by the automobile, and factories regularly gave birth to new models: the Apperson 'Jack Rabbit,' the Essex, the Owen Magnetic, the Mercer Raceabout. At approximately five hundred dollars Henry Ford's Tin Lizzie was revolutionizing transportation for the masses and would bring its producer a profit of twenty million dollars that year. In aeronautics, it was enough for thrill-hungry crowds to watch exhibition fliers race against an automobile, or for local aero clubs to put on minor meets. Only in the realm of hydro-aeroplanes and flying boats, where Glenn Curtiss led the way, was America ahead.

Nevertheless, when inscriptions for the Gordon Bennett closed on 28 February the Aero Club of America had entered a team of two in the hope of wiping out the ignominious experience of the year before. Despite the absence of competition at Chicago, international rivalry was still keen, and a total of eleven entries from six nations were received, in the following order: Belgium, one; United States, two; France, three; Great Britain, three; Italy, one; and Germany, one.

The race was scheduled for Monday, 29 September. It was organized by a committee of the Aéro Club de France under the direction of the lighter-than-air veteran Surcouf as the concluding feature of another great tournament at Rheims. Choice of the familiar town was certain to revive nostalgic memories of the first Gordon Bennett, certain to bring out a large attendance. A poster advertized the event with a soaring, princely eagle—symbol of strength of purpose, of farsighted vision, of boldness in flight—reminding the public of the heights to which man had ascended in the intervening four years. The meet itself would open on Saturday the twenty-seventh with elimination trials to pick the defending team for France, followed by a competition for altitude and a slow-speed contest. Sunday the twenty-eighth was set aside for competitions in speed and altitude and a cross-country race of 150 kilometers.

The airplanes of 1913 were a far cry from the pioneer vehicles that had made their début at the Rheims meeting of 1909. Almost gone by now were the Wright biplane, the fabulous Antoinette, the once ubiquitous Blériot. Better understanding of the principles of flight had resulted in designs that incorporated elements of streamlining, while new domains in engineering technique were under active research. The tractor biplane had largely displaced the pusher. Spruce, ash, or other light woods were giving way to thin, high-alloy steel tubing; steel joints were becoming common; stronger body frames were tolerating increased engine power. With the lessons of lift and control more fully grasped, the problem of power was in fact paramount; although motors still had a habit of failing in flight, they were generally more reliable and delivering more horsepower in relation to weight. Nowhere could the evolution of aircraft design be observed better than in preparations for the Gordon Bennett race.

Progress in speed had been greater than any other change, and with it had come a potential new role for the airplane. Military commanders had hitherto been served by scouts on horseback or on foot; but with a machine that could travel a hundred miles an hour they would be able to glean information about enemy positions that might alter a whole campaign plan. Europe in the summer of 1913 was a powder keg. Large scale maneuvers were being carried out in Germany, France, England, and Austria, and it was taken for granted that should hostilities break out the airplane would be put to use for reconnaissance. Prelude to the coming conflagration, the Balkan wars had started up again, involving Bulgaria, Serbia, Greece, Rumania, and Turkey; there was increasing fear that war with Germany was inevitable. In several countries military authorities eyed the speeds brought forth by the Gordon Bennett as an argument in seeking appropriations for their aerial squadrons.

While biplanes were said to be structurally safer and more stable than monoplanes—the monoplane could lose a wing if bracing was inadequate—monoplanes were rapidly coming into their own. Because they did not have the struts and wires of a biplane and thus offered less head resistance, they obviously could slip through the air faster. True, England had temporarily banned the monoplane from its military programs because of an alarming number of fatalities due to structural failure, and France had followed suit. The Deperdussin racer, however, was a perfect example of the exception that proved the rule, its robust monocoque construction refuting the view that all monoplanes were dangerous. Combining speed with safety, it was selected by the first pilot to register for the 1913 Gordon Bennett, a fair-haired, unassuming young man named Henri Crombez, representing the Aero Club of Belgium.

Only twenty years old, Crombez had the distinction of having flown higher than any other Belgian, with a record of 3,000 meters, and of having been the first in his country, during the recent international exposition at Ghent, to demonstrate the possibilities of carrying mail by air. He had made his first flight as a passenger with Louis Paulhan in 1909 and from then on was obsessed with the sport of flying. At Nieuport-Bains, a small coastal resort where his well-to-do family spent their vacations, he began experiments with a makeshift machine; these terminated when the primitive apparatus capsized. He then importuned his father to send him to the flying grounds at Kiewit near Hasselt, where the chevalier Jules de Laminne was giving instructions to a pioneer group of military pilots on a Henry Farman biplane. After a few lessons he went to France and enrolled in the Farman school at Etampes. There, on 18 October 1910 he passed the tests for a license, which was granted to him as Belgian No. 26.

The elder Crombez was an indulgent father. He made a present to his son, probably the youngest flier in the kingdom, of a Sommer biplane equipped with a 50-horsepower Gnôme motor. Not realizing that the oil-spitting Gnôme had to be disassembled and overhauled at frequent intervals, Crombez underwent his first crash when it stopped abruptly in midair. A second lesson he learned at that time was that an airplane was normally capable of gliding to earth when the power failed. The machine repaired, he tried to fly from Kiewit to Nieuport but was twice forced down by carburetor trouble, the second time capsizing when taking off from a field that was too short. In 1911 his father provided him with a Sommer monoplane and, when that too crashed, with yet another of the same make. Undeterred and unafraid, Crombez fitted this machine with a more powerful Gnôme—of 70 horsepower—but wrecked it the first time he tried to get it into the air. He was hospitalized for a fortnight, at which point, on the advice of his supportive parent, he switched to a Deperdussin and made a two-way crossing of the English Channel—the first such exploit carried out from Belgian soil.

"My father," Crombez confided to the famous pilot Willy Coppens, "has played a great part in my life as an aviator. You might say he has really been my manager." That was something of an understatement, for without the funds to buy the planes on which he gained experience, Crombez might never have become the proficient flier he was on the eve of the Gordon Bennett. He had acquired a new Deperdussin monocoque with a 140-horsepower Gnôme, but at the last minute he found a Gnôme of 160 horsepower that he thought would give more speed. There had barely been enough time to try out the machine, and the

CROMBEZ
sur monocoque Deperdussin

Henri Crombez, Belgium's entry in the 1913 race, with his Deperdussin monocoque. Photograph in author's collection.

mechanics had to work through the night to change the engine. So great was the solicitude of father for son that Crombez senior would stay up all night to supervise the job.

As had happened before, entrants backed out one by one as the day of the race drew nearer. It was one thing to signify an intent to participate, quite another to design and construct a worthy contender and bring it to the starting line. For the second year in succession, Great Britain was unable to furnish a single machine—let alone a team—to dispute the title to the trophy, for the industry had produced nothing to match the high standards of the French. Top speeds for most current models varied between 60 and 70 miles per hour; motors rarely exceeded a rating of 80 horsepower. No one was building aircraft of advanced streamlined design with 160-horsepower Gnômes for superior performance. Whether it was a lack of financial inducement, a loss of initiative, insufficient encouragement by the government to develop a machine suitable

175

for military purposes, or merely a low threshold of public interest as in the United States that was responsible, the fact remained that English manufacturers trailed their counterparts on the continent by a wide margin. Even the Howard-Flanders S2 monoplane, with an 80-horsepower Gnôme, supposed to be capable of 82 miles per hour, could not be expected to stand up to the latest French product. Only the Sopwith Tabloid, a small two-seater biplane designed by Harry Hawker and F. Sigrist (also driven by an 80-horsepower Gnôme) was giving an impression of speed. At 92 miles per hour it could have made a creditable showing in any race.

Germany, too, dropped out, perhaps for similar reasons. Although German airplanes had set records in most categories they had not excelled in speed. Undoubtedly, a contributing factor was the country's continued preoccupation with the airship. Kaiser Wilhelm was still backing the dirigible against heavier-than-air craft, losing no opportunity to hail Count Zeppelin as "the greatest man of the century," taking pains to send the venerable inventor a warm telegram on his birthday, 8 July: "The Emperor and the Empire are proud of their gallant conqueror of the air." It would take the crushing loss, later that year, of the L2—the count's newest and the world's largest airship—for the London *Times* to call on Germany for a reconsideration of "the relative merits of the Zeppelin and other types of aircraft." Meanwhile, with the official emphasis on dirigibles, less attention than ever was likely to be given to developing a challenger for the Gordon Bennett Cup.

Actually, there seemed good cause to favor the airship. In tests over the North Sea the Zeppelin had demonstrated its usefulness as a naval arm, and tourist excursions out of Frankfurt and Baden-Baden with the *Viktoria Luisa,* organized by the Deutsche Luftschiffs Aktien Gesellschaft, were being run with a high degree of success. Ultimately, ocean crossings were envisaged, under management by the Hamburg–Amerika steamship line. To the airship belonged the future: the commodious passenger-carrying dirigible that could stay up all day and if necessary all night would be vastly more efficient than risky heavier-than-air craft of limited range and capacity. Those who had made

176

flights, claimed one colorful prospectus, "were profuse in their expressions of admiration and absolute faith in the airship. Their senses were completely given over to the enjoyment and appreciation of the beauties of the earth below and the sky above." Absolute protection and safety had been combined with luxurious comfort. Polished mahogany, rich carpets, comfortable wicker chairs provided a feeling of security and restfulness, causing the passenger "to banish all fear or trepidation" and to relax completely into the enjoyment of the "exhileration [sic] produced by the splendid panorama" spread before his eyes.

"Women trust themselves to the aerial cruise with the utmost confidence," the travel folder went on. "The almost natural assumption of a hazardous undertaking in making a flight is instantly dispelled even among the most timid, when one views the immense fabric, the strength of its construction, and becomes acquainted with the wonderful capabilities and scientific precautions ensuring the safety of the Zeppelin airship and its passengers." Yet, with prophetic insight into the disaster of a later generation, the company saw fit to add a disclaimer: "Participation in any excursion is entirely on the responsibility of the person participating. The German Airship Navigation Company is not responsible for any consequences or unexpected occurrence that may happen during an excursion."

In any case, few German airplanes could be considered as racers. The original Etrich Taube—the nation's early favorite—equipped with either a Mercedes or Argus motor of 100 horsepower had a top range of not more than 71 to 75 miles per hour (118 to 125 km/hr). The construction of a racing monoplane was begun early in 1913 by the Johannistahl-based flier Emile Jeannin but it was not expected to do better than 87 miles per hour (145 km/hr). Two torpedo-bodied monoplanes had been flown successfully, one with a 90-horespower Mercedes motor, built by the long-established motorcar firm of Kühlstein in Charlottenburg, which had turned to flying machines in 1911, and the other an Argus-powered Kondor monoplane from the Essen factory of the aviator-constructor J. Suvelack. Neither was noted for speed. One of the more important aviation works in Germany, the Deutsche

Flugzeugwerke of Leipzig, had brought out a formidable-looking mono-plane equipped with a 95-horsepower N.A.G. motor, yet its speed did not exceed 75 miles per hour. None of these could be regarded as even the prototype of a Gordon Bennett racer. Furthermore, what German talent there was was going into building up an air force, leaving little time for such frivolities as sporting aviation. It was not surprising that in the face of the likely French competition, by the time September rolled around the German entry was withdrawn.

Nor did anything in Italian aviation justify the hope that the entry of the Aero Club of Italy could compete with success. Aviation in that country was largely in the hands of the military, which did not encour-age racing for sport. At the beginning of 1913 no more than eighty-four civilian pilots had been registered, only one of whom had made a name for himself in speed flying. Mario Cobianchi, who had been granted license No. 24, held all Italian speed records for distances between 200 and 300 kilometers, but the Caproni monoplane that he flew was hardly in the same class as a Deperdussin or a Nieuport. At the end of March a scant handful of manufacturers were in existence: about forty-five machines were in use at various private schools and about fifty more were available to the army. Six or seven machines were assigned to naval aviation, including a hydro-airplane conceived by Italy's leading flier, Mario Calderara, the first Italian to qualify for a license. Had his machine been designed for use over land instead of for the navy, Calderara might well have been nominated for the second time to repre-sent his country in the Gordon Bennett. As it was, Italy's entry was cancelled, perhaps in the realization that none among its miscellany of imported and domestic craft could equal the forthcoming French repre-sentation.

As for the United States, no amount of hand-wringing could bring a machine on the line. Half-hearted efforts by the Aero Club of America to make good on its two entries were unavailing: aviation continued to be in the doldrums, far eclipsed by developments in Europe, and public interest was difficult to arouse in a contest remote from America's shores. Norman Prince, however, was still in the ring, and as the months sped by with no tangible results in finding a racer he offered to underwrite the cost of any machine that would represent the United States. During the summer, Harold Kantner, chief pilot of the Moisant school, went to France with Prince's backing to investigate the purchase of a suitable craft. Born at Meadville, Pennsylvania, on 23 February 1886, he was the holder of license No. 65, obtained at Hempstead Plains on 6 September and 14 October 1911. Kantner was highly regarded as an exhibition flier, instructor, and demonstrator of the Blériot-type, Gnôme-powered Moisant monoplane. He had made some test flights in 1911 for W. L. Fairchild, builder of a monoplane embodying steel-tube construction and equipped with a 100-horsepower Emerson engine. In the winter of 1912–13 he designed and built a new Moisant Military Scout. Known as the Kantner–Moisant Bluebird, the machine could be taken apart in four minutes and reassembled in eight. Superbly constructed, the Bluebird was successful from the start. Kantner interrupted tests and demonstrations before representatives of foreign governments to go to Europe on his Gordon Bennett quest. Though he lacked experience in racing, he stood in the front rank of American aviators and had the reputation of being a careful and conscientious pilot. But time was running out. When September arrived, no American entry had materialized.

Only Belgium fulfilled its commitment to send a machine to Rheims. Aviation in that country benefited by the open encouragement of King Albert I, whose interest had been stirred at the *Grande Semaine de la Champagne* in 1909. Subsequently, he had been given a ride on a Farman biplane, which led the company to advertize its product as "The king of aeroplanes and the aeroplane of kings." Following the success of the Circuit of Europe in 1911, a Circuit of Belgium was organized, with ten of an original twenty entrants crossing the starting line and five finishing the 1,000-kilometer contest. On 16 April 1916 the king signed an important decree establishing four aerial combat squadrons, whose pilots carried out extensive reconnaissance flights in ensuing military maneuvers. A few experimental machines had appeared by 1913, but for the most part Belgian fliers imported Blériots, Farmans, or Deperdussins—the last a natural choice for Crombez because of its speed.

On 21 September, a week before the tournament was to open at Rheims, Adolphe Pégoud had performed the almost unbelievable feat of looping-the-loop. This sensational stunt put aviation at the top of the news and whetted the public's appetite for the fifth Gordon Bennett speed contest. Pégoud had parachuted from an old Blériot on 19 August—the first pilot to abandon a plane in full flight—and on 2 September, to the amazement of onlookers, had deliberately turned a specially reinforced machine on its back and flown upside down. These topsy-turvy antics were to show the way to complete maneuverability in the air, to the strengthening of machines so they would not crack up under stress, and, sooner than anyone thought, to the development of techniques essential in aerial combat. Jules Védrines's views notwithstanding, acrobatics, like the Gordon Bennett itself, were to become a testing ground of an airplane's capabilities.

Perfect weather conditions awaited the thousands of spectators who, as in 1909, converged on the plain of Bétheny for an exhibition of flying that would have no equal anywhere in the world. Again the dusty roads were clogged with vehicles of every description, again the flying machine was the talk of the town. Few were aware that a heated wrangle behind the scenes at the Aéro Club de France had nearly caused the show to be transferred elsewhere. Shortly after the French victory at Chicago in 1912, Armand Deperdussin, in a characteristically generous gesture, had offered the flying grounds he had acquired at Bétheny as a site for the 1913 race, together with cash prizes for the preliminary events, and the Aéro Club had accepted the arrangement with alacrity. But the Deperdussin empire, over-extended and financially unsound, had begun to collapse in 1913 and the ensuing furor caused one faction among the club's membership to agitate for annulment of the plan. Henri Deutsch de la Meurthe proposed that the War Office be asked for permission to hold the Gordon Bennett on army grounds at Châlons; at the same time he proffered the sum of 100,000 francs as a substitute for Deperdussin's proposal. But when the club met on 26 August to discuss

Table 9
1913 • Entry List
French Elimination Trials

Pilot	Machine
Georges Chemet	Borel monoplane
P. H. Dancourt	Borel monoplane
Henri Brégi	Bréguet biplane
Dr. G. Espanet	Nieuport monoplane
Marcel Prévost	Deperdussin monoplane
Eugène Gilbert	Deperdussin monoplane
G. Rost	Deperdussin monoplane
Emile Védrines	Ponnier monoplane

the question, an overwhelming majority was found to be in favor of adhering to the original plan. Although in a fit of pique such prominent members as Louis Blériot, Alfred Leblanc, and the Comte de la Vaulx walked out and tendered their resignations from the club, Rheims remained the chosen site.

The elimination trials for the Gordon Bennett on the morning of 27 September over ten laps of the 10-kilometer course—in other words, half the distance of the race itself—attracted an entry list of eight of the best pilots and the speediest machines to be found in France (table 9). Five manufacturers were represented, in striking contrast to the lack of racing machines produced in other countries. Only one of the machines was a biplane.

One after another, Chemet, Dancourt, Brégi, and Espanet withdrew, after which selection of the team became easy. Prévost took first honors by covering the course in 31 minutes $22\frac{2}{5}$ seconds, equal to a speed of 191 kilometers per hour, with Emile Védrines second in 32 minutes 38 seconds (184.8 km/hr) and Gilbert third in 33 minutes $45\frac{4}{5}$ seconds. Rost, who was born in Germany on 4 March 1874 and had obtained French license No. 126 with a Grade monoplane on 26 October 1911, took 37 minutes 4 seconds and was named as alternate. It was an all-star combination.

The program on the afternoon of 27 September and the following day, Sunday, the twenty-eighth made the fliers at the first Rheims meeting look like neophytes indeed. It brought out clearly the immense progress aviation had made, and it filled the crowd with enthusiasm for French accomplishments. Deperdussins dominated the events, taking all three places for monoplanes in the cross-country race. In the biplane class the brothers Gaston and René Caudron were first and second, respectively, and Moineau on a Bréguet was third. One had only to recall that four short years before, Latham had set the altitude mark with his Antoinette at 508 feet. Now Gilbert on a Morane–Saulnier climbed to 19,008 feet and, with a passenger, to 14,381 feet, topping off this display with a *vol-plané* lasting a breathless 28 minutes. Brindejonc des Moulinais, whose long-distance dashes around Europe had put him in the recent limelight, won the 30-kilometer speed contest, also using a Morane-Saulnier. In the slow-speed contest, or SLOTH, as the British called it, competitors had first to show that they were capable of at least 56 miles per hour, then cover a course of 2 kilometers and, after a stop of 2 minutes, fly back to the starting point, the slowest to be the winner. In this oddity, Derome's 160-horsepower Gnôme-motored Bréguet was first with a bare 32 miles per hour and Gaston Caudron second at 36 miles per hour. The stage was set for the main attraction next day—the Coupe Internationale d'Aviation— which would show what speed, the opposite of SLOTH, was like.

Each Gordon Bennett had produced a new world record. What could one expect this time? In 1909 Curtiss had flown at 47¾ miles per hour; Grahame-White had raised that figure to 61.5 miles per hour in 1910; Weymann had touched 78 miles per hour in 1911; and then in 1912 Védrines had broken the century mark with an incredible 105.5 miles per hour. Already in the trials Prévost had exceeded 114 miles per hour; favored in the betting, he was expected to go even faster in the race. To put it in kilometers, the Gordon Bennett in 1910 had brought out for the first time a speed of 100 kilometers per hour. Would it now see that doubled, with 200 kilometers crowded into an hour? The weekend throng that spilled over until Monday the twenty-ninth could hardly wait to see.

Marcel Prévost, winner of
the Gordon Bennett Cup in
1913. Courtesy National
Air and Space Museum.

Table 10
1913 • French Team

Pilot	Machine	Motor
Marcel Prévost	Deperdussin monocoque	160-hp Gnôme
Eugène Gilbert	Deperdussin monocoque	160-hp Gnôme
Emile Védrines	Ponnier monoplane	160-hp Gnôme

The powerful French team, chosen on the basis of the elimination trials, is shown in table 10. Recognized as one of the nation's top performers, Prévost had been awarded the Grand Vermilion Medal of the Aéro Club de France for taking second place in the 1912 Gordon Bennett at Chicago. Modest to a fault, he was never one to discuss his achievements, preferring to let deeds speak rather than words. He had an excellent chance to do so in April 1913 at Monaco, when the inaugural race for the Schneider seaplane trophy took place. In February, he had walked away with the Concours Militaire in Spain. Then, fitting his Deperdussin with floats and installing the newest 160-horsepower Gnôme, he took part in a variety of events at the Riviera resort, including a rigorous 2½ nautical miles of surface navigation that brought him up against most of the nautical-minded constructors of the day, who had turned their land machines into *hydro-avions* by the simple expedient of substituting pontoons for wheels. The Deperdussin showed itself thoroughly at home on the water and the high esteem in which its pilot was held by company officials proved more than justified. On 16 April Prévost took the Schneider cup for France, sweeping around the 270-kilometer course in 3 hours 48 minutes 22 seconds. He had faithfully followed the construction of Deperdussins from their earliest triumphs into the world-famous monocoque design and entered the Gordon Bennett lists at Rheims with the reputation of a master pilot, the acknowledged standard-bearer of the firm.

The 1913 Gordon Bennett Deperdussin showed a remarkably clean profile, embodying several improvements over the 1912 model that emphasized the streamlined form that aircraft design was to follow in the future. Years ahead of its time, like Latham's progressive Antoinette of 1911, it had a wing span of 28 feet 2½ inches; its length was 19 feet 8 inches and its height about 7 feet 3 inches; the wing area was 107 square feet and the maximum speed of the machine was optimistically calculated at 130 miles per hour. Loaded, the weight was 1,500 pounds. Scrupulously designed for speed, the monocoque had a padded cone melding into the fuselage against which the pilot's head rested, minimizing strain on the neck caused by the wind at high speeds.

Eugène Gilbert, who also bore the surnames of Adrien and Amable, flew the same type of monocoque as Prévost. Born at Riom in the province of Puy-de-Dôme on 18 July 1889, he was educated at the Carnot school in Vichy and at the college of Brioude, where he was captain of the football team. He took part in numerous regional cycling events, as a boy setting something of a record by driving a petrol engine tricycle of 2¼ horsepower between Brioude and Vichy, a distance of 125 kilometers, repeating the performance in the reverse direction three years later with a Clément–Bayard voiturette of 2¾ horsepower. Known as the "demon driver," he became a mechanic at the Auto-Garage in Clermont-Ferrand at the age of sixteen; at twenty he was building a 100-horsepower monoplane with Louis Besseyre when the project foundered on the accidental death of his friend. In August 1910 Gilbert entered the Blériot school at Etampes and on 24 September was granted pilot's license No. 240. He was inducted into the ninety-second infantry regiment on 5 October, transferring to the air services in April 1911 and making many flights at Satory, Châlons, and Etampes. On 24 October of that year he suffered a severe crash, which put him out of action for six months.

By March 1912 Gilbert had recovered sufficiently to make what was then considered a danger-fraught city-to-city flight, over mountainous territory from Clermont-Ferrand to Brioude and back, in which he used a Morane–Saulnier monoplane. With the same machine he passed the first test for a military license on 31 May; on 31 August he took the second test and was awarded military brevet No. 160. In September, as member of an escadrille attached to the first army corps, he took part in maneuvers in Northern France. On 28 October he amazed and excited Paris by putting on a memorable acrobatic exhibition over the Champs-Elysées.

His military service concluded, Gilbert joined the Rhône motor company and on 12 December 1912, with a Morane–Saulnier equipped with a 50-horsepower Le Rhône motor—destined to be a rival of the Gnôme—he broke the speed record over distances of 350, 400, 500, and 600 kilometers. By way of variety, he began the year 1913 by try-

185

ing for altitude with passengers, turning in fine performances with a Henry Farman biplane. Returning to his Morane in March, he flew from Melun, near Paris, to Lyons, a distance of 400 kilometers, at an average speed of 100 kilometers per hour, coming back to land at Villacoublay in 3 hours 10 minutes at 126 kilometers per hour. During the first two weeks of April he participated in the elimination trials for hydro-airplanes at Monaco. On the twenty-sixth, in a dawn-to-dusk bid for the Pommery Cup, he flew from Paris to Medina del Campo in Spain—1,020 kilometers—with a stop for fuel at the small Basque town of Vittoria, 825 kilometers from the start, in 8 hours 25 minutes air time. It was the first flight of more than 1,000 kilometers in a day and set a new world record for both distance and duration. Gilbert continued to flash across the sky like a meteor that summer. In June he flew from Villacoublay to Folkstone and back; in July he received the Médaille Militaire for outstanding aeronautical exploits, and on 2 August on a two-seater Morane-Saulnier he linked Villacoublay with Cáceres, Spain, not far from the Portuguese border, a distance of 1,325 kilometers in a day. It was not surprising that he should next be found at the controls of one of the fast new Deperdussins entered in September's Gordon Bennett.

Younger brother of the redoubtable Jules, with much the same flair for flying, Emile Védrines was born at St.-Denis on 27 December 1886, and held license No. 536, awarded to him on 1 July 1911, flying a Morane monoplane. He had then cast his lot with the Copin–Revillard school at Juvisy-sur-Orge, where he served as chief instructor, flying their monoplane at numerous meets and races. This machine, with its slim fuselage and sweeping tail assembly, closely resembled the Antoinette and made an impressive appearance in flight; but it was not fast enough to satisfy its pilot. In the early part of 1913, Emile left Copin–Revillard and joined the entourage of Alfred Ponnier, who was associated with the construction of Hanriot monoplanes at Rheims. Ponnier, born at Fontenay-sous-Bois in 1888, was a wealthy, bespectacled Parisian addicted to sports and physical exercise, given particularly to riding horseback and driving motorcycles and automobiles. He was

1658. — Monoplan Hanriot, piloté par FREY
A ailes et empennages repliables. Envergure 8 m., surface 14 mq., longueur 6 m.
poids 300 kgr, moteur Gnôme 50 HP, enfreinage des patins, permettant l'arret en
10 m
J. H.

M FREY

Hanriot monoplane of Alfred Frey, third member of the French team at
Chicago. Photograph from a postcard in the author's collection.

an inveterate traveler as well, spending a year and a half in the study of
chemistry at Crefeld-Posse in Germany and six months in England,
where his restless energy led him to investigate automobile construction
at Brooklands.

After completing his military service, Ponnier became engrossed in
the technical aspects of aviation and, with only five lessons, obtained a
pilot's license, No. 620, on 8 September 1911. He considered the
machines he had observed at meetings and exhibitions too slow and too
frail, so he decided to become a constructor himself. But before taking
this step, he prudently sought a connection with an established firm to
gain some practical experience in design, and his affiliation with
Hanriot was the result. Successful as he was as a flier-constructor, René
Hanriot lacked the means to extend his operations and welcomed the
infusion of fresh capital that Ponnier supplied. The first machine produced under this arrangement was known as the Hanriot–Pagny, a
speedier version of the Nieuport, conceived by Hanriot's engineer Alfred
Pagny. Subsequent models showed more of Ponnier's influence and the

187

Hanriot–Ponnier quickly gained a reputation for being stoutly built and very swift. Here was a monoplane which Emile Védrines thought could not only beat the Deperdussin made famous by his brother but win the Gordon Bennett as well. He placed an order with Ponnier for a machine to be specially designed and constructed for the race and equipped it with a 160-horsepower Gnôme. Aerodynamically, in purity of outline, the Ponnier—though stockier—was as forward-looking as the Deperdussin. Its configuration was based on data supplied by an expert named Maignan on the flight of birds. Included was the padded cone for a headrest in anticipation of high speeds. The wing span of only 8 meters was regarded as the minimum consistent with stability. Obviously fast when first tested, the monoplane was finished too late to permit alterations that might have made it even faster.

Weather conditions overnight did not look promising for the day of the race, but dawn dispelled the clouds and, in the words of one enthusiast, it turned out "gloriously fine." There was no wind and the sun shone with unseasonable warmth. When a group of Deperdussin employees arrived very early in the morning to put the finishing touches on Prévost's plane, they found their rival, the Ponnier, already on a test flight. One of them, a twenty-year-old graduate of the Ecole des Arts et Métiers at Châlons named André Herbemont, recalled years later what happened: "Mechanics had been up half the night working on the Ponnier's motor. It occurred to me that I ought to time the machine—which revealed the fact that it was slightly faster than our Deperdussin." He clocked it at an astonishing 2 minutes 58 seconds for the course. Herbemont had been told by his superior, Béchereau, to have a pair of wings constructed incorporating the young engineer's personal ideas, to be used only in case of strict necessity. Smaller and flatter than the usual surfaces, they were noticeably thicker at the trailing edge than elsewhere.

Less than two hours remained before the race. Acting on his own initiative, Herbemont ordered the new wings installed at once—a decision that met with the full approval of Béchereau when he reached the scene and that had a decisive effect on the outcome. Actually, three pairs of wings were on hand. Those with the widest span had been used in the elimination trials; another pair, considerably smaller, had a left-hand surface that was smaller than the right to offset the torque of the whirling engine; but there was no need to use them.

By the luck of the draw, Crombez had secured the right to be sent off first. Shortly before ten o'clock a squadron of gendarmes galloped across the field to chase away photographers too near the line of flight, and precisely on the hour the signal to depart was given. Amid cheers from the crowd, Crombez's mechanic swung the propeller and the monoplane shot forth from its restraining hands like a cannonball. Moments later the Belgian entry was circling the first pylon, as prescribed by the rules; then the pilot drove it across the starting line on its initial dash around the 10-kilometer circuit.

Recently, the utility of pylon racing had come under criticism. Wasn't distance in a straight line more important than competing against the clock? *Flight* had first raised the question after the race at Eastchurch in 1911. "We hardly think," the journal had then commented, "that after the present year's contest the Gordon Bennett Cup will be competed for under similar conditions again, and it is well that this should be so as the mere circling of an aerodrome for hours at a time is not likely, beyond the attainment of higher speeds, to advance the science in any material way." The attainment of higher speeds, of course, was designed to make the airplane more practical and to improve the quality of its construction, while if there was anything monotonous about the "mere circling of an aerodrome," the crowd never gave the slightest indication it was bored. On the contrary, cheers swelled into a roar each time the Deperdussin rushed past the grandstand, leaving in its wake a sonorous trail; attention was complete.

The official time of Crombez's first round, announced on large placards visible to all, was 3 minutes 29 seconds—actually the slowest of a day marked by speeds never seen before. In view of what was expected from the other contenders, it was apparent that the Belgian would have to do better if the cup was to be lifted from France. Flying with great regularity but approaching the pylons with noticeable caution, he com-

189

pleted the full course of 200 kilometers in 1 hour 9 minutes 52 seconds, which was 1 minute 3 seconds better than Védrines's time over the same distance at Chicago the year before.

Contestants were spaced at intervals of one hour and a quarter: at 11:15 Prévost was flagged away. Officials had warned him, as they had Crombez, that he would have to keep count of each lap for himself, though his mechanic would be allowed to give him a signal when the twentieth and last round had been finished. Starting like a thunderbolt unleashed, he took an enormously long run to get off. Once aloft, he quickly showed that the new, medium-span wings—still untested in flight—were increasing the speed of the Deperdussin. Prévost covered the first lap in 2 minutes $56\frac{3}{5}$ seconds, shattering all records, at what the French called the "stupefying" speed of 204 kilometers per hour (126.67 m/hr). This and the sixth lap, which he completed in the same time, were the fastest in the race.

"No words can describe adequately the impression created by velocity of the French machine," declared the Paris *Herald* in a special dispatch from the airfield. It was a sporting event of top-most importance, its international flavor preserved, as the paper pointed out, by the presence of a Belgian competitor; and what made the sport a healthy one was the absence of commercial exploitation. No billboards advertized a motor, a propeller, a spark plug, or different brands of tires, oils, and cigarettes—a practice that had helped undo the amateur standing of the Gordon Bennett automobile races and led to their demise. Such products could legitimately be extolled in the press after the event, but not before a captive audience of aviation racing fans.

Banking steeply at the turns and flying very low, Prévost made his circuits of the course like clockwork, the second and third rounds in exactly 2 minutes 58 seconds and the fifth in a fraction less, at the speed of 202.4 kilometers per hour. On the back stretch, the wings appearing so reduced in size as to be almost invisible, the machine looked like a projectile. At the end of the twentieth lap a "deafening roar" from the spectators nearly drowned out the noise of his motor. He had flown the 200 kilometers in the extraordinary time of 59 minutes $45\frac{3}{5}$ seconds,

Prévost's victorious monocoque rounding a pylon at the 1913 Rheims race. For the first time an airplane flew faster than 200 kilometers per hour. Courtesy Musée de l'Air.

an average of 204 kilometers per hour (124.5 m/hr). A wild ovation greeted the new hero when, after an extra lap to slow down, he brought his sleek, fleet machine safely to earth. Even so, he took nearly a mile, rebounding in a number of tremendous hops, before he could bring the craft under control and come to a halt.

Gilbert, who had never given much thought to pylon racing, was the next to start. His monocoque, too, was fast but not fast enough to equal Prévost's record. Again the crowd was regaled with the spectacle of an airplane, advanced in every detail save for its rigid undercarriage and rakish disc wheels, completing lap after lap at prodigious speed with pendulum-like precision. But the first lap took 3 minutes 2 seconds, perceptibly slower than Prévost's, and the full course required 1 hour 2 minutes 55 seconds for an average speed of 192 kilometers per hour.

Minutes and seconds now counted heavily as Emile Védrines, the last to get away, took to the air at what was described by one reporter as "an

191

Table 11
1913 • Results

Place	Pilot	Country	Time	Speed
1	Prevost	France	59m 45$\frac{3}{5}$s	124.5 m/hr
2	E. Védrines	France	60m 51$\frac{2}{5}$s	123 m/hr
3	Gilbert	France	1h 2m 55s	119.5 m/hr
4	Crombez	Belgium	1h 9m 52s	106.9 m/hr

alarming rate." A prolonged shout went up when the time for his first lap was hurriedly displayed: 2 minutes 59$\frac{1}{5}$ seconds. Anything under 3 minutes was within striking distance of the pace set by Prévost. The sturdy little Ponnier seemed just as fast as its main rival; surely it would close the gap. But no. Védrines's pylon turns were wide, losing him priceless seconds. Although his average speed only once dropped below 195 kilometers per hour, he could not quite nose out the Deperdussin for first place. For the full circuit his time was 60 minutes 51$\frac{3}{5}$ seconds, a rate of 198 kilometers per hour(123 m/hr). Less than a minute and a half separated him from the winner, and only a shade of difference could be found in the times for Gilbert, in third place, and Crombez in fourth. The official results are seen in table 11.

All four contestants flew faster than the mark set by the last Gordon Bennett. To Prévost went the honor of winning the cup. The others, after entrance and other fees had been deducted, received the following amounts in cash: Védrines, 2,250 francs; Gilbert, 1,500 francs; Crombez, 750 francs.

Védrines was unstintingly praised for a valiant effort, which, had it not been for the chance that caused Prévost's wings to be changed at the last moment, might have brought him the cup. Though he had never piloted a machine of more than 100 horsepower or raced over the course before, his neck-and-neck performance against Prévost would be long remembered. He shared with the victor a triumphal welcome when both arrived at the buffet-bar to celebrate in the best French style with the finest champagne of the region. France's clean sweep for the second time in a row was hailed by an uproarious, jostling throng. The "glorious trophy—the most noble dream of the aviator"—would remain on French soil: and if France should win again the next year it would stay there for good. For France, winning both the Gordon Bennett Cup and the Schneider Trophy would make the year 1913 famous as "La Glorieuse Année." For the house of Deperdussin it was the pinnacle of pride before its financial fall.

GREATEST AIR RACE EVER KNOWN burbled the *Herald,* "the winner's speed being the fastest ever made by man in this mode of locomotion. . . . " In England, the *Daily Mail* agreed that "the performance eclipses anything of the kind yet achieved," adding that "if the speed could be maintained the Atlantic itself could be crossed at its narrowest part in a fraction over fifteen hours." *Flight* noted, "All speeds were well over 2 miles per minute, especially after allowing for turning corners. It is . . . the first time any human has traveled 120 mph in an hour round a set course, and no vehicle except an aeroplane has done so even in a straight line, though Guillaume has done 140 mph with the wind." Only the *Daily Telegraph* was restrained in its outlook: "It is doubtful whether, under next year's regulations . . . such velocities will be equaled, or for several years to come."

The failure of the United States to participate again pointed up the slow rate of progress in the country that had defeated the best France had to offer in the first Gordon Bennett. Alan R. Hawley, newly elected president of the Aero Club of America, admitted what was wrong in a blunt statement to the press: "We could not send an American monoplane or biplane over, because none of our machines are half speedy enough." The French openly regretted the lack of foreign competition. As *L'Aérophile* made plain, the Gordon Bennett had become almost exclusively a French affair; even when Weymann won the cup for America it was with a French machine. Understandably, said the magazine, Germany's interests may have lain elsewhere—but where were the Anglo-Saxons? Bemoaning the lack of official or unofficial support "which might have brought at least one British racer" to Chicago in

1912 or to Rheims in 1913, Claude Grahame-White accused the sporting circles of England of not meeting their responsibility:

> Many of us would have given an eyetooth to have been in the race. I'd have been there like a shot if a machine had been provided for me . . . and so here I am, sitting at my desk and reading about the precious victory for France.
>
> England should have been represented and America, too, and I daresay American aviators were as anxious to compete as we were, but those upon whose backing we relied were dead asleep.
>
> Sportsmen in England and America should have prepared for suitable representation months ago. . . . It would seem that if aviators can be had to pilot machines some organization like the Royal Aero Club might show a little interest, but the entire burden of putting out money is shifted to the shoulders of the aviator himself. I am not speaking of France, for there the real sportsmen's spirit is shown.

Grahame-White would give substance to his concern by embarking on a tour of the country, his airplane decked with the slogan WAKE UP ENGLAND, but its orientation was more toward military preparedness than sport. A new look would have to be taken at the problem of catching up with France in the next race.

Chapter 7 THE WAR YEARS • 1914-18

France had no sooner celebrated the country's second consecutive win in the Gordon Bennett than critics began openly to question the utility of a competition whose only criterion was speed. Should the race continue purely as a sporting event, every year faster than before, or should the rules be changed so it would contribute more to the development of the airplane as a practical vehicle of the future? As a closed circuit contest, had it not outlived its usefulness? Should it not be turned into a straight-line contest, for example, aiming at distance rather than speed?

Incontestably, said *L'Aérophile,* the Gordon Bennett had been a tremendous triumph for the French aeronautical industry, proving that as far as speed was concerned the flying machine was well on its way to surpassing all other forms of locomotion. How often was it necessary to demonstrate that fact? Had not Gabriel Voisin averred, half facetiously, that given a good motor and a good propeller even a paving stone could fly? Now, with even more powerful motors and wing areas of less than ten square meters, it should be possible to attain speeds as high as 300 kilometers per hour or more. Constructors seemed to have been seduced by the Goddess of Speed, to the neglect of everything else. It was high time that the cup should stand for something of more general benefit to mankind. Maurice Farman, Henry's older brother, whose pusher biplane had earned a reputation for reliability and safety, was in hearty accord. "I should like to see the competition enlarged," he declared when interviewed by one of Bennett's reporters, "It should include some kind of trial beside that of speed."

Taking account of growing sentiment along these lines, the Fédération Aéronautique Internationale decided that for 1914 a new condition would have to be met: to qualify as an entrant, a machine, as well as being fast, should be able to fly at a certain *minimum* speed. A special rule was introduced, to be applied in tests preliminary to the race itself; it contained the following innovative provisions.

> Each contestant shall complete a straight-line course of approximately 2 kilometers and return, without touching the ground, at a height discernably less than 5 meters. The average of the time each way shall be less than, or in any event not more than, 70 kilometers per hour (42 m/hr).
>
> Each contestant shall be entitled to three trials. Machines shall be rotated at intervals of 10 minutes so that all contestants shall be treated as fairly as possible.
>
> After completing the qualifying trials, machines will be permitted no modifications. Nevertheless, they may undergo repairs with the authorization of, and under the supervision of, stewards of the course.
>
> Only while in full flight are contestants allowed to modify the wings [of their machines], whether as to surface area, shape or angle of incidence, and, in general, all [other] parts of their machines, and always with the proviso that they are able, while still in flight, to bring their machine back to its former configuration.
>
> The winning contestant shall be the one who, having satisfied the qualifying conditions, completes the 200-kilometer course in the shortest space of time over a minimum circuit of 5 kilometers.

The dates selected for the competition were Sunday, 27 September, and Monday, 28 September, the place to be the airfield at Buc, just beyond Versailles, where the R.E.P. and Maurice Farman schools had been long established. No better site could be found from the airman's point of view, though for spectators it was another matter. Buc (later Toussus-le-Noble) had no grandstand or racecourse, no facilities for the convenience of the public. The huge crowds that had gathered for the predawn start of the Paris–Madrid race in 1911 had simply camped on the grounds overnight. On the other hand, the wide-open countryside, flat and devoid of all obstacles, was ideal for flying, easily marked out into turns for the circuit and safe for emergency landings at high speed. When the time came, adequate provisions would be made for the large attendance expected.

Five nations signified their intention to compete: France, Great Britain, the United States, each with a team of three, Germany and Italy with a single representative apiece. The race would be a crucial one, for if the seemingly invincible French won again they would keep the cup for good. Now or never was the time for another country to break their winning streak, and if for no other reason excitement was running high. Whether determination and resolve would be enough to bring victory was the question. The quality of a machine and the skill of its pilot were at stake as never before.

The war clouds piling up that fateful summer had made little impression on the sporting world, and preparations for the race went on as usual. How seriously the politicians had taken the threat of armed conflict between France and Germany is still debated today, but analysts of the arms race such as Albert de Mun of the *Echo de Paris* had predicted that the two nations were moving toward a clash "with the implacable certainty of destiny itself." A small incident in the Bennett balloon race of 1913 had illustrated the prevailing tension. Flying the German flag, a contestant descended close to French soil at Châteaudun in order to ask directions of a group of peasants. But instead of being helpful the group seized the balloon's guide rope and held on to it firmly while a messenger was hastily dispatched to summon the gendarmes. When the police arrived they found the aeronauts' papers in order and allowed them to proceed—but the balloon was out of the race. According to the regulations, touching the guide rope by persons other than the pilot or his aide constituted a technical landing and disqualified the competitor.

Better than most, the international-minded members of the aeronautical industry with their innumerable foreign contacts were quick to perceive in such acts of chauvinism the way the wind was blowing. But their warnings—at least in London—that hostilities might erupt at any time and would include the participation of aircraft were in large part discounted in official circles.

As the defending champion, France was expected to produce the fastest airplane yet, and speculation spread as to what type of machine it might be. Speeds had reached nearly three times that attained by Curtiss in the first Gordon Bennett: what mark would be set in the sixth? Nothing faster had appeared than the Deperdussin, but the chances were slim that a record-breaking monoplane by that name would ever race again. Its manufacturer, to the dismay of the nation, was a bankrupt accused of illegal financial practices (some said embezzlement) to the tune of twenty-eight million francs. The entire industry was shaken to its foundations and Armand Deperdussin would never get over the scandal. Though a new firm rose, phoenix-like, from the ashes of the old, its greatest fame would come not from another racer but from the fighter plane it was to produce in the war about to break out. The Société Provisoire des Aéroplanes Deperdussin, of which Louis Blériot became president, soon changed its name to Société Pour l'Aviation et ses Dérives, with the famous initials S.P.A.D. If the original company had not collapsed, the machine that had won the two previous Gordon Bennetts would no doubt have been favored to win again. In its place the choice of top-caliber contenders was limited: Nieuport, Hanriot, Morane–Saulnier were the leading possibilities. A decision could not be made immediately; time would be required for the aircraft business to recover from its disarray.

British manufacturers had at last shown signs of exercising their inherent skills, aroused by a patriotic sense of duty to take part in the competition. Toward the end of July word went out that the empire would be represented by a team chosen from the following firms: Sopwith Aviation Company, A. V. Roe and Company, Vickers, and Cedric Lee.

Of these, the Sopwith company was in the best position to turn out a challenger for the cup. Founded at Kingston-on-Thames in the autumn of 1911 by the well-known aviator T. O. M. Sopwith, holder of British license No. 31, it had a production capacity of about fifty machines a year. Its proposed 1914 *Gordon Bennett Racer* was derived from the Sopwith Tabloid, which had created a sensation on 20 April by winning the second Schneider Trophy race for seaplanes. It had a very clean design and with a fully cowled Gnôme motor was thought capable of at least 105 miles per hour.

Alliott Verdon Roe also had an outstanding reputation. In 1906 he had designed the first British machine to leave the ground, a biplane, and had since experimented with triplanes and monoplanes as well. An early version of the completely enclosed monoplane, the AVRO Type F, had set a British record on 24 October 1912 by flying 450 miles in 7 hours 31½ minutes, and further development of its advanced contours might have been expected to put such a craft in the racing class. Vickers Ltd., with an established factory at Westminster, had produced an interesting two-seater Gnôme-powered monoplane with rectangular fuselage in 1912–13; while far from approaching progressive French designs, it might have served as a model for a fast machine with Gordon Bennett capabilities.

Whether a serious attempt was made in America to find a suitable entrant is open to question. After the disheartening experience of the two preceding years, the prospect of coming up once more against the seemingly unbeatable French, coupled with the cost of building and shipping an airplane to distant Europe, was enough to give the Aero Club pause. The collective conscious of its members was centered elsewhere. Lord Northcliffe and his *Daily Mail* had offered a 10,000-pound prize in 1913 to the aviator who made the first transatlantic flight, with landings permitted to refuel at sea. Prodded by the indefatigable Henry Woodhouse, who saw an opportunity to gather more laurels in a field where America already was ahead, the club was actively supporting the construction of a giant, twin-engined flying boat with an upper wing span of 76 feet—the largest of the day—especially designed by Glenn Curtiss for the crossing. The project was backed by Rodman Wanamaker, of the Philadelphia department store fortune, to commemorate one hundred years of peace between Great Britain and the United States; if successful it would go far to alter the image of the United States as lagging the world in aviation. Lt. John Cyril Porte of the Royal Navy, one of the first in Britain to fly a Deperdussin, was named as pilot of the huge machine; copilot and engineer was to be George E. A. Hallett, later of the U.S. Army. Assembled by the Curtiss factory on the shores of Lake Keuka at Hammondsport, the craft was christened the *America* on 22 June. A route was mapped out from Newfoundland to the Azores, thence to Lisbon and on to Plymouth, England. In an era when horse cabs had not yet disappeared from New York City streets and gas light was still in use, the idea of flying across the Atlantic was like a Jules Verne fantasy about to become fact, beside which the annual Gordon Bennett contest lost some of its attraction. Moreover, Americans were as ever preoccupied with the automobile. For thrills they were content to watch Lincoln Beachey loop-the-loop or race Barney Oldfield in a monster car built by Walter Christie. Or they went to the movies to participate vicariously in the cliff-hanging serials *The Perils of Pauline* and *The Exploits of Elaine.*

During the first half of 1914 interest in sports—the last bastion of peaceful competition among nations—remained high. But the fuse to the powder keg was ignited on 28 June at Sarajevo when the heir to the Austro-Hungarian throne and his wife were assassinated by a young Serbian nationalist. Austria accused Serbia of plotting the murder; an ultimatum was issued, and like automatons the governments of Europe began putting into effect their plans for mobilization. Yet an atmosphere of calm, deliberately fostered by the Germans and the Austrians, encouraged promoters of events like the Gordon Bennett to believe up to the last minute that their racing schedules would suffer no interference.

Throughout the critical month of July, monarchs and their ministers ostentatiously proceeded with their summer vacations. No wonder that a sports-loving public continued to think in terms of racing. Though the continent might be tottering on the brink of war, the headlines on 5 July were shared with the Automobile Club de France's Grand Prix at Lyons; in England *The Autocar* devoted seven full pages to the contest, with a list of eighty-two addresses in the United Kingdom where telegraphic reports would be available lap by lap. There was every reason to expect that when September rolled around the fans would find full scope for their enthusiasm in the Gordon Bennett race at Rheims. *Flight* perceived no reason why the competition should not be held even after hostilities had begun: members of the Royal Aero Club were reminded in the magazine's issue of 31 July that "those wishing to attend should send in their names to the secretary as soon as possible, for if enough are registered arrangements will be made for reduced railway fares and hotels."

But the gods of war had decreed there should be no Gordon Bennett in 1914. On 28 July the conflagration suddenly broke out: Austria-Hungary declared war on Serbia. Germany declared war on Russia on 1 August, invaded Luxembourg on 2 August, declared war on France on 3 August, and invaded Belgium on 4 August, causing Britain to declare war on Germany the same day. It would be a short, quick war, everyone thought—six months at the most.

Six years were to elapse, however, before there would be another contest for the blue ribbon of the air. Instead, there would be combat in the skies, as many had predicted. In a sensational novel, *The War in the Air,* published in 1908, H. G. Wells imagined a surprise attack by Zeppelins, the superseding of the airship by the airplane, the extension of the air war to the whole world, and the collapse of civilization. Four years earlier, in 1903—the year the Wrights first flew—a commission headed by the French Minister of War André, after inspecting Santos-Dumont's diminutive airship, was reported to be considering the use of dirigibles for military purposes. "The world is fast approaching an era," the Paris *Herald* commented, "when men will fight not only on land and beneath the surface of the sea, but also among the clouds." The

201

prophecy was the subject of much debate. Describing the Wrights' flying machine to the press in 1906, Charles S. Rolls said, "It is an aeroplane, not a balloon. From the aeroplane you can drop a bomb on any fort you like . . . there is no doubt that this particular aeroplane will play a very great part in future warfare."

At a time when many people saw no future for the airplane other than as a sportsman's plaything, least of all as an instrument of warfare, Grahame-White showed remarkable prescience in a book he wrote, again with Harry Harper, in 1912, *The Aeroplane in War*:

> Ceasing to be fair-weather craft, powerful, modern-type aeroplanes can combat high and gusty winds, and are already capable of being used, for reconnoitring flights, on at least 80 per cent of the days of the year. No longer unreliable, they have become practical weapons.
>
> A squadron of war aeroplanes, carrying pilots and observers, can, as has been shown again and again, lay bare the disposition of a wide-spread battle-front. In one hour, they can perform the reconnoitring work which has hitherto been carried out in a day, and in a necessarily hit-or-miss fashion, by cavalry and other scouts.
>
> The use of well-trained corps of military airmen will revolutionize the tactics of war. No longer will two Commanders-in-Chief grope in the dark. They will sit, so to speak, on either side of a chess-board, which will represent the battlefield. Each will watch the other's moves; nothing will be concealed. From a blundering, scrambling moving about of masses of men, modern warfare will become—through the advent of the aeroplane—an intellectual process.
>
> The Commander-in-Chief who has no proper air-corps, in the next great war, will be in a hopeless position. He will have lost a battle practically before it begins. Whereas his opponent will know exactly what *he* is doing, he will be able to obtain nothing but vague and confusing tidings as to the movements of the enemy. Imagine two armed men approaching each other, one being blindfolded. The Commander-in-Chief without aeroplanes will be like a blindfolded man.
>
> At present, [the war aeroplane's] work has been confined to scouting. But it has other, and grimmer possibilities. It can, and without doubt will, be used as an engine of destruction—not by means of the bomb-dropping attacks of a few aeroplanes, but by the organized onslaught of large squadrons of weight-lifting machines, which will be able to rain down tons of missiles over any given spot.

And there is another possibility, also. Machines are carrying heavier loads every day. Soon the practicability of aeroplanes to transport troops—particularly in regard to hurrying up reinforcements in an emergency—will be demonstrated.

When two opposing armies both have large fleets of war aeroplanes, and these machines take the air in squadrons, prior to a battle, what will happen when they come in contact with each other?

Back in 1908, as a dedicated aeronaut who put his trust in a "steerable balloon," Comte Henri de la Vaulx chose to disagree with such a vision: "For the life of me, I cannot see what an aeroplane can do which is likely to be of any practical utility in warfare. . . . [It] would be shot down like a bird." Lt. Ferdinand von Hiddessen, who had taken his license No. 47 in a Euler monoplane on 27 January 1910, put an end to conjecture on 30 August 1914 by dropping bombs and tracts from his Taube in the first aerial bombardment of Paris.

Even so, the world's military establishments had shown little interest in developing aerial weapons before the war. Even the Germans had failed to grasp their significance and to realize that the advent of three-dimensional warfare would revolutionize strategy and tactics. In France, junior officers were enthusiastic about the airplane but army and navy chiefs were generally apathetic and inclined to snub the air arm. "Aviation is good sport," was the opinion of General Foch, former commander of the Ecole Supérieure de la Guerre, "but for the army it is useless." Only with regard to reconnaissance was it conceded that aircraft might be of some use. New and unproven, they were looked on as ancillary weapons, perhaps to obtain information on troop movements, railheads, or the like. For the most part air services were trained with no specific objective in view, with only the vaguest idea of the tasks they were expected to perform.

The United States was the first country to contract for an airplane intended for military use. On 1 August 1907 the Army Signal Corps established an Aeronautical Division, responsible for "balloons, air machines, and kindred subjects." It acquired a small dirigible built by

Capt. Thomas S. Baldwin in 1908 and, in September of that year, a two-seater Wright biplane, which was tested by Orville Wright at Fort Myer, Virginia, until it crashed with fatal injuries to its passenger, Lt. Thomas Selfridge. In August 1909 a flying field was opened at College Park, Maryland, where Wilbur Wright provided instruction for Lieutenants Lahm, Humphreys, and Foulois. At the same time experiments were conducted in antiaircraft missiles at Sandy Hook, New Jersey. On 12 September 1910 at the Harvard–Boston meet, Lt. J. N. Fickel, an army sharpshooter, rode with Charles Willard in a Curtiss pusher and demonstrated before President Taft the possibility of using aircraft in war. While Willard circled Squantum Field, Fickel fired at targets on the ground. He scored a large percentage of hits, and from an experimental standpoint the demonstration was considered highly satisfactory. Progress, however, was slow. At the end of 1911 only eight pilots had been commissioned; between 1908 and 1913 Congress appropriated a mere 430,000 dollars for aviation, despite the support of President Teddy Roosevelt. Not until 18 July 1914 was a separate air corps recognized.

Considered primarily a civilian sport, European aviation began to assume a military aspect in 1910 when France allocated funds that provided for twenty-nine aircraft—Blériots, Farmans, Voisins, Bréguets, and Antoinettes—and thirty-nine military pilots. Spurred by the long-distance competitions of 1911, the army instituted trials for the first time in the autumn of that year, with England following suit. In 1912 public interest outran skepticism in high places, with the result that a national aircraft fund organized by *L'Auto, Le Matin,* and the Association Générale Aéronautique succeeded in raising a total of 2,771,000 francs for French military aviation. Germany raised the equivalent of two million dollars to train pilots and establish prizes for a budding national industry. Too often its manufacturers had copied foreign, especially French, designs with or without license. Uncertain of the airplane's place, the army air services were apparently regarded as a form of conveyance and placed under the inspector-general of military transport. Britain, approaching military aviation with reserve, had formed an air battalion of the Royal Engineers in 1911; in 1912, notwithstanding the apathy of most military officials, the Royal Flying Corps came into being—a joint service with military and naval wings and a central flying school at Upavon on Salisbury Plain. Two years later the admiralty established a separate Royal Naval Air Service.

Italy was the first to use airplanes in warfare. An expeditionary force against Turkey that landed in Libya in the autumn of 1911 included a flotilla of two Blériots, two Nieuports, two Farmans, and two Etrichs, as well as two small dirigibles. Its commander, Capt. Carlo Piazza, in a single-seater Blériot made the first officially recorded reconnaissance flight over enemy lines, and on 1 November Lt. Giulio Gavotti became the first to drop live bombs from the air—four modified Swedish grenades weighing two kilograms (4.4 lbs) each—sowing panic, if not greatly damaging an Arab encampment. In the Balkan wars of 1912-13 Bulgaria made use of an air corps hastily organized with machines of Russian, French, British, and German manufacture. Col. Radoul Milkopf broke into the headlines when he bombed the fortifications of Adrianople from a military base in European Turkey. Rumania and Turkey boasted of a dozen machines each and Serbia of seven. All were of foreign origin with the exception of Rumania's two Vlaiclu's—a tail-first monoplane with a propeller at either end of the main planes, which had won first prize at the Vienna meeting in 1912 for accurate bomb-dropping.

When hostilities began in 1914 the average speed of machines used for military purposes was not much more than 60 miles per hour, their ceiling from 3,000 to 12,000 feet. Estimates varied considerably as to the number of aircraft available on each side, one source being about as reliable as another. One generally accepted table of the relative strength of the combatants' air arms follows:

Country	Airplanes	Dirigibles
France	138	5
Germany	295	4
England	48	
Italy (1915)	86	
Japan	14	
United States	6	

Recently, the British writer Alan Clark in *Aces High* gave France 160 airplanes and 15 dirigibles, Germany 246 airplanes and 7 Zeppelins, and England 113 airplanes and 6 dirigibles. The discrepancy is as great in most other tabulations, making it impossible to arrive at an exact figure. But there seems little doubt that the French were outnumbered by the Germans at the start.

"Romance, adventure and opportunities for glorious achievement," recruits of Britain's Royal Flying Corps were promised. "War in the air recalls the olden times, when knights rode forth to battle and won honor and glory by their deeds of personal heroism." Many of the volunteers were cavalrymen, discarding their horses for winged steeds in the skies, learning to spy out enemy movements, locate targets for the artillery, strafe trenches, and duel in the air. "They recall the legendary days of chivalry not merely by the daring of their exploits but by the nobility of their spirit" was the sentimental view of Prime Minister Lloyd George. But chivalry soon gave way to shooting an opponent dead to prevent disclosure of information obtained over the battle lines. Desultory duels gave way to multiple dogfights, where no quarter was expected or given. Losses were appalling: on the Western front life expectancy was from three to six weeks. France had a combat loss of 77 percent over the war; Germany in the first month lost 100 planes, mostly due to accidents or malfunction; of 180 American volunteers before their country entered the fray, one half were killed or captured.

The war was scarcely ten days old when James Gordon Bennett, the inveterate bachelor, was married at the age of seventy-three to the former Maud Potter of Philadelphia, widow of his good friend Baron George de Reuter, son of the founder of Reuter's news agency. Always a Francophile, Bennett threw himself wholeheartedly into the French cause and campaigned for America's entry into the conflict. Through the dark days of September 1914, when the tide was running against the French, he stayed in Paris, predicting that the Germans would never reach the capital. Because of the pro-French attitude of his paper it was boycotted by organizations favorable to the Germans, who derided it as a French journal and supplied funds to opposition publications. Bennett sold his luxury yacht, the *Lysistrata,* to Russia's czarist government in 1916, the year he made his last visit to the United States. The *Herald* remained in Paris throughout the war, never missing an issue despite censorship and earning the gratitude of the populace and government.

On 28 September, instead of acclaiming the competitors in the Gordon Bennett scheduled for that day, the front page of the *Herald* was devoted to heavy fighting on the heights of the Meuse. GERMANS VAINLY MAKE DESPERATE EFFORT... ENEMY NIGHT AND DAY TRIES UNSUCCESSFULLY WITH UNPARAL-LELED VIOLENCE TO END BATTLE... BRITISH REPULSE ENEMY WITH HEAVY LOSSES. On the same day there was another air raid on Paris. Lt. G. von Detten dropped several bombs, killing one man and injuring a girl near the chancery of the American embassy on the rue Chaillot and giving Ambassador Myron T. Herrick a close brush with death. War in the air had taken over the headlines reserved for the classic annual speed contest.

No true fighter plane had appeared by the end of 1914 but in the battle of the Marne, which saved Paris, the value of aerial reconnaissance had been fully demonstrated. Warring nations began to take another look at the possibilities of air power. Stalemated on the ground, both sides started to build bombers along with scouts and fighters to protect them. Rudimentary at first and combat-oriented, the new generation of aircraft was looked upon as one means of effecting a breakthrough. On 6 October 1914 a Voisin piloted by Joseph Frantz, armed with a machine gun fired by his observer Sergeant Quenault, brought down a German Aviatik. Before long the Voisin, together with the Caudron, was carrying out bombing attacks like the Germans, while the Maurice Farman Longhorn, was extensively used for scouting. All were pusher biplanes.

But these were slow machines, hard to handle in an emergency; obviously, speed was a prime requisite. It was only natural for the French to turn to the Nieuport, which had proved itself so convincingly in the

207

Gordon Bennett of 1911. A two-seater version, the Nieuport 10, soon made its début, followed by the Nieuport 11—the Bébé—with a single seat and a machine gun mounted on the upper wing to fire above the propeller. The Morane–Saulnier "parasol," with an 80-horsepower Gnôme or Le Rhône motor—copied by the Germans in their Pfalz scout—was approximately the Nieuport's equal with a speed of 118 kilometers per hour (71 mph) Germany's Rumpler–Taube, powered by a six-cylinder, 120-horsepower Mercedes motor, was somewhat faster and the mainstay of German military aviation until 1916, when it was replaced by biplanes that were swifter, stronger, and more maneuverable.

The year 1915 was marked by the invention of a machine gun that fired through the propeller, by the beginning of Anthony Fokker's work for the Germans, and by the formation of the Lafayette Escadrille, a corps of American volunteers whose leading spirit was Norman Prince—his patriotic efforts to provide a racer for the Gordon Bennett now channeled into flying for the French. Germany boldly played the Zeppelin card in nighttime bombing raids, frightening Londoners and inspiring the use of a lurid recruiting poster that told the British "It is Far Better to Face the Bullets than to be Killed at Home by a Bomb—Join the Army at Once and Help to Stop an Air Raid." At a banquet of the Aero Club of America honoring Santos-Dumont in 1916, Henry A. Wise Wood, the toastmaster, pointed out, "A few years ago they smiled at the dirigible, and it is shaking the World's imperial city; they laughed at the aeroplane, and it is directing the armies of Europe." But the dirigible did comparatively little damage; cumbrous, slow, and highly inflammable, it was largely ineffective as a weapon.

Under the imperatives of war, manufacturers strove mightily for better design and ever faster production. From a scattering of workshops at the start, Germany alone developed an industry that turned out 1,600 planes a month in 1917. The French supplied not only their own squadrons but the air forces of Belgium, Italy, Russia, Great Britain, and eventually the United States. As the fortunes of war fluctuated on the ground, so they did in the air; first one side, then the other would gain the ascendancy. The names of aces would become immortal in the history of military aviation: Guynemer, Nungesser, Fonck, Bishop, Ball, Manneck, Rickenbacker, Luke, Campbell, Lufbery; and on the German side Boelcke, Udet, Immelmann, Voss, and the "Red Baron" Manfred Freiherr von Richthofen. The planes they flew were not only progressively faster, but their rate of climb was ever higher, their bomb load ever heavier. War birds that became legendary were the SPADs and the Nieuports, the de Havillands and the Bristols, the Fokkers and the Sopwith Camels, the Albatroses and Aviatiks, the Bréguets, the Gothas, the Halberstadts and Pfalzes, the Handley Pages and Capronis; to mention but a few.

Bennett did not live to see the jubilation at the end of the war, which he had followed closely from embattled Paris. NEWS FIRES CAPITAL WITH FRENZIED JOY announced the *Herald* when the armistice was signed on 11 November. Nor was he destined to know which nation would become the final winner of the cup he had donated in the infancy of flight. In November 1917 he caught a severe cold in the autumnal dampness and at the beginning of December decided to leave Paris for milder temperatures in the south of France. At his Villa Namouna in Beaulieu, however, he caught another chill, which developed into bronchial pneumonia. For the next several months he was ailing. In April 1918, apparently on the road to recovery, he suffered a relapse. Specialists were summoned from Paris, but on 14 May, four days after his seventy-eighth birthday, the famous publisher died of heart failure.

To the end, Bennett maintained an unflagging interest in the news, attending personally to the business and editorial details of running his three newspapers. In a black-bordered, full-page obituary the *Herald* described how, throughout his illness, he had followed "with penetrating insight all the developments of the war, discussing with keen insight all the fluctuations of the battle now raging and exulting patriotically in the magnitude of America's participation in the war and every reported action of the American forces—'our men,' as he always called them with affectionate pride." His death swiftly brought condolences from the French government, from residents along the length of the Riviera, and from the American consul and vice-consul at Nice; tributes from around the world were legion.

The Aero Club of America marked the passing of Bennett, whom it called the "First Patron Saint of International Aeronautics," with a resolution adopted at a meeting held on 15 May:

WHEREAS: Through the death of James Gordon Bennett, which occurred at Beaulieu, France, on the 14th day of May, 1918, the Aero Club of America has lost one of its most revered honorary members, and the aeronautical movement one of its most devoted patrons, and

WHEREAS: Since the earliest days of ballooning as a sport, he encouraged international competition by offering the Coupe Gordon Bennett, which resulted in bringing the aerial sportsmen of the different countries together in friendly competition, thus uniting them in closer harmony and better understanding, and resulting in the greater perfection of the aerostat, and

WHEREAS: By his clear vision of the tremendous possibilities of the aeroplane and realizing the important results to be gained by international competition, he offered the Gordon Bennett Aviation Trophy, which did more than any other one thing to develop aviation to the point where it became a factor in military operation, and

WHEREAS: He has, at all times given the invaluable assistance and support of his papers, the NEW YORK HERALD and the PARIS HERALD, to the aeronautical movement,

THEREFORE, BE IT RESOLVED that in expressing our deep sorrow at the loss of so valued an associate, we emphasize our unbounded admiration of those qualities of heart and mind which made him such a beloved member of the aeronautical fraternity, and

BE IT FURTHER RESOLVED that a copy of these resolutions be suitably engrossed and presented to his family.

"Mr. James Gordon Bennett created the most celebrated sporting events the world has known," said the Paris *Journal,* leading the press in lamenting the loss of a friend. "There were innumerable Gordon

210

Bennett cups and all were destined brilliantly to justify their founder's enterprise."

> Two of these cups stand out pre-eminently from the others, however: the Automobile Cup and the Gordon Bennett Aviation Trophy. The latter was first won at Rheims by the American aviator Glenn Curtiss, defeating Blériot; then in America by the Englishman Grahame-White, on a Blériot machine; in 1911 by C. T. Weymann, on a Nieuport machine in England; in 1912 by Jules Védrines, and finally, in 1913, by the Frenchman Prévost, who was the first to exceed 200 kilometers in the hour. Two years later the engineer M. Béchereau, who constructed Prévost's machine, constructed the famous Spad on which the victories of Guynemer and Fonck have been won.
>
> For James Gordon Bennett had seen clearly ahead. He knew that it was sport that created the intense energy which in peace time wins races and in war times wins battles.

Bennett would be remembered, agreed a writer in *Le Figaro,* as "the first to encourage aviation." The *Excelsior* said: "His foresight was remarkable." Many others came to the same conclusion "that by initiating the idea of racing between nations" he had awakened an interest in the sport that led to steady improvement in the airplane's design and construction.

Where the Gordon Bennett races left off, interrupted by the guns of August 1914, the war carried on over four momentous years until in its final months aerial accomplishments reached a stage few had ever thought possible. More than 8,000 military aircraft were in action along the Western Front in the summer of 1918. Every offensive and counteroffensive was accompanied by massive air battles in which dozens if not scores of machines participated at speeds of 130 miles per hour and altitudes up to 20,000 feet. Germany alone was planning to increase production to 2,000 planes a month, to find 24,000 recruits, and to double the output of fuel.

So recently a sportsman's toy, the airplane had become a potent weapon of war—but with the prospect of immeasurable usefulness when peace was restored. That end would be served by one more race for the Gordon Bennett Cup. With the score at two victories in a row for France, the outcome still hung in the balance.

Chapter 8 THE LAST RACE · 1920

The war left France a recognized leader in aircraft design and production, ready and more than willing to lay claim to supremacy in the realm of speed by reviving the postponed Gordon Bennett. Racing enthusiasts had never lost sight of the international series, their anticipation heightened by the knowledge that France had only to win one more time to clinch possession of the trophy. It was the last chance for another country. Who would rise to the challenge?

Circumstances were very different from previous contests. The war had given birth to planes of extraordinary versatility, capable of much more than the single-purpose, made-to-order monocoques of Védrines and Prévost—planes that made earlier Gordon Bennett racers look quaint by comparison. Distance, duration, rate of climb, acrobatics had all become hallmarks of a new kind of flying machine. More than ever, it seemed that a test of speed alone was not enough to merit the accolade Blue Ribbon of the Air. Before the annual event's prestige should wane, the French prepared to assert final claim to the honor.

Shortly after the armistice was signed in 1918, the Aéro Club de France let it be known that it wished to hold the next contest in the summer of 1919. That date was premature, however, for the Treaty of Versailles, remaking the map of Europe, held the center of the world stage. To give ample time to prepare, the race was rescheduled for Tuesday, 28 September 1920. The place selected was the Villesauvage airfield at Etampes, a short distance south of Paris, an area chosen first by Henry Farman for his school of flying and also by Blériot. Following the railroad for virtually the entire route, the 50-kilometer course lay between Villesauvage and the farm of La Mormorgne in the commune of Gidy, 12 kilometers from the city of Orléans. It would have to be covered six times—that is, three times out and three times back, or three full laps—for a total distance of 300 kilometers (186.4 mi). A pole with a flag at the top indicated the further pylon. Each competitor would be allowed but one start, at a time of his own choosing between the hours of 7:00 A.M. and 6:00 P.M. on the day of the race. Final arrangements were made at a meeting of the Fédération Aéronautique Internationale held at Geneva, Switzerland, 8 to 10 September.

To comprehend fully the enormous strides made by aviation since the first race for the cup at Rheims, one had but to remember that in 1909 the course was only 10 kilometers in length and had only to be covered twice for a total distance of 20 kilometers, about 12½ miles!

As in the past, France, Great Britain, and the United States entered teams of three. Defeated Germany had been stripped of its aviation industry at Versailles and would probably not have been accepted as a contestant by the victorious Allies. No other country signified a desire to compete.

America used the interval to the best advantage. Although it had contributed none of its own aircraft to aerial combat, save for a handful of SE–5s and two-seater de Havillands built under license, manufacturers were geared to the large scale production of training planes—the Liberty-motored Curtiss JN–4, or Jenny, in particular. With the advent of peace, there seemed no place to go; while no one now questioned the importance of air power, to sustain public interest and promote government support was another matter. Realization that the racing craft of today could become the pursuit plane of tomorrow suggested a new market, however, and both military and civilian circles busied themselves with prospective entries for the Gordon Bennett.

Maj. Rudolph W. Schroeder of the U.S. Army Air Service, American entrant in the 1920 Gordon Bennett. Courtesy National Air and Space Museum.

Symptomatic of the wartime just ended were the number of military titles among the officers and governors of the Aero Club of America. The president was Col. Jefferson DeMont Thompson; Rear Adm. Bradley A. Fiske and Lt. Godfrey L. Cabot were vice-presidents; Col. Charles Eliot Warren was treasurer; and the governors included Col. James A. Blair, Jr., Brig. Gen. Robert K. Evans, Lt. Col. F. L. V. Hoppin, and Maj. Albert Bond Lambert. Maj. Charles J. Glidden was acting chairman of the Contest Committee. Hardly surprising, therefore, seemed a formal request by Maj. Rudolph W. Schroeder of McCook Field, Dayton, Ohio, to be entered in the race as representative of the U.S. Army Air Service. "Shorty" Schroeder, who was 6 feet 3 inches tall, was in the limelight. He had broken the world altitude record on 27 February by rising to a height of 33,114 feet (10,093 meters) using a Lepère biplane powered by a 400-horsepower super-

215

charged Liberty motor. He informed the Club, by permission of his commanding officer, that he had been designated as pilot of a standard Verville Scout biplane VCP-1—the army's first purely racing plane. From then on he wished to obtain "all information . . . pertaining to the race," including elimination trials and other time-consuming operations. The major was anxious to sail for France by 14 August, so much so that he enclosed a check for 500 francs to cover the entry fee in case Washington (which intended "to pay all expenses pertaining to the entry") delayed payment. He asked only that he be reimbursed if the government should forward the fee later.

Rudolph William Schroeder was born at Chicago on 14 August 1886 and began glider experiments in 1909. He was a mechanic for Otto Brodie, one of the earliest exhibition flyers, until 1913, when he joined Mickey McGuire and his Curtiss pusher in exhibitions. McGuire was killed in 1914 flying with the Mexican army, and 1915 found Schroeder giving exhibitions on his own. In 1916 he was associated with the aviatrix Katherine Stinson as an expert on rotary motors. He enlisted in the aviation section of the U.S. Army Signal Corps in October 1916 and was rapidly promoted, becoming a major in September 1918. Schroeder was the chief test pilot at McCook Field, where he insisted on the development of a free-type parachute pack as invented by Floyd Smith and in 1919 was the first air service aviator to wear one. He was credited with being the first to fly with a supercharged engine and the first to open a night-flying school. On 6 September 1919 he set a new altitude record at Dayton with Lt. G. Elfrey as passenger, reaching 28,900 feet in a Lepère biplane built by the Packard Motor Car Company of Detroit and equipped with a 400-horsepower supercharged Liberty motor. On 4 October he pushed the mark up further to an uncorrected altitude of 33,335 feet (McCook Field, where the flight was made, reported corrections later that brought the figure down to 31,796 feet). Schroeder placed first in the 1919 New York–Toronto reliability race.

Schroeder exuded confidence in his chances of winning the Gordon Bennett. In his letter to the Aero Club, he said: "From all indications, it looks to me as though the next Gordon Bennett will be held in America."

Army interest in the Gordon Bennett dated back to 1912, when the acting chief of the Signal Corps, Col. George P. Scriven, traveled to Chicago to attend that year's contest and Capt. Charles Chandler, Lt. George H. Arnold, and Lt. Thomas de Witt Milling accepted an invitation of the Illinois Aero Club to officiate at the meet. Maj. Samuel Reber had served as an official at the 1910 Belmont Park race. At the same time a move got under way in Washington to induce "all officers from the Chief of Staff down" to undergo the experience of flying. According to *Aero and Hydro,* "All of the practical aviators in the service agree that it is absolutely essential to get the higher officers of the army to ride in the army aeroplanes as passengers. The army machines are always free to officers wanting to ride, but so far the volunteers have been rather scarce. It seems ridiculous for a commanding officer who does not know a flying machine from a sewing machine to be picking camp and landing fields for practical aviators to risk their necks on. . . . Such a course may be looked back on a decade hence as a remarkably funny necessity, for the chances are that a rudimentary training in aviation will be considered by that time quite on a plane with compulsory vaccination."

Whatever the number of officers who had taken a ride by 1920, the army knew as well as anyone that it was now or never for the United States to regain the trophy. The machine with which it thought this could be accomplished was designed by Alfred Vincent ("Fred") Verville, one of the earliest aeronautical engineers, who had been born in Atlantic, Michigan, in 1890. After working briefly for the Hudson Motor Company and the Fisher Body Company in Detroit, Verville went to the Curtiss plant at Hammondsport as an apprentice in 1914. There he put in time on the Jenny and the Wanamaker transatlantic flying boat *America,* following which he formed his own firm, the General Aeroplane Company of Detroit, to build the Verville flying boat. It was a short-lived venture; he then moved to the army's base at McCook Field, where he became a member of the Lockhart Commission, an official group that was sent to France to study the French aeronautical industry. Returning to McCook Field, Verville developed the racing plane that bore his name; it was constructed to his specifications by the Lawrence Sperry Aircraft Company. Made entirely of wood and plywood, its tapered wings and movable surfaces fabric covered, the Verville Scout was normally powered by a Hispano–Suiza engine. But for the Gordon Bennett it was equipped with an outsize new twelve-cylinder V–type Packard motor rated at no less than 638 horsepower—nearly double that of most other entries in the race. With slightly staggered wings, the pilot's head barely showing above the strongly streamlined fuselage, the Verville–Packard was the picture of a scientifically constructed racer, for which no expense had been spared. In fact, when all the returns were in, it was estimated that 1,500,000 dollars had been spent in building and shipping the machine to Paris and furnishing it with a staff of experts and mechanics.

The army was not alone in its determination to bring the trophy back to America. Sponsored and financed by S. E. J. Cox, a Texas oil tycoon not at all averse to personal publicity, who hoped to heap glory on the Lone Star State by backing a sure winner, not one but two unusual aircraft were constructed for the race by the Curtiss company: one, the *Cactus Kitten,* was a thick-winged monoplane; the other, a biplane with unusual double-cambered wings, was christened the *Texas Wildcat.* Each had an all-plywood fuselage 19 feet 6 inches long in which the only metal was the motor mount, a fully enclosed cockpit, and a water-cooled Curtiss V–12 engine of 435 horsepower whose rectangular honeycomb radiator along each side was reminiscent of the Antoinette. These aircraft were probably the first ever to have transparent cockpit hatches, which had to be installed after the pilot was seated. The *Wildcat* had a span of 25 feet, and its gross weight was 2,300 pounds; top speed was estimated at well over 200 miles per hour. The *Kitten,* on the other hand, was built with two optional sets of wings, the shorter in span considerably thicker than the other, with extending ailerons; it had a wide-bladed wood propeller of extremely high pitch for top speed—but the long takeoff run this required would be found incompatible with the shorter than expected airfields of France. Both the *Wildcat* and the *Kitten* were designed solely for speed, solely for winning the Gordon Bennett.

Not to be outdone by its longtime Curtiss rival, the Dayton–Wright Company, with Orville Wright now an engineering consultant, decided to build an advanced type of plane for the contest. Breaking with its biplane tradition, the firm produced a full cantilever-winged monoplane with a very slim, extremely deep fuselage. Designed by Milton C. Bowman and designated as the RB Racer, it was 22 feet 8 inches in length, had a span of 21 feet, and was powered by a water-cooled six-cylinder in-line Hall–Scott Special motor of 250 horsepower with a radiator in the nose cone. A top speed of 200 miles per hour was thought to be attainable. The single wing was of balsa, with chunks removed for lightness, and its structural strength was such that it easily supported the weight of twelve men standing on it. Leading and trailing edges were hinged to permit the pilot, by means of two actuating rods on each side of the wing top, to change the camber on takeoff and landing.

The entire aircraft was covered with plywood, including the movable control surfaces. Linen was glued on the plywood and given several coats of varnish, much in the manner of the prewar Deperdussin monocoque. From the totally enclosed cabin, which was entered by a trapdoor above the cockpit, the pilot could see only through windows at the side; he could open these by hand or, on landings, by leaning a shoulder against the back of the window frame and pushing forward, thus leaving his hands free. The most interesting feature of the Dayton–Wright, however, was its retractable undercarriage, operated by a hand crank in the center of the instrument panel—one of the first such landing gear to be seen in any country, but not the very first. The American Matthew B. Sellers incorporated a retractable undercarriage in a primitive machine that he tested in 1908; the device was patented in 1911. In the Dayton–Wright the same crank was used to actuate the mechanism that adjusted the wing camber. Nothing further in design from the original Wright biplane that had taken part in Gordon Bennett contests a short decade before could possibly be imagined. Such technical innovations were years ahead of their time; eventually they would be embodied in airplanes throughout the world.

By letter dated 3 August 1920 the Contest Committee of the Aero Club of America notified the Fédération Aéronautique Internationale that the club had "accepted and confirmed" three entries for the Gordon Bennett the week of 27 September.

> Army Air Service. (Capt. R. W. Schroeder has been entered as the pilot of this aeroplane in the race).
> Mr. S. E. J. Cox, through the Aero Club of America.
> Dayton–Wright Company, through the Aero Club of America.
> The above three representing the United States in the Contest.

For once, club members believed, America had the machines as well as the men to ensure victory. Four aircraft of advanced design would be sent to France: one of them would be sure to win. Experience accumulated during the war years and reflected in the aerodynamic skills of the manufacturers, in addition to the necessary financial resources, would make an irresistible combination against any racers Europe could put up—which would be reworked pursuit planes carried over from the war. The pilots, too, were the very best. Howard M. Rinehart, holder of the club's certificate No. 266, was a top-ranking, seasoned flier for the Wright organization. He had been an instructor for the Wrights at their winter headquarters in Augusta in 1911 and had flown for the Mexican revolutionary Pancho Villa in 1914. He was in charge of all tests for the de Havilland–4s that Dayton–Wright produced in large numbers during World War I and had spent many years in research work, which gave him the title of aeronautical engineer on the company's list of executive officers. Major Schroeder clearly was the army's first choice to handle the powerful Verville–Packard. And blond, level-headed Roland Rohlfs had a fine reputation as chief experimental pilot for the Curtiss Aeroplane and Motor Company of Garden City, New York.

Rohlfs had broken the world record for altitude on 18 September 1919 by climbing to 34,910 feet in a Curtiss Wasp triplane even without the use of a supercharger for its 400-horsepower Curtiss–Kirkham K–12 engine. Born in Buffalo, New York, on 10 February 1892, he was the son of a noted fiction writer, Anna Katherine (Green) Rohlfs. He was educated at local schools and, like Glenn Curtiss, began by designing and building racing motorcycles. When Curtiss moved part of his factory to Buffalo in 1914, Rohlfs answered an advertisement for a mechanic to work at Hammondsport and remained there until transferred back to Buffalo in the spring of 1915. As a pupil of Victor Carlstrom, who was to win the New York–Toronto Air Race in 1919, Rohlfs learned to fly at Newport News, Virginia. He qualified for license No. 699 on 25 April 1917 at Miami, Florida, after which he became an instructor, as well as a demonstrator and tester, of Curtiss airplanes at the Mineola field near Garden City. On 13 April 1919 he made headlines by carrying a Broadway actress, the wife of cartoonist George McManus, in a training plane over the Polo Grounds in New York, where a game was in progress; a baseball was dropped from a height of 300 feet, autographed, and auctioned off for the benefit of the Actors Fund of America. A year later he set a seaplane speed record of 138 miles per hour at the Rockaway Naval Air Station on Long Island with one of the two Wasp triplanes owned by the U.S. Navy. His association with the Cox family, to fly the Curtiss-built machines it had financed, followed.

The British also were resolved to try for the trophy, counting on their industry's wartime experience to make a good showing. At the outbreak, British military aircraft were far from being the equal of the French, but by September 1916 the highly efficient Sopwith Pup, derived from the Sopwith Tabloid, the company's 1914 entry in the cancelled Gordon Bennett, had arrived to support the embattled troops in France. The next two years saw the production of some excellent machines, notably the Sopwith Camel and the SE–5. Manufacturers had hit their stride, so that at the end of hostilities prospects seemed favorable for nominating a team of three. Sopwith was clearly in the lead with its Sopwith–Hawker Rainbow, a land version of the seaplane that had competed for the Schneider Trophy in 1919. Named as pilot was the experienced Harry G. Hawker, whose attempt to fly the Atlantic with Lt. Comdr. K. Mackenzie-Grieve and dramatic rescue at sea on 18 May 1919 had electrified the world. The series of machines that Sopwith had produced since 1914 were of the highest order. Now, however, the firm was about to go into liquidation owing to war-related debts and heavy losses incurred in the attempted manufacture of motorcycles.

The Martinsyde *Semiquaver* of F.P. Raynham, British entry in the final Gordon Bennett. Courtesy National Air and Space Museum.

A modified Nieuport–Goshawk pursuit plane was also entered, with Henry P. Folland, its chief designer, as pilot. As a single-seater racing biplane, it was the last machine to be turned out by the Nieuport and General Aviation Company, which had been formed to build Nieuport designs in Britain. The Goshawk was fitted with a 320-horsepower A.B.C. Dragonfly engine. Entered in a number of races in 1920, for various reasons it had not so far met with any great success.

Britain's third entry was a Martinsyde *Semiquaver* biplane, adapted from the F–4 Buzzard fighter, with staggered wings, a wing span of 20 feet 2 inches, and a length of 19 feet 3 inches—the recent winner in Britain's 200-mile Air Derby. It was assigned for the race to the likable, lanky pioneer pilot F. P. ("Freddie") Raynham, the holder of license No. 85, obtained at Hendon on a Roe biplane on 9 May 1911. Among his other qualifications, Raynham was on record as having been the first aviator to recover from a spin—an event, according to the authoritative Charles Gibbs-Smith, that occurred on 11 September 1911. Not long

222

after the end of the war in 1918, Raynham announced that he would be among the competitors for the *Daily Mail*'s 10,000-pound prize for a transatlantic flight. With Captain C. W. F. Morgan as navigator, he arrived in Newfoundland in April 1919, along with Harry Hawker and others, to attempt the west–east crossing in a Martinsyde biplane named the *Raymor* (a combination of his name and that of his partner). After testing the machine on 16 April, the airmen crashed in a wind gust while trying to take off on 18 May, fortunately without great harm to themselves. The small *Semiquaver* that was to carry the British colors in the Gordon Bennett looked to one reporter like a "chubby, self-reliant red sparrow." It was believed by many to have more than an even chance for the cup with a rated speed of 165 miles per hour.

France was represented by a three-man team flying two late-war-model Nieuports and a SPAD—top scorers in elimination trials held on Saturday, 25 September, two days before the race. Georges Kirsch, a heavyset, beetle-browed, former mechanic, had started his career in late 1910 with Edouard Nieuport after a short apprenticeship with the Société Antoinette. At the modest Nieuport factory on Paris's rue de Seine, he was put to work on the construction and assembly of three types of monoplane: (1) a 100-horsepower Gnôme-equipped single-seater ordered by Charles Weymann for the 1911 Gordon Bennett, (2) a similar machine of 70 horsepower to be used by Edouard Nieuport himself in the same race, and (3) a three-place model driven by a 100-horsepower Gnôme designed to meet the exacting requirements of the 1911 *Concours Militaire*. It was a gratifying year for Kirsch, who watched Weymann win the Gordon Bennett and Nieuport take third place, then saw Weymann's triumph in the military trials. Kirsch never swerved in his allegiance to the house of Nieuport and was rewarded by being named the pilot of one of its entries in the 1920 Gordon Bennett. The conventional Nieuport Model 29, with a V–8 320-horsepower Hispano–Suiza motor, had a wing span of 19 feet 6 inches and a length of 20 feet 3 inches. Empty it weighed 1,521 pounds, while its gross weight was 2,060 pounds. But Kirsch's plane, displaying the racing number 11, wasn't strictly a stock model. At first glance it appeared to be a standard open-cockpit biplane, but closer inspection showed a peep-hole in the shape of a teardrop directly below the cockpit from which the pilot could peer out the side. It was believed this configuration might give the machine an extra touch that could prove decisive.

As the pilot of a postwar two-seater production line SPAD–Herbemont with the rear cockpit covered for the race and, like the Nieuport, fitted with a 320-horsepower Hispano–Suiza motor, Bernard-Henry Barny de Romanet had a wealth of war experience behind him. Born on 28 January 1894 at Saint-Maurice de Sathonay to a military family, he showed exceptional brilliance in his studies as a youth. He joined the cavalry in 1914 and departed for the front in August as a sergeant in the Eighth Army Corps; he was cited on the twentieth of that month for taking the place of a wounded comrade under heavy enemy assault. During the winter of 1914–15 he participated in the battles of Sarrebourg, the Meuse heights, and Apremont; in April he was assigned to the Fifty-Sixth Regiment of Infantry and obtained a license to fly at Pau. By August he was conducting reconnaissance flights and serving as liaison with the infantry. His machine riddled with bullets after each sortie, he was finally downed by German infantry fire.

De Romanet was made an adjutant in 1916 and on 17 October was again cited for bravery. On 12 March 1917, mentioned in army orders for the consistent success of his missions, he was transferred to a pursuit squadron. He engaged two German airplanes near Rheims on 3 May and shot down one of them for his first aerial victory; for this he was awarded the Medaille Militaire. In numerous other encounters his opponents either escaped or crashed too far away to be confirmed as kills but on 17 October he was credited with a "probable" victim. He earned a fifth citation on 31 March 1918 when he brought down a German plane over the French lines at Rollot. In May he destroyed an observation balloon—his second such exploit—and on 1 June downed a two-seater biplane over the forest of Villiers. In the course of a patrol on 29 June he scored his fifth victory, shooting down a Fokker D. VIII in flames. On 15 July he downed a two-seater D.F.W. and the next day still another adversary, for which he was made a chevalier of the Legion

224

of Honor. Three more German airplanes were his prey in August, and in October nine more—including a redoubtable three-passenger Gotha bomber escorted by four Fokkers. That brought the total number of his official kills to thirty. De Romanet ended the war with the grade of lieutenant, credited with 855 hours of flight over enemy territory, and rounded out the year 1918 by adding an eleventh citation to the Croix de Guerre he had so richly earned. The Aéro Club de France on 6 June 1919 presented him with its Grande Médaille Militaire. A more respected and decorated war ace would have been hard to find.

De Romanet joined the Bréguet company in 1919 but entered the race for the Deutsch de la Meurthe Cup on 14 October with a Nieuport equipped with a 300-horsepower Hispano–Suiza motor; he was forced down only 20 kilometers from the finish. A week later with the same machine he set a closed-circuit speed record of 268.631 kilometers per hour. Going back to the Bréguet and its 300-horsepower Renault motor, he flew on 7 April 1920 from Villacoublay to Madrid, a distance of 1,200 kilometers in eight hours. Then, at the spring meeting at Monaco on 25 April he piloted a Hispano–Suiza-powered SPAD–Herbemont on floats to victory in the first of a series of speed tests at the rate of 211.712 kilometers per hour; he finished second in a race on 2 May over an 80.5-kilometer course.

As a result of his many combat missions, de Romanet had become a past master of the SPAD. Wartime reincarnation of the Deperdussin, acknowledged by the experts to be among the finest *aéroplanes de classe,* the SPAD was renowned for its high speed and climbing power. The most recent model had a wing spread of 28 feet 6 inches and was 21 feet 9 inches long; the fuselage was of plywood, the wing and tail surfaces were built up of wood spars and ribs, and the whole was fabric covered; weight empty was 1,950 pounds and the gross weight was 2,875 pounds. To the designation SPAD was appended the name Herbemont in recognition of the engineer who became associated with the original Deperdussin concern in 1913. De Romanet's plane bore the number 8 for the race. A sister ship, flown by Lt. Jean Casale of the French army, failed to qualify in the elimination trials, though on 28

Sadi-Lecointe of the 1920 French team. In this autographed photo he pays tribute to the manufacturers of the Hispano–Suiza engine that enabled him to break nine world records. Courtesy National Air and Space Museum.

February at Villacoublay its pilot had set a world record of 176.111 miles per hour (283 km/hr). A Borel biplane piloted by Barrault also did not qualify.

The clear-cut winner of the French trials was a jovial Joseph Sadi-Lecointe, born on 1 July 1891 at Saint-Germain sur Bresie in the valley of the Somme. His family were farmers but such an occupation had no appeal for a young man enthralled by the feats of Blériot and his contemporaries. Instead, he found employment as mechanic with an aspiring airplane constructor named Minet, whose brainchild was the Zenith monoplane. Working enthusiastically from dawn to dusk, Sadi thought of nothing but becoming a champion flier, vowing even to win the Gordon Bennett some day. When the Zenith was completed in 1910 with no pilot in sight, he offered his services—which were accepted on condition that he confine himself to "grass-cutting." After several sessions of rolling along the ground at Issy-les-Moulineaux, the Zenith unexpectedly took off one morning and the nineteen-year-old novice at an altitude of 10 meters found the Paris fortifications suddenly straight ahead. He cut the motor and the monoplane landed by itself. Proud of this first flight, he determined then and there to devote the rest of his life to aviation.

The Zenith project having finally been abandoned, Sadi-Lecointe scrimped and saved to pay for flying lessons at an informal school run by the Italian-born motor manufacturer Alessandro Anzani, who was also based at Issy. Using an Anzani-powered Blériot, he was granted the Aéro Club's license No. 431 on 11 February 1911 and spent the rest of that year making flights in the Midi, at Carmaux where he broke an arm in a bad landing, at Argentan, Alençon, Falaise, Mamers, and many other places in France. A medium-sized man with a jaunty upturned moustache, he was called to military duty with the First Engineers at Versailles on 12 October 1912 and spent the following six months at the Satory camp; in 1913 he was sent to the Blériot school at Etampes, where he obtained military license No. 373; he was then assigned to the BL10 squadron at Belfort. Demonstrating unusual proficiency as a pilot, he was given the grade of corporal in 1914 and on

3 August, at the outbreak of war, was mobilized with the rest of his squadron.

Sadi-Lecointe's war record also was a distinguished one. As a spotter for the artillery and a far-ranging scout, he often returned from missions with his machine full of bullet holes but invariably with important intelligence. Promoted to sergeant, he was attached to the staff of General Foch; he became an adjutant on 15 March 1915, twice cited in army orders for his virtuosity and for the resolute carrying out of his missions. In 1916 he reached the rank of *sous-lieutenant* and was sent to Avord to the school to train fighter pilots. At the end of 1917 his familiarity with the Blériot led to an assignment as test pilot for the new 200- and 300-horsepower SPADs. By the time the war was over, he had been awarded the Croix de Guerre.

For the first part of 1919 Sadi-Lecointe went in for altitude, successively raising the French record to 8,155 meters, 8,585 meters, and 8,900 meters—the ceiling of his SPAD–Herbemont. He then joined the firm of Nieuport–Delage and began to concentrate on speed, turning in marks from 247 to 270 kilometers per hour. The year 1920 opened auspiciously for him. On 3 January he won the Deutsch de la Meurthe Cup—a 190-kilometer race around Paris—in 42 minutes 53⅘ seconds or at a speed of 266.314 kilometers per hour. At Villacoublay on 7 February he broke the world straight-line record for 1 kilometer with a speed of 275.862 kilometers per hour. From then until the Gordon Bennett in September he was variously engaged in challenging the altitude record, in competing in the hydro-aeroplane meet at Monaco, where he was awarded the Grand Prix, and in a circuit that took in points in French North Africa and Spain, and in winning the speed trophy at the Olympic Games in Antwerp. For the blue ribbon contest at Étampes he was at the controls of a Nieuport 29 identical to that of Kirsch, with the number 10 painted in black on its silvery sides.

The prospective lineup for the 1920 race is shown in table 12.

A few days before the race, America's choice of entries was reduced by one. The Curtiss–Cox monoplane, *Cactus Kitten,* painted red with silver wings and tail had been shipped to the Morane–Saulnier airfield

Table 12
1920 • Prospective Entry List

Country	Pilot	Machine	Motor
United States	Maj. R. W. Schroeder	Verville Scout biplane	638-hp Packard V–12
	Roland Rohlfs	Curtiss *Texas Wildcat* biplane	435-hp Curtiss V–12
		Curtiss *Cactus Kitten* monoplane	435-hp Curtiss V–12
	Howard Rinehart	Dayton-Wright monoplane	250-hp Hall-Scott
Great Britain	Harry Hawker	Sopwith Rainbow biplane	
	Henry Folland	Goshawk biplane	320-hp A.B.C. Dragon-fly
	F. P. Raynham	Nieuport Martinsyde *Semiquayer* biplane	320-hp Hispano-Suiza
France	Georges Kirsch	Nieuport biplane	320-hp Hispano-Suiza
	Bernard de Romanet	SPAD-Herbemont biplane	320-hp Hispano-Suiza
	Joseph Sadi-Lecointe	Nieuport biplane	320-hp Hispano-Suiza

at Villacoublay for assembly along with its mate, the *Wildcat*. But it was not even removed from the crates. Built for high performance and all-out speed seemingly without regard for the type of landing and take-off facilities to be encountered in Europe, it was obviously unsuitable for the relatively limited field at Etampes.

Only one of the British entries reached France for the race—the Martinsyde *Semiquaver*; with the company close to bankruptcy, Raynham towed it behind his car. Serious financial problems confronted an industry that had reverted to civilian status. Sopwith, in voluntary liquidation after being presented with a huge tax bill by the government, was in the process of reorganization as the Hawker Engineering Company. Henry Folland's Goshawk, beset by bureaucratic red tape, could not reach the continent in time. At the last minute an attempt was made to replace it with a Nieuport flown to Le Bourget by L. R. Tait-Cox. But it was too late: the rules stipulated that all contenders had to be on the field at least twenty-four hours before the race.

Conscious of this requirement, the American team's Dayton–Wright and Verville–Packard had been transported by truck to Etampes from the staging area at Villacoublay three days in advance to be assembled at the Villesauvage airfield. Not so with the Cox entry, the *Texas Wildcat*. Late in the afternoon of Sunday, 26 September—the deadline was 7:00 A.M. on the twenty-seventh—the machine was still at Villacoublay, giving rise to uncertainty as to whether America would field its full complement of three entries. For several days Cox and his contentious publicity director had been at odds with representatives of the Aero Club of America (Colonel Jefferson DeMont Thompson, the president; Captain V. E. Brandeis; and the durable Cortlandt Field Bishop), creating a small furor in the press. Claiming that he was entitled to two of the club's three entries, Cox and his wife went further and insisted on calling their cup defender a Cox, not Curtiss, machine, alleging they had directed every detail of its construction. Adding to the commotion was a foolish rumor that whoever piloted a Cox entry in the Gordon Bennett would leap from his machine with a parachute at the finish because the Curtiss planes were considered too fast to land safely. French Air Minister Flandin had published a notice that anyone making such an attempt would face both criminal and civil charges. Finally, the millionaire Texan declared he would not trust his entry to a bumpy ride over the roads in a truck but that he would have it flown over from Villacoublay at four o'clock on Sunday afternoon in time to complete the American team's formal entry into the contest. A sizable crowd was on hand to await the plane's arrival.

When the *Wildcat* had not shown up at ten minutes to six, Capt. C. C. Moseley, military attaché at the American embassy, volunteered to fly to Villacoublay to ascertain the reason for the delay. At half past six he returned with word that Roland Rohlfs and the *Wildcat* were poised for takeoff. What ensued was graphically described by the Paris

230

Herald's reporter in a story that would take up more space than the race itself.

A loud roar was heard from the direction of Villacoublay, and then a speck appeared. The speck was coming with the speed of lightning. The little biplane swept by on the opposite side of the road from the field like a flash. Such speed drew a gasp of astonishment from the crowd of professional aviators.

"He can walk rings around the British," they exclaimed. Rohlfs took two sweeping rushes around the field, locating himself. The crowd dashed to the fence, holding its breath for the landing. Down the field he came, lower and lower. Now he was almost touching the ground. Then the roaring motor stopped for an instant and the wheels just skimmed the turf as a seagull's feet will skim the deck of a vessel when it has not made up its mind whether or not to come to rest. Then the motor roared again for an instant the machine took a little lift and again the roaring was silenced. The machine came to rest on an even keel. It looked like a beautiful landing and the crowd breathed again with relief.

At that instant something seemed to crumple under the plane. The machine plunged forward on its nose and then turned turtle, pinning the plucky aviator underneath.

Pandemonium was loosed. The crowd dashed frantically on the field. The United States Army emergency truck, which always waits with fire extinguishers and wrecking tackle whenever there is a plane coming down, was on the scene in a jiffy. Rohlfs was dragged out from beneath the fuselage. He was unconscious. It was apparent that he was grievously hurt and at first it was thought he was dead.

Not only was pandemonium loosed but confusion and indignation as well. A hurry-up call had been despatched to the sheds and barracks for a doctor, a stretcher and nurses, which the American committee had been informed would be in attendance at all times. The messenger returned with the information that none was to be found. After the injured man had been lying beside his machine for twenty-five minutes, someone found some bandages in the pack of a French soldier, and a mattress and a sort of stretcher were located in barracks about half a mile away. A French soldier with a knowledge of first-aid bandaging did what little he could.

In the meantime, Rohlfs had become conscious. Seeing Captain

231

Schroeder . . . bending over him, he whispered:

"Hello, Shorty. This is my first crash, but I guess I'm not hurt very bad." That was before he had tried to move.

A truck had been procured by this time, and Rohlfs was bundled into it by aviators and mechanics, who then set off toward the town of Etampes, eight kilometers away, to look for a hospital and a physician. At this point, Mr. Bishop took affairs into his own hands.

Speeding ahead of the truck in his fast machine, he made arrangements for the injured man's care at the Sisters' Hospital, and then rounded up the local medical man. As Rohlfs was placed upon the operating table, where his clothes were cut away, he pleaded with Captain Schroeder that his wife, who is in New York and highly wrought up over her husband's fate, should not be unnecessarily alarmed.

At nine o'clock Mr. Cox arrived at the hospital with a physician. Rohlfs had miraculously escaped death, but his shoulder, back, and left arm had been badly hurt and he had suffered head injuries.

Someone had blundered, charged the *Herald,* in allowing Rohlfs to fly in "a veritable death trap." He had gone into the air "under no misapprehensions as to the unfitness" of the widely heralded Cox airplane, after repeated warnings "by other experts" and "tentative trials which he had undertaken at Villacoublay had convinced him that the machine was structurally unsound. It had been conclusively demonstrated that the landing gear was as brittle as china and that it was not equipped with shock absorbers or any of the other safety appliances for coming to earth", which, the newspaper added indignantly, "for several years have been considered ABC's of aeroplane construction." But Rohlfs had loyally taken "the one chance in a hundred of coming through with a whole skin in a valiant effort to enable the United States to have its full representation" in the Gordon Bennett. It was plain where the *Herald*'s sympathies lay.

The entrants were now down to six—two American, one British, and three French. Reversing the trend toward monoplanes of the prewar years, all but one flew biplanes.

The weather in late September was unpredictable, morning mist more than likely to obscure the ground. Weather permitting, therefore,

232

Starting Sadi-Lecointe's Nieuport with an Odier air starter. Courtesy National Air and Space Museum.

said the *Herald* in its edition of 28 September, the race would be held as scheduled; otherwise, the rules specified, it would take place next day, with no provision for further postponement. Entrants were expected to fly at as early an hour as possible, for the air was calmest then or in the evening, and shortly after 7:00 A.M. spectators began to arrive. Among the Americans was the injured Rohlfs, head and face bandaged, arm in a sling. Present also were reporters from the United States, France, Great Britain, Italy, Spain, and Portugal and, underlining the importance of the occasion, military observers not only from America but from practically every country in Europe as well as Japan.

But the weather was not encouraging. A heavy fog hung over the field—visibility was almost nil—and it was feared the race would have to be put off. As the day wore on, famous personalities in the aviation world motored out from Paris and waited in groups, discussing the war-spawned aircraft lined up at the far side of the airfield or reminiscing about former contests: Henry Farman, Louis Blériot, Louis Bréguet,

233

René Caudron, Robert Morane, Marcel Hanriot, Delage and Barzaine of the Nieuport company, previous competitors such as Charles Weymann, Marcel Prévost, and Alfred Leblanc. Some had been an integral part of the Gordon Bennett story from its inception; now they would witness a new and technically advanced chapter in the eleven-year history of the great race.

Around midday scouts for the American and French teams were despatched to determine the condition of the course, Captain Moseley acting for the United States. Their reports were gloomy, as the fog seemed thicker at the end of the route. But at one o'clock the sun abruptly pierced the haze. Half an hour later the last wisp was gone and the contenders wasted no time in getting away. At eight minutes past two Kirsch started in his Nieuport; first circling the field to warm up his engine, then saluting with his wings, he crossed the starting line and was off. He was followed into the air twenty minutes later by de Romanet in the SPAD, then by Sadi-Lecointe in the second Nieuport.

With all three French entrants up, it was the turn of America to bid for the crowd's attention. Everyone watched in fascination as Howard Rinehart got the Dayton–Wright off the ground and began retracting the wheels into the fuselage by hand crank. That accomplished, the unconventional-looking monoplane, conspicuously numbered 2, flashed across the starting line, as the *Herald* put it, "like a great silvery aerial porpoise." The plane had done 165 miles per hour on a practice lap, its Hall–Scott motor not fully open, and its reputed capability of reaching 200 kilometers per hour confirmed the impression that it had a theoretical edge over the other contestants.

Last to leave was Schroeder. He and his wife—who, it was noted, was constantly at his side until he climbed into the cockpit of the Verville–Packard—were required to pose for the press and eleven insistent "cinema operators, fifteen camera men, and an Annamite." There was difficulty in starting the big engine. Ten men, working in relays, were needed to set off its thunderous roar, but at length the army entry too was off and away.

Raynham's *Semiquaver* would stay behind until the air was cooler later in the day, for the pilot was well aware of its motor's propensity to overheat.

Kirsch completed two full laps of the course in 48 minutes $53\frac{3}{5}$ seconds, the first lap at a speed of 181.5 miles per hour—the fastest time of the day. Misfortune, however, was just around the corner. On the second round he was compelled to land with badly fouled spark plugs, which then and there put him out of the race. It did not augur well for France.

Averaging 162 miles per hour, de Romanet was on his second lap when all eyes were diverted to the spectacle of the Dayton–Wright coming in for a landing with its wheels extended. Minutes later, to the consternation of America's fans, Rinehart was rolling to a stop, also out of the running. What could have caused his abrupt descent? The question eluded an immediate answer. A broken rudder cable, making it impossible to turn left, according to one report. Sabotage, said another; someone had applied acid to the cable, which ate away the wire in flight. More likely was the pilot's inability to crank the wing to its flat, high-speed contour (and at the same time to fully retract the landing gear). The plane had entered the race with only one actuating rod on each side of the wing top instead of two—the original configuration. If the mechanism was not working properly and the wing camber could not be changed in flight, it would no doubt have been dangerous to continue.

America's chances went glimmering when the Verville–Packard too dropped out of the race, even though its speed indicator showed better than 210 miles per hour when Schroeder chose to bring it down. The explanation was simple enough: not enough radiator area to cool the oversize engine. Besides, there was a risk of fire as the carburetor intake was not functioning normally at full throttle, causing flames to shoot out the exhaust pipes. Critics after the race asserted that adequate radiator surface had been sacrificed to considerations of weight and air resistance and blamed America's poor showing on the failure to make enough practice flights—as the French had been doing for days before

235

the race—when the faults "could have been discovered and easily remedied." Unable to complete a single lap, the costly machines from America were an embarrassing disappointment.

Near his starting point, at the end of his second lap, de Romanet was forced down for repairs. The motor of the SPAD was giving trouble. Mechanics working frantically for thirty minutes enabled him to resume the race—but luck was still against him. An oil leak developed on his last lap, black fluid spewing into the cockpit and drenching his face and shoulders. Raising his goggles, he was almost blinded. Gamely, he kept on and succeeded in landing safely downwind at "terrific" speed, his machine rolling hundreds of yards after alighting. His elapsed time was 1 hour 39 minutes 6.6 seconds for an average speed—slowed by the forced landing—of 113.5 miles per hour.

Sadi-Lecointe meanwhile was flying a steady, smooth, and consistent course, rounding the pylons in steeply banked turns that drew cheers from the onlookers. He had been over the route again and again in practice, and the results showed in the precision of his flight. To a storm of applause he crossed the finish line for an average speed of 168.5 miles per hour. The fast little Nieuport had functioned to perfection, though the motor was boiling when he landed. For the first 100 kilometers his time was 21 minutes $36\frac{3}{5}$ seconds; for 200 kilometers it was 43 minutes $42\frac{3}{4}$ seconds; and for the course it was 1 hour 6 minutes $17\frac{1}{5}$ seconds. No records were broken, but all agreed that he had given a superlative exhibition of flying.

Table 13
1920 • Results

Place	Pilot	Country	Machine	Motor	Speed
1	Sadi-Lecointe	France	Nieuport biplane	320-hp Hispano-Suiza	168.5 m/hr
2	B. de Romanet	France	SPAD-Herbemont biplane	320-Hispano-Suiza	113.5 m/hr

236

Sadi-Lecointe carried off by his admirers after winning the 1920 race, thus giving France permanent possession of the Gordon Bennett Cup. Courtesy Roger-Viollet, Paris.

Only Raynham and the Martinsyde remained to dispute French possession of the cup and the crowd waited impatiently to see if Great Britain's representative could improve on the Nieuport's mark.

At half past four the British biplane, which had evoked high praise when tested the day before, was brought onto the field and the engine started. Expectancy ran high as it roared into the air after a short run. England's contingent of spectators shouted wild support as it completed the first lap in masterful style and sped into the second. Then ill luck struck again: a broken oil pump brought the *Semiquaver* down in a humiliating anticlimax. Like the United States, Britain failed to stop the French from gaining the cup they had so long sought. The Gordon Bennett trophy passed permanently into possession of the country where the blue ribbon contest had originated. The score (table 13) was conclusive proof of French predominance.

237

A popular hero, Sadi-Lecointe was hoisted on the shoulders of his admirers and carried off to the ovation that awaited him. Champagne flowed freely at the party that followed; glasses clinked and toasts were repeatedly made. Besides winning the celebrated competition for France, the doughty, self-made aviator would receive a prize of 10,000 francs and the unstinted acclaim of his deliriously exultant countrymen. Illustrated with pictures, his triumph was spread across the front page of all newspapers on 29 September, dwarfing the latest despatches from Belfast that told of rioting in Ireland and the use of British troops to put it down. He had shown that it was not only speed that counted in a racing craft but mechanical fitness and piloting skill as well. Sheer horsepower was not the answer, as the American effort had demonstrated, nor was the amount of money spent on construction. The right combination of man and machine, as represented by the conscientious, thoroughgoing French airman and his finely tuned Nieuport was an example to the world of aviation at its best.

And so came to a close the glorious Gordon Bennett races, symbol of international sportsmanship, blue ribbon of the air. Their originator would have been content: their objective had been achieved. Speed alone had proved to be no final goal—development of the airplane had gone with it. But by dedicating his trophy to the encouragement of speed, James Gordon Bennett took the first step toward a design that enables us to fly faster than sound today.

Epilogue

The Gordon Bennett Cup now occupies an honored place in a spacious salon of the Aéro Club de France at 6, rue de Galilée in Paris, the owner in perpetuity by virtue of three successive wins. Resting on a marble pillar in the form of a fluted Greek column, it has the added decoration of a band of silver engraved with the name of each year's winner, his machine and motor, and the speed that brought him victory:

1909	Curtiss	USA	Curtiss	Curtiss
	75 Km/H 492			
1910	Grahame White	Gr Br	Bleriot	Gnome
	98 Km/H 552			
1911	Weymann	USA	Nieuport	Gnome
	125 Km/H			
1912	Vedrines	France	Deperdussin Bechereau	Gnome
	169 Km/700			
1913	Prevost	France	Deperdussin Bechereau	Gnome
	204 Km			
1920	Sadi Lecointe	France	Nieuport	Hispano
	271 Km/H 547			

The trophy may seem slightly top-heavy today because the obsolete Wright biplane with its forward elevator contrasts with the sleek contours of a modern racer, but this in no way detracts from the fine work-manship or the unique composition that brought such wide acclaim as an example of the silversmith's art. Frenchmen like to point out that all the races except the first were won with French machines and French motors. Nevertheless, the airplane chosen to represent man's most exalted aspiration—the conquest of the air—is American and the primitive Wright model confirms for all time the fact that America showed the way.

Those who participated in the series were a special class of airmen, chosen to fly for their country against the strongest international competition. In that era there was no higher honor, no greater ambition for an aviator than to win the Gordon Bennett. Thinking of the men immortalized on the silver band, you wonder what became of them and the other contestants—those whose names flashed across the aviation firmament once a year like meteors in the night skies. What were their later lives? Their deaths?

Little more than a week after the 1909 race at Rheims, Eugène Lefèbvre, who had finished fourth for France, fell to his death while testing a new Wright machine—one of the first to be fitted with wheels in addition to the skid undercarriage. On 7 September at a relatively low altitude, the plane went into a nose dive and struck the earth with such force that Lefèbvre perished instantly. It was difficult to determine what caused the crash but most witnesses thought the controls had jammed.

Two months after he had taken second place for the United States in the 1910 Gordon Bennett, John B. Moisant suffered a fatal accident at New Orleans, Louisiana. After the race, he had organized a group of itinerant exhibition fliers—Moisant's International Aviators Ltd.— whose travels across the country and into Mexico and Cuba signaled the birth of barnstorming. On the last day of the year Moisant decided impulsively to try for the Michelin non-stop distance prize. Coming in for a landing, a gust of wind up-ended the tail of his 50-horsepower Blériot. It was not then the fashion to wear seat belts and Moisant was pitched forward and out, breaking his neck. His exploits are kept alive today in the name of the international airport at New Orleans.

240

Arch Hoxsey, appointed a substitute pilot in the 1910 race, also lost his life on 31 December. He had become famous for his "Dive of Death," hurling the "headless" Wright of which he was a proficient exponent vertically down from the sky to pull out and land at the last moment. At the second meet held on Dominguez Field at Los Angeles, Hoxsey strove for altitude, hoping to break the world record of 10,204 feet set by Georges Legagneux in France three weeks earlier. On his last such attempt, a blustery wind was blowing. Hoxsey's biplane broke in midair and spun to earth from a height of 600 feet directly in front of the grandstand, its pilot thrown out and crushed by the engine behind him.

Edouard Nieuport, who placed third in the contest at Eastchurch in 1911, was fatally injured in an accident two and a half months later. During the French military trials at Charny on 16 September he came down in a *vol-plané* with a series of sharp turns. Caught by the wind at the moment of landing, he tried to switch on the motor. But his Gnôme—flooded with gasoline—failed to respond. In the crash that followed Nieuport was flung heavily forward. With internal injuries he lived only a few hours thereafter.

The year 1912, marred by Wilbur Wright's death on 30 May from typhoid fever, saw as well the premature decease of Hubert Latham, contender in both the 1909 and 1910 races. On 16 July while on a big-game hunt near Fort-Lamy in French Equatorial Africa, Latham was killed in the charge of a Congo buffalo he had shot but only wounded. The idolized twenty-nine-year-old sportsman was universally mourned as one who could have made an ever more substantial contribution to the science of flight.

Less than two months after the 1912 race at Chicago, André Frey crashed to his death at Rheims while completing a course of instruction as corporal. Struck by a violent gust of wind, his machine fell to the ground from a height of 50 meters on 21 November, the pilot sustaining mortal injuries.

Despite his prediction that "we shall all be killed if we stay in this business," Charles K. Hamilton, member of the American team in 1910, who was fond of boasting that he had broken every bone in his body, continued to fly until 22 January 1914, when he succumbed to an internal hemorrhage, probably caused by tuberculosis, at his New York apartment. Emile Védrines, pilot of the Ponnier in the 1913 contest, lived a scant six months after finishing second in that event. He died in a crash on 1 April 1914 at Rheims where he had come so close to defeating Prévost and his Deperdussin. Seven weeks later, Gustav Hamel—Britain's unlucky representative at Eastchurch in 1911— vanished over the English Channel in a new Morane–Saulnier monoplane he was to fly in the *Daily Mail's* "aerial derby" Circuit of London. He had helped to ferry the first English air mail between Hendon and Windsor in September 1911 and had won the 1912 derby carrying as passenger an adventurous young lady named Trehawke Davies. He had earned a reputation as regular commuter between London and the continent with his Blériot and on 17 April 1914 had flown a distance of 340 miles into the heart of Germany to rouse his countrymen to the need of defense against aerial attack. On 23 May 1914 he set out for England after meeting France's Roland Garros in a match of virtuoso flying at Juvisy; his body was found by fishermen but lost again when they attempted to retrieve it from the sea. Only his goggles were recovered. It was assumed that Hamel had miscalculated his drift in patches of fog and had fallen into a watery grave when his fuel gave out.

World War I claimed the life of Norman Prince, backer of the Burgess *Cup Defender* in 1912. He was instrumental in organizing the Lafayette Escadrille and flew for France before America joined the conflict. On 12 October 1916, coming in to land after escort duty on a bombing raid, his Nieuport hit a high tension cable. Prince incurred injuries from which he died three days later. In less than six months he had flown 122 sorties against enemy planes and was officially credited with five kills.

Another war casualty was Eugène Gilbert, who had taken third place at Rheims in 1913. He was awarded the Coupe Michelin for 1914 by covering 3,000 kilometers in a "tour de France" with fourteen mandatory stops in 28 hours of flight, his elapsed time being 39 hours 35 minutes. Early in the war he became an ace. Interned after a forced landing in neutral Switzerland, he escaped on his third attempt. Ear trouble prevented him from flying at high altitudes; accordingly, he was put in charge of a group that tested and took delivery of new military machines. On 16 May 1918 Gilbert met death on the airfield at Villacoublay when a stabilizer broke on a machine he was putting through its trials.

Two days earlier, on 14 May, James Gordon Bennett had died at his villa in Beaulieu. In a tribute in *Le Figaro*, Pierre Véber pointed out that the publisher had always declined honors, decorations, and ribbons of all sorts; even so, he could not prevent a boulevard being named for him in the early years of the century, any more than he could have foretold that at the resort town of Menton in August 1967 the Quai James Gordon Bennett would be dedicated to his memory. The Villa Namouna was eventually turned into a select apartment house, known today as the Residence Gordon Bennett; its sunny site, the garden flanked by mimosa, cypress, and olive trees, is exposed to a stream of coastal traffic undreamed of by a man who preferred a four-in-hand to a motor car.

Jules Védrines was the only winner of the Gordon Bennett to die in a subsequent crash. The victor at Chicago in 1912 added to his laurels the year war broke out by flying, between 20 November and 29 December 1914, from Nancy to Cairo via Central Europe, Constantinople, Syria and Beirut. He accomplished the journey in ten stages, using a Blériot equipped with an 80-horsepower Gnôme. He served his country well during the war, landing French agents behind the German lines and picking them up again. Impressed by the commercial possibilities of the airplane after the war, he made up his mind to demonstrate the feasibility of a Paris–Rome route. On 19 April 1919 Védrines set out on a nonstop flight to the Italian capital but fell to the ground near the small town of Saint-Rambert-d'Albon. Both he and his mechanic Guillaud were instantly killed.

Bernard de Romanet improved his image as second best in the Etampes race by setting a world speed record of 309.012 kilometers per hour with his SPAD in the course of a meeting at Buc on 4 November

1920, a performance that won him a prize offered by the Ministry of War. In July 1921 he was promoted to the grade of officer of the Legion of Honor. On the twenty-seventh of that month he was slightly injured when a new machine he was testing for the navy capsized on landing in the water. Earlier, he had taken up for its first test another ill-fated product—the de Monge monoplane, equipped with a 300-horsepower Hispano–Suiza motor. Then on 23 September, while competing for the Deutsch de la Meurthe Cup at the Villesauvage airfield, he met disaster. At 300 kilometers per hour a wing of the machine began to disintegrate. Despite the pilot's best efforts to effect a turn and bring it under control, de Romanet crashed to his death. Member of the Aéro Club de France's board of directors, honored by the kings of Belgium and Spain, a brilliant consultant on aviation, he was also the recipient of the Aero Club of America's gold medal. A monument was erected to his memory at Le Bourget in 1927.

De Romanet seems to have been the last of those associated with the Gordon Bennett to die a violent death. Save for Armand Deperdussin, who, in the most dire financial straits, took his life with a revolver in a Paris hotel in 1924, the rest passed away from natural causes. René Hanriot, builder of the machine flown by André Frey in the 1912 race at Chicago, saw his firm fill orders after World War I in the principal countries of the world, including China, Turkey, Brazil, and the Soviet Union; manufacturing licenses were granted to Italy and Japan. Officer of the Legion of Honor, recipient of Belgium's Order of Leopold and other foreign decorations, Hanriot had just been decorated by the Italians when he died of a heart attack on 7 November 1925 at the age of fifty-eight.

As a manufacturer of airplanes, Glenn Curtiss, following his victory at Rheims in 1909, enjoyed a success equaled in the United States only by the Wrights. But the patent litigation in which both firms were involved left Curtiss an embittered and vindictive man, dissociated from aviation. During the Florida real estate boom of the 1920s, while preserving his ties with Hammondsport, he developed the subdivision of Hialeah near Miami. In July 1930 Curtiss was stricken with appendici-

244

tis and was operated upon at the General Hospital in Buffalo, New York. Complications set in and his death from peritonitis ensued on 23 July at the age of fifty-two. His great rival in the Gordon Bennett, Louis Blériot, died in Paris of heart failure on 2 August 1936, serene in the knowledge that the widely copied machine he invented had carried his name to the most distant corners of the earth, bringing him fame and fortune as maker of the most popular monoplane of its day.

A heart ailment also ended the life of James C. Mars, picked as a member of the American team at Belmont in 1910. As a first lieutenant in the aviation section of the Signal Corps in World War I, Mars trained soldiers to fly. After his discharge from the army in 1918 he built an airport in Westchester County, New York, and acted as instructor there until the airport was bought by the Westchester Park Commission in 1924. For a time he was a real estate operator in New York and Florida, then he went into the gas engineering business. He lived in Los Angeles until 1942, when he moved to South Pasadena. Mars died in the Los Angeles Veterans Hospital on 25 July 1944 at age sixty-eight.

Sadi-Lecointe sped from one record to another after nailing down the Gordon Bennett Cup for France. At Buc in October 1920 he flew against de Romanet at 302.529 kilometers per hour, and at Villacoublay he beat his rival with a speed of 309.092 kilometers per hour, which brought him the Vermilion Medal of the Aéro Club de France. He was made a chevalier of the Legion of Honor in 1921 and at a meeting in Brescia in September he successfully carried the French colors with his Nieuport–Delage against an array of Italian competitors, one of them using a 700-horsepower engine. On the twenty-sixth of that month at Villesauvage he broke the world straight line record for speed over a distance of 1 kilometer, registering 330.275 kilometers per hour. Trying for the Deutsch de la Meurthe Cup in October, his propeller shattered in flight and he suffered injuries to his legs and an eye in the total wreck of his machine. The following year, at an international meeting at Brussels, he placed second with a Nieuport–Delage "limousine" in a reliability contest for commercial transports.

Pushing for speed with the firm's "sesquiplane," Sadi-Lecointe broke the world record at Istres on 15 February 1923 with a speed of 375 kilometers per hour. Turning next to altitude, he established a new world mark on 5 September of 10,741 meters, for which he was awarded the Lamblin armband and its accompanying pension of 50 francs a day. On 30 October he broke his own record, reaching an altitude of 11,145 meters. These exploits earned him further honors from the Aéro Club, but more was to come. With a Nieuport on floats he surpassed by 2,612 meters the existing world altitude record for hydro-aeroplanes, attaining 8,980 meters at Meulan on 11 March 1924. For his numerous record-breaking performances he was promoted to the rank of officer of the Legion of Honor. He won the Beaumont speed trophy on 22 June, covering the distance of 300 kilometers at 311.299 kilometers per hour, and the next day he set a speed record of 306.696 kilometers per hour over a 500-kilometer course. In 1925 he served as a volunteer in Morocco in the war against Riffian tribesmen and was promoted to captain after receiving three citations. He competed again for the Beaumont cup that year and then resumed his post as chief test pilot for Nieuport–Delage. The year 1929 saw him taking part in several meetings; on 30 January 1933 he was made a commander in the Legion of Honor.

While testing the prototype of an 800-horsepower Nieuport monoplane on 26 April 1934, Sadi-Lecointe was forced to bail out when the machine caught fire; landing in a garden, he escaped with minor injuries. He was called in by the Air Ministry in 1936 and in 1937 was made inspector general of aviation, a title changed in 1938 to inspector general of civil aeronautics and public aviation. Mobilized on the outbreak of World War II in 1939, he was named inspector of flying schools. During the German occupation of Paris he was actively engaged in a news service, *Aviation*, directed against the enemy. On 21 March 1944 he was arrested by the Gestapo and secretly held in the notorious Fresnes prison for two months. The treatment he received there exacted its toll: Sadi-Lecointe died suddenly and tragically on 15 July. In addition to his other honors and prizes, he was the recipient of the Lahm Cup, the Rateau Cup, the Roland Garros Cup, the Jean

Casale Cup, the Grand Prize of Italy (at Brescia), and the Deutsch de la Meurthe Cup. Between 1919 and 1924 he had broken the world altitude record six times and between 1920 and 1923 the speed record seven times. A true national hero, his place in history was recognized in a ceremony on 8 December 1955, when a street in Paris's nineteenth arrondissement was renamed the rue Sadi-Lecointe.

Marcel Prévost died at Rheims on 27 November 1952, an officer of the Legion of Honor and, in addition to his other honors, holder of the Military Medal and the Aeronautical Medal. Mobilized on 1 August 1914, he spent the war years taking delivery of Deperdussins and their SPAD successors, as well as Nieuports, and organizing three American pursuit squadrons at Orly, Domrémy, and Toul. He continued to fly after the armistice, giving several exhibitions. On 17 July 1922 he passed the tests for touring license No. 154 and on 4 August took transport pilot's license No. 705. He devoted himself thereafter to industrial and commercial interests, among them Kellner airplanes and a French petroleum company. He was remembered in the United States as a member of the Early Birds of Aviation, an organization of pioneers who flew solo before 17 December 1916.

Glenn Martin, the to-be-or-not-to-be pilot of the Burgess racer at Chicago, went on to a highly prosperous career as a designer and manufacturer of airplanes. He received his first order from the United States government in 1913 and produced several models for the army. One of his earliest deliveries was to the government of the Netherlands, for which he built twenty-four planes. His factory expanded and by the time America entered the First World War he was employing 150 men. Within the next three decades he had designed and built hundreds of machines, including the first army bomber and the famous American Clipper. Many honors were bestowed upon him; in May 1933 President Franklin D. Roosevelt presented Martin, then forty-six years old, with the Collier Trophy, most coveted of all American aviation awards. He died of a cerebral hemorrhage on 4 December 1955 at age sixty-nine.

Henry Farman, his name a household word in the aeronautical industry, lived in Paris until 17 July 1958, when at the age of eighty-four he succumbed to a long illness. He was a commander in the Legion of Honor and in 1955 was awarded France's gold medal for arts, sciences, and letters. Claude Grahame-White, too, died in bed; for the winner of the 1910 Gordon Bennett the end came at Nice on 17 August 1959 three days before his eightieth birthday. He had been commissioned in the Royal Naval Air Service in 1914 and took part in the first air raids on German bases in Belgium. But he was soon discharged to superintend the manufacture of airplanes for military use and the training of pilots. Married three times, his postwar aviation activities proved lucrative; at one time he owned homes in both England and the United States. Grahame-White was a founder of the Royal Automobile Club and, with Harry Harper, the author of several books on aviation. At the time of his death he was working on an autobiography, which was completed by his friend Graham Wallace in 1960.

Another competitor who died after a long illness was Henri Crombez. Following the 1913 contest, the Belgian flyer began his military service and was put in charge of a squadron of monoplanes when war erupted in 1914. Promoted rapidly from sergeant to adjutant to *sous-lieutenant*, he was assigned to fly one of the first two-seater Nieuport pursuit planes, with which he specialized in aerial photography. During one such flight he was wounded by a bullet in the kidneys. After the war, his reputation as a modest, reliable airman resulted in his being chosen on frequent occasions as the personal pilot of King Albert; honored throughout his country as well as abroad, this was the distinction in which he took the most satisfaction. Crombez died on 17 January 1960 in his sixty-seventh year.

Two others who came to a peaceful end were Louis Paulhan, reserve pilot in the original contest, and Alfred Verville, designer of the Verville–Packard for the last race in 1920. Paulhan's life ended at his home in Saint-Jean-de-Luz on 11 February 1963. Verville's innovative airplane, after failing in the Gordon Bennett, was the winner of the first Pulitzer Race, on Thanksgiving Day, 25 November 1920. He himself remained at McCook Field until 1925, when he formed the Buhl–Verville Aircraft Company. From 1933 to 1945 he worked with the

Bureau of Air Commerce in Washington, D.C., and from 1945 to 1961 he was associated with the Navy Department and the National Air Museum. In recognition of his contribution to aviation, a scholarship was established in his name by the National Air and Space Museum, and a thirty-three-cent airmail stamp bearing his likeness and a sketch of the plane that brought him renown was issued by the United States Post Office.

Roland Rohlfs died of cancer at his home in Manhassate, New York, on 22 March 1974. Charles Weymann's life came to a close at the advanced age of eighty-seven in the summer of 1976. Chevalier of the Legion of Honor, recipient of the Croix de Guerre for the 1912–18 war, he remained an expatriate in France after winning the Gordon Bennett Cup for America in 1911. He applied himself to business pursuits, at which he was eminently successful, but he never lost interest in aviation. In 1975, the year before he died, he was fêted at a banquet by the Vieilles Tiges, an association of aeronautical pioneers in Paris, and given its gold medal.

The day since these names were front page news is long past, for the role of the individual aviator has given way to that of the impersonal technocrat in the business of flying. Yesterday the daring pilot was the star in the realm of aeronautics, today the machine is all important. Pioneers in swiftness of flight, forerunners of travel in space, the contestants in the Gordon Bennett were truly international heroes. They were the best ambassadors in a challenging new world that a country ever had.

Appendix 1
The Burgess Company's Statement
on Its Cup Defender

Marblehead, Mass., September 14.—In regard to the Chicago Syndicate Cup Defender, the Burgess Company and Curtis have issued the following statement:

Early in July Mr. Norman Prince, representing the Syndicate in Chicago, visited Marblehead for the purpose of finally closing an order with the Burgess Company for the design and construction of the Cup Defender. For more than four months preceeding overtures were made in various forms by the Aero Club of America and individual clubs and members looking towards interesting American manufacturers in the construction of a racing machine.

Great pressure, however, was brought to bear upon the Burgess Company to design and build an aeroplane suitable for the 160-horsepower Gnome power plant which had been purchased. Considerations of friendship finally prevailed upon Mr. Burgess and the Burgess Company agreed to design and build the aeroplane in six weeks, but at the same time took no responsibility whatever with regard to the furnishing of the aviator either for the test flights, or for the race.

This work was done at a great sacrifice to the company at this time of the year, the busiest one in a really very short season of activity. However, the machine was turned out and delivered within the time specified and shipped to Chicago with a large quantity of spare parts, also furnished. At the request of a member of the syndicate, Mr. Burgess went to Chicago and placed himself at the disposal of the committees there without recompense, remaining in Chicago until after the race.

When the machine arrived, there was at once a question as to who should drive it. No definite arrangements seem to have been made and conditions were aggravated by the fact that contrary to the company's advice, the Wright system of control had been installed. After a number of days' delay, it was finally decided that Mr. Glenn L. Martin, of Los Angeles, would undertake to drive the machine. He, with a number of others interested in aviation, of course, immediately began to criticize certain details of design and construction. The use of single wires with a factor of safety of over six was criticised, and at the same time the large wing surface, 130 square feet, was said to be too large for the horsepower. Some did not like the landing gear and others thought the tail was incorrectly designed, and so on.

Mr. Burgess has designed seven distinct types of aeroplanes in the last four years, every one of which has been sold to and flown by the purchasers successfully. The last previous design was the tractor biplane built for the United States Signal Corps, which passed its entire tests, including climbing 200 feet a minute and landing and leaving plowed ground without the slightest difficulty, even though other standard machines in this country ordered under the same specifications required from one to three months of adjustment and correction before acceptance.

Naturally when the request was made that smaller wings be furnished, the company believed that this was contrary to good judgment and was reluctant to aid in any changes made by those who perhaps lack the experience and skill which has been evident in the Burgess products. Small wings were hastily put together in Chicago to meet Mr. Martin's requirements, even though the large wings had never previously been tested out. If it had been possible to thoroughly train a man with large wings the question of smaller wings would have been, of course, in order, but with the horsepower furnished the original design was by no means excessive in amount of surface and limited time naturally prevented the highest possible development which can only be reached by experiment.

In the meantime, day after day passed in Chicago without any real work being accomplished, other than racing back and forth between Chicago and Clearing and the exchange of endless dissertations on racing by so-called experts.

The aeroplane arrived on August 20 and from that time until the day of the race, was not actually tried out, although the motor was found to be entirely satisfactory. The Burgess Company finally built a small set of wings, extra propellers and shipped sufficient spare parts there to build an entirely duplicate machine should it have been necessary.

The real difficulty in the whole episode is boiled down to three general criticisms:

First: The lack of any real support by the Aero Club, looking towards the constructions of a Cup Defender. As usual, the Aero Club was quite willing to encourage others to spend their money, but actual support was lacking.

Second: The disqualification of the best flyers in this country at a time when the choice of an aviator was quite as important as the choice of a machine.

Third: The construction of an aeroplane at the eleventh hour without any arrangements for the training of the aviator in the two weeks which remained between the date of delivery and the race.

The relations between the leading members of the Syndicate and the Burgess Company have been most friendly and it is with the sincere regret of all concerned that the machine was not actually in the race.

Source: *Aero and Hydro* (21 Sept. 1912).

Appendix 2
James Gordon Bennett Cup 1909–1920

Course and Place	Place	Pilot	Nation
1909	1	Glenn Curtiss	U.S.
2 laps—12.43 mi.	2	Louis Bleriot	France
Rheims, France	3	Hubert Latham	France
	4	Eugene Lefebvre	France
		George Cockburn	Great Britain
1910	1	Claude Grahame-White	Great Britain
20 laps—62.137 mi.	2	John B. Moisant	U.S.
Belmont Park,	3	Alec Ogilvie	Great Britain
Long Island	4	Hubert Latham	France
		Alfred Leblanc	France
		J. Armstrong Drexel	U.S.
		James Radley	Great Britain
		Walter Brookins	U.S.

254

Aircraft	Engine	HP	Avg. Speed
Curtiss *Rheims Racer*	Curtiss V-8	50	47.65
Bleriot XII	Gnome	50	46.83
Antoinette	Antoinette V-8	50	42.5
Wright	Bariquand et Marre	25	35.7
H. Farman	Gnome	50	
Bleriot XI bis	Gnome	100	61.3
Bleriot XI bis	Gnome	50	31.5
Wright "C"	Wright	36	29.4
Antoinette	Antoinette V-16	100	17.8
Bleriot	Gnome	100	
Bleriot XI	Gnome	50	
Bleriot XI bis	Gnome	50	
Baby Wright racer	Wright V-8	50	

Course and Place	Place	Pilot	Nation
1911	1	Charles Weymann	U.S.
25 laps—94 mi.	2	Alfred Leblanc	France
Eastchurch, England	3	Edouard Nieuport	France
	4	Alec Ogilvie	Great Britain
		Louis Chevalier	France
		Gustav Hamel	Great Britain
1912	1	Jules Vedrines	France
30 laps—124.8 mi.	2	Marcel Prevost	France
Chicago, Illinois		Andre Frey	France
1913	1	Marcel Prevost	France
20 laps—124.3 mi.	2	Emile Vedrines	France
Rheims, France	3	Eugene Gilbert	France
	4	Henri Crombez	Belgium
1920	1	Joseph Sadi-Lecointe	France
3 laps—186.4 mi.	2	Bernard de Romanet	France
Etampes, France		Georges Kirsch	France
		F. P. Raynham	Great Britain
		Maj. R. W. Schroeder	U.S.
		Howard Rinehart	U.S.
		Roland Rohlfs	U.S.

Source: *Racing Planes and Air Races 1909–1923*

256

Aircraft	Engine	HP	Avg. Speed
Nieuport	Gnome	100	78
Bleriot	Gnome	100	75.83
Nieuport	Gnome	70	75.07
Wright	N.E.C. V-8	50	51.31
Nieuport	Nieuport	28	
Bleriot	Gnome	100	
Deperdussin	Gnome	160	105.5
Deperdussin	Gnome	100	103.8
Hanriot	Gnome	100	
Deperdussin	Gnome	160	124.5
Ponnier	Gnome	160	123
Deperdussin	Gnome	160	119.5
Deperdussin	Gnome	160	106.9
Nieuport	Hispano-Suiza V-8	320	168.5
SPAD-Herbemont	Hispano-Suiza V-8	320	113.5
Nieuport	Hispano-Suiza V-8	320	
Martinsyde *Semiquaver*	Hispano-Suiza V-8	320	
Verville-Packard	Packard V-12	638	
Dayton-Wright	Hall-Scott	250	
Curtiss *Texas Wildcat*	Curtiss V-12	435	

Notes

INTRODUCTION

The story of the Gordon Bennett races has been pieced together from a myriad of sources—newspaper files, notes and clippings, articles in magazines, personal records and recollections, and the books on the history of aviation and publications relating to the subject that are listed in the bibliography. A principal source has been, naturally, James Gordon Bennett's own aviation-minded newspaper, the Paris edition of the New York *Herald*. Its pages not only record the competition for his trophy in its travels back and forth across the Atlantic, but they bring to life the exciting achievements of the airplane in speed, duration, and altitude from 1908 to 1920, not to speak of the valiant men who made those achievements possible. Indeed, the *Herald* and the Gordon Bennett Cup are part of the same story, for together they reflect the dramatic progress in aeronautics during the heroic pioneer years.

Because the cup was launched and eventually won in Europe, much of the story unfolds there. Publications such as the French *L'Aérophile* and the British magazines *Flight* and *The Aeroplane* have been heavily drawn upon, but American sources—especially *Aerial Age, Aero and Hydro,* and *Flying*—have not been neglected.

Aviation historians know different sources sometimes give different versions of an event, different figures for a record mark, different spellings for a name, even different dates on which an event occurred. To be confronted with a choice between two or more apparently reliable sources is frustrating for the researcher, but for the reader minor discrepancies should not detract from the larger picture. The Gordon Bennett races were among the most famous sporting events of their time. In the author's opinion they have not been treated as fully in historical works as they deserve. *Blue Ribbon of the Air* attempts to remedy that.

1 THE AIRPLANE COMES OF AGE

For a fuller treatment of early French attempts to fly and of Wilbur Wright's success in France, see Charles H. Gibbs-Smith's works *Aviation* and *The Wright Brothers* and Fred C. Kelly's *The Wright Brothers*, a biography authorized by Orville Wright. Biographical information about James Gordon Bennett can be found in Oswald G. Villard's *Some Newspapers and Newspapermen* and in Richard O'Conner's *The Scandalous Mr. Bennett.* The May incident is also described in André Cane's *James Gordon Bennett*, a biography spiced with anecdotes in more or less questionable taste. Cane, a resident of the Riviera, appears to have had an intimate knowledge of Bennett's personal life. *La Belle Epoque* is concisely summarized in Jacque Chastenet's *La France de M. Fallières.* For a complete account of the Gordon Bennett races for automobiles, see the author's *The Great Road Races, 1884–1914* and also Lord Montagu of Beaulieu's *The Gordon Bennett Races.* The best source for background about the Rheims meeting is the files of the Paris *Herald.*

2 RHEIMS • 1909

The Paris *Herald* for 28 and 29 Aug. 1909 reported the scene at Rheims *in extenso*; see also author's *Contact! The Story of the Early Birds* and "Les Meetings d'avant Guerre" in *Icare*, vol. 51. Curtiss's part at the Rheims meeting, as well as his previous career, is more fully covered in *The Curtiss Aviation Book*, which he wrote in collaboration with Augustus Post; Louis S. Casey's useful *Curtiss—The Hammond-*

sport Era, 1907–1915 contains technical details and pictures of the various Curtiss aircraft of the period. Good accounts of Blériot's duel with Latham to be the first across the Channel, and descriptions of his famous monoplane, are found in Tom D. Crouch's *Blériot XI: The Story of a Classic Aircraft* and Michael Lhospice's *Match pour la Manche*. Collin's version of the outcome at Rheims is found in E. J. LaSalle's *Les 100 Premiers Aviateurs Brevetés au Monde et la Naissance de l'Aviation*. This rare publication is also a valuable source of biographical information about the first French and other early aviators. Early Italian pilots are covered by Carlo Montu's *L'Aviazione in Italia*. Information about Esnault-Pelterie and Latham was kindly furnished to the author by the families of these aviators, and details of Latham's Antoinette are included in Kenneth Munson's *Pioneer Aircraft*, illustrated in color.

3   BELMONT PARK • 1910

The author witnessed the Belmont meet and many details are the subject of vivid recollection, especially the impression made on the public by Latham and his Antoinette. See his "Fabulous Belmont Park" in the *Journal of the American Aviation Historical Society* 1 (Spring 1984) and his *Contact! The Story of the Early Birds*. His *Great Road Races, 1884–1914* further treats America's fascination with automobiles. French criticism of the course was covered as sensational news by the New York press; the "revolt" can be followed in the New York *Herald*, the *Telegram*, and the *Evening Sun*. Biographical data regarding members of the French team, including pictures, are found in LaSalle's *Les 100 Premiers Aviateurs Brevetés au Monde*. For British fliers see Graham Wallace's *Claude Grahame-White* and two publications, *Heroes of the Air* and *The Aeroplane, Past, Present and Future*, by Grahame-White and Harry Harper; the last-named contains the first attempted directory of the men and women known to have flown up to that time (1911)—a total of 729 names. The Curtiss monoplane is described in Casey's *Curtiss—The Hammondsport Era* and in Munson's *Pioneer Aircraft*. Information about the American team is drawn from *Popular*

Mechanics (Dec. 1910) and Kelly's *Wright Brothers*; see also *Contact! The Story of the Early Birds*. Blériot's views on the possibilities of flight are set forth in Section VII of *The Aeroplane, Past, Present and Future*.

4 EASTCHURCH • 1911

For a comprehensive description of Eastchurch, see Maj. C. C. Turner's *The Old Flying Days*; chapter 2 recalls the spirit and atmosphere of the first phase of practical aviation in England. Aviation as a principal subject of social conversation is mentioned in numerous books dealing with the Edwardian era. James Gordon Bennett's activities can be followed in Cane's biography. Hamel's career in aviation is covered in, among other sources, Turner's *Old Flying Days*. The name of Graham-Gilmour, whose life was to terminate prematurely in a cross-country flying accident, occurs frequently in the pages of *Flight* and *The Aeroplane* during this period; his loss was a severe blow to British aviation. In their respective June 1911 issues, both *Flight* and *The Aeroplane* discussed the clipped wing Blériot XXIII. The description of Nieuport and his machine is based on information supplied by the Musée de l'Air at Le Bourget and *Les 100 Premiers Aviateurs Brevetés au Monde*, and the former is also the source of information about Védrines. *L'Aérophile* and other French sources assert that Weymann flew exhibitions in the United States in 1910–11, but no evidence to confirm this has been found. *The Aeroplane* and *Flight* provide the basis for the account of Hamel's crash, but they do not agree on the details.

5 CHICAGO • 1912

For much of the material relating to the 1912 Gordon Bennett, the author is indebted to aviation buff and writer Bill Hannon of Escondido, Calif. Griffith Brewer was the first Englishman to be taken up by Wilbur Wright and was entrusted with the formation of the British Wright Company by Orville after Wilbur died. He was a member of the Royal Aero Club from its inception in 1901 and was one of its delegates to F.A.I. meetings. An experienced balloonist, in 1908 he won an international race from Hurlingham, which, with a field of 31 starters, was the largest ever held in the United Kingdom. The author, elected in 1914, was the youngest member of the Aero Club of America. The club's tribute to its members lost with the *Titanic* was reported in *Flying* (June 1912). The experiences of Norman Prince in the service of France and the perils he met in aerial warfare were published in 1917, a year after his death, by Houghton Mifflin. The Burgess *Cup Defender* was described and illustrated with drawings and photographs in *Aeronautics* (Sept. 1912), *Fly* (Sept. and Oct. 1912), and other publications. For further information about construction of the monocoque, see Gibbs-Smith's *Aviation*, and *L'Aérophile* (Sept. 1912); *Flying* and *Aeronautics* were among other magazines also publishing details. *Aerial Age* did not respond to Védrines's joke with similar humor. "Needless to say," observed E. Percy Noel, the editor, "there was no button on the cap when the race started."

6 RETURN TO RHEIMS • 1913
Good information about the early fliers can be found in the French review *Pionniers*, an organ of the Paris-based "Les Vieilles Tiges," composed of pioneer airmen and others interested in aviation. Further sources for the aviators of the 1913 race are the biographical files in the National Air and Space Museum, Gibbs-Smith's *Aviation*, and, for the elimination trials and composition of the French team, *L'Aérophile*.

7 THE WAR YEARS • 1914–18
Rules for the anticipated 1914 race were published in *L'Aérophile* (15 Mar. 1914). For details about the *America*, see Casey's *Curtiss— The Hammondsport Era*. For a description of the Grand Prix and the nationalistic fervor it engendered on the eve of the war, see the author's *Great Road Races*. Retrospective accounts of the Great War, notably that published serially by the London *Times* in 1983, give a good idea of the events and circumstances of the era.

8   THE LAST RACE • 1920

Schroeder's letter, dated 18 June 1920, is in the collections of the National Air and Space Museum. Biographical information about Verville can be found in *W.W.I Aero* magazine (Sept. 1984), and details about his machine were published in the Paris *Herald* of 29 Sept. 1920. The Curtiss aircraft are described in Reed Kinert's *Racing Planes and Air Races*. According to the *Aircraft Yearbook* for 1920, Rohlfs's barograph was read, for purposes of international comparison, without air temperature corrections, thus conforming to European practices. After calibration by the Bureau of Standards, the barograph showed a maximum corrected altitude of 32,450 feet. These readings gave Rohlfs the official record in both corrected and uncorrected classes, his nearest rival being French Lieutenant Casale, who was reported to have reached an uncorrected altitude of 33,100 feet. Rohlfs's birthdate is listed as 10 Feb. 1892 in the biographical section of the *Blue Book of Aviation*; in an article written for *W.W.I Aero* in 1985, the respected authority Edward Peck gives it as 25 Sept. 1891. Biographical details about de Romanet and Sadi-Lecointe were supplied by the Musée de l'Air. There are several discrepancies in accounts of the final race itself; see Kinert's *Racing Planes and Air Races*, Gwynn-Jones's *The Air Racers*, and the Paris *Herald* for 29 Sept. 1920.

Selected Bibliography

The American Heritage History of Flight. New York: Simon and Shuster, 1962.

Angelucci, E., and P. Matricardi. *Les Avions 1/des origines a la première guerre mondiale*. Paris-Bruxelles: Elsevier-Séquoia, 1978.

Babbit, George F., with memoir by. *Norman Prince: A Volunteer Who Died For The Cause He Loved*. Boston and New York: Houghton Mifflin Company, 1917.

Bacon, Gertrude. *Memories of Land and Sky*. London: Methuen & Co., 1928.

Berget, Alphonse. *The Conquest of the Air*. New York: G. P. Putnam's Sons, 1911.

Bowen, Ezra. *Knights of the Air*. Alexandria, Va.: Time-Life Books, 1980.

Brett, R. Dallas. *History of British Aviation, 1908–1914*. London: John Hamilton, 1934.

Cane, André. *James Gordon Bennett*. Saint-Paul-de-Vence: Editions Bernard de Gourcéz, 1980.

Casey, Louis S. *Curtiss—The Hammondsport Era: 1907–1915*. New York: Crown Publishers, 1981.

Chastenet, Jacques. *La France de M. Fallières*. Paris. A. Fayard, 1949.

265

Crockett, A. S. *When James Gordon Bennett was Caliph of Bahdad.* New York: Funk & Wagnall, 1926.

Curtiss, Glenn H., and Augustus Post. *The Curtiss Aviation Book.* New York: Frederick A. Stokes Company, 1912.

Crouch, Tom D. *Blériot XI: The Story of a Classic Aircraft.* Washington, D.C.: Smithsonian Institution Press, 1982.

Demand, D., and H. Evude. *Conquest of the Air: The Evolution of Aircraft, 1903-1945.* New York: Viking Press, 1968.

Gibbs-Smith, Charles H. *Aviation.* London: Her Majesty's Stationery Office, 1970.

_____. *The Wright Brothers.* London: Science Museum, 1963.

Gibbs-Smith, C. H., W. J. Tuck, and W. T. O'Dea. *Aeronautics: Early Flying up to the Rheims Meeting.* London: Science Museum, 1966.

Grahame-White, Claude, and Harry Harper. *The Aeroplane: Past, Present and Future.* Philadelphia: J. B. Lippincott Company, 1911.

_____. *The Aeroplane in War.* London: T. Werner Laurie, 1912.

_____. *Heroes of the Air.* New York: Hodder and Stoughton, 1912.

Gwynn-Jones, Terry. *The Air Racers: Aviation's Golden Age.* London: Pelham Books 1984.

Harris, Sherwood. *The First to Fly.* New York: Macmillan and Co., 1970.

Hawkins, Eric. *Hawkins of the Paris Herald.* New York: Simon and Shuster, 1963.

Hoagland, Roland W., ed. *Blue Book of Aviation: A Biographical History of American Aviation.* Los Angeles: Hoagland Company, 1932.

Issy-les-Moulineaux, Commune of. *Issy-les-Moulineaux.* Paris, 1984.

Jane, Fred T. *All the World's Aircraft.* 1908-20 ed. London: Sampson, Low, Marston & Co.

Kelly, Fred C. *The Wright Brothers.* New York: Harcourt, Brace and Company, 1943.

Kinert, Reed. *Racing Planes and Air Races, 1909-1923.* Fallbrook, Calif.: Aero Publishers, 1967.

Lasalle, E. J. *Les 100 Premiers Aviateurs Brevetés au Monde et La*

Naissance de l'Aviation. Paris: Editions Nautiques et Aérospatiale.

Lhospice, Michel. *Match Pour La Manche.* Paris: Editions Denoël, 1964.

Lewis, Peter. *British Racing and Record-Breaking Aircraft.* London: Putnam, 1970.

Lieberg, Owen S. *The First Air Race.* New York: Doubleday & Company, 1974.

Manufacturers Aircraft Association. *Aircraft Year Book.* New York: Doubleday, Page and Company, 1920.

_____. *Aircraft Year Book.* Boston: Small, Maynard & Co., 1921.

McMahon, John R. *The Wright Brothers: Fathers of Flight.* Boston: Little, Brown and Company, 1930.

Montagu of Beaulieu. *The Gordon Bennett Races* (motor cars) London, n.d.

Montú, Carlo. *L'Aviazione in Italia.* Rome: Armani e Stein, 1911.

Munson, Kenneth. *Pioneer Aircraft.* London: Blandford Press, 1969.

O'Conner, Richard. *The Scandalous Mr. Bennett.* New York: Doubleday & Company, 1962.

Prendergast, Curtis. *The First Aviators.* Alexandria, Va.: Time-Life Books, 1980.

Turner, C. C. *The Old Flying Days.* London: Sampson, Marston & Co., 1927.

Villard, Henry Serrano. *Contact! The Story of the Early Birds.* New York: Thomas Y. Crowell Company, 1968.

_____. *The Great Road Races, 1894–1914.* London: Arthur Barker, 1972.

Villard, Oswald Garrison. *Some Newspapers and Newspapermen.* New York: Alfred A. Knopf, 1923.

Wallace, Graham. *Claude Grahame-White.* London: Putnam, 1960.

Whitehouse, Arch. *The Early Birds.* New York: Doubleday and Company, 1965.

Year editors of. *A Pictorial History of Aviation.* Vol. 2. New York: Year, 1961.

Index

268

LIB CIRCULATING COLLECTION

GV 759.2.G67 V55 1987

Villard, Henry Serrano, 1900-
Blue ribbon of the air :the Gordon
Bennett races /

9000052275